THE IMAGINARY TIME BOMB

Why An Ageing Population Is Not A Social Problem

PHIL MULLAN

I.B.TAURIS *Publishers*
LONDON • NEW YORK

Paperback edition published in 2002 by I.B.Tauris & Co Ltd
6 Salem Road, London W2 4BU
175 Fifth Avenue, New York, NY 10010
www.ibtauris.com

In the United States and Canada distributed by St. Martin's Press
175 Fifth Avenue, New York, NY 10010

First published in 2000 by I.B.Tauris

ISBN 1-86064-778-2

A full CIP record for this book is available from the British Library
A full CIP record for this book is available from the Library of Congress

Library of Congress catalog card: available

Typeset in Ehrhardt 10 on 12pt by Q3 Bookwork, Leicestershire
Printed and bound in Great Britain

Contents

Abbreviations

CFS	Completed family size
DHSS	Department of Health and Social Security
DoE	Department of Employment
G7	Group of Seven countries (US, Canada, Japan, Germany, France, Italy, Britain)
GDP	Gross Domestic Product
GHS	General Household Survey
ILO	International Labour Organisation
IMF	International Monetary Fund
NHS	National Health Service
OASDI	Old Age, Survivors, Disability Insurance
OECD	Organisation for Economic Co-operation and Development
ONS	Office for National Statistics
OPCS	Office of Population Censuses and Surveys
PAYG	Pay-as-you-go pension scheme
SERPS	State Earnings Related Pension Scheme
TPFR	Total period fertility rate
UN	United Nations
WHO	World Health Organisation

Charts, Tables and Diagrams

Foreword

In recent years ageing has been transformed into the new population problem of our times. Numerous demographers and social and political commentators have pointed to the growth in the numbers of the elderly and have warned of the danger facing the world in general and the West in particular. According to one account we are facing a 'Global Aging Crisis', which will 'daunt the public policy agendas of developed countries and force the renegotiation of their social contracts'.[1] The combination of a world wide decline in birth rates and an increase in the life expectancy of people has created a so-called gerontological drift. It is claimed that it is only a matter of time before Western societies will find it impossible to carry the burden of an ever-growing population of elderly people.

Concern with the greying of society is often linked to a preoccupation with apprehensions about declining fertility rates. 'Where are children?', asked one British commentator before adding that 'not having children must represent some sort of vote of no-confidence in the future'.[2] Concern with the decline of birth rates in the West is reinforced with fears about societies where fertility rates still remain high. Old preoccupations about competitive fertility have been recast as the threat faced by an ageing West from the younger and faster growing societies of the South.[3] Paradoxically, Malthusian fears about overpopulation in developing societies co-exists with anxieties about the low rate of fertility in the West.

The discussion about the so-called problem of ageing is not merely confined to the international sphere. Indeed, there is a much more developed debate which is focused on the apparent negative socio-economic impact that the growth in the numbers of elderly poses for Western societies. As Phil Mullan points out in this book, the increase in

the proportion of elderly is seen as the source of some of the difficulties faced by the Welfare State. Many contributors argue that as the proportion of (young) people shrinks further, it will not be possible to support the growing army of society's elderly. Economists have claimed that the growing population aged over 65 will make it impossible to sustain the present system of old age pensions.

As we argued elsewhere, population problems are rarely about numbers.[4] Whenever demography is politicised, emotions become highly charged and the protagonists in the debate carry a heavy ideological baggage. Experience suggests that it is often difficult to separate the facts about population from the perceptions of those concerned about the subject. Often, what is presented as a population problem is better understood as a moral or ideological problem which assumes a demographic form.

In the past, concern with an ageing population reflected deep-seated anxieties about the direction of society and loss of national power. In inter-war Britain, fears about imperial decline converged with a strong sense of insecurity about the trajectory of the world economy. Many leading economists blamed the economic crisis and the coming of the Great Depression on the stagnant rates of birth in the West. During this period, most economists and demographers defined the population problem as one of falling birth rates. John Maynard Keynes informed the Eugenics Society in February 1937 that the problem of overpopulation had been solved and that, instead, society was 'threatened by another danger'. The danger that Keynes alluded to was the lack of demand for goods caused by a declining population.

Today, the problem of ageing is rarely presented in the terms that Keynes constructed the issue during the inter-war years. In contemporary times it is difficult to be openly concerned with falling birth rates. Why? Because, such a diagnosis would seem to contradict the emphasis which the population lobby places on combating high birth rates in the developing world. It would appear too much of a double standard if the South were advised to reduce its rate of population growth while the North was worried about its shrinking numbers. Consequently in international fora, population policy advisors refer discreetly to the 'greying' of society rather than the danger of falling birth rates.

Nevertheless, the double standard towards the issue of differential fertility rates is not entirely absent from the public domain. The European Union is continually confronted with the tension that is the product of its policy of promoting population control policies abroad whilst decrying the danger represented by falling birth rates in Europe. Numerous resolutions passed in the European Parliament have indicated that it considers the decline in the growth rate of its people to be a serious problem for the future.

The issue of ageing is most widely discussed in relation to domestic questions. While the emotion that drives this discussion is very clear, it is not always evident what actually constitutes the problem of ageing. In Britain, the problematization of the elderly often has a tactical role in welfare discussions. As Raymond Jack argues this tactic has been widely deployed in the post-war years since the 'development of social policy and social services are inextricably bound up with the growth of the aged population'.[5] However, it is mainly since the 1980s that the problem of the elderly has been promoted in order to consolidate an anti-welfarist consensus in Anglo-American societies.

It is worth noting that the problematization of the elderly reflects some very important trends in society. In particular it coincides with the tendency to marginalize the elderly from the labour market and from society at large. The real issue is not so much the fact that there aren't enough people capable of working to support an elderly population. Rather, increasingly older people find it difficult to find employment. According to recently published figures, employment for older men has declined faster than for any other age group. As a result, a third of the men between 50 and 65 are now jobless in Britain.[6] Demography has little to do with the growing trend of forced early retirement. It is this shortening of the average period of working life rather than demographic patterns, which is likely to create difficulties for the economic position of the elderly.

The marginalization of the elderly from the labour market coincides with the construction of a much wider crisis concerning this section of the population. It is widely acknowledged that contemporary society is not hospitable to the elderly. Terms like 'vulnerable' and 'at risk' are often used to describe the position of elderly people. One symptom of the recognition that not everything is right in this respect is the wide usage of the term **elder abuse**. The term elder abuse is used to describe the regime of mistreatment experienced by older people from their family members and carers. This brutalised lifestyle faced by some of the elderly is sharply at variance with the traditional image of people living a dignified life in their old age.

Contemporary society is faced with a major dilemma. On the one hand people are living longer and longer but at the same time society is less and less certain about what role it ought to assign to the elderly. The erosion of traditional communities and of family networks further adds to the difficulty of establishing a harmonious relationship between the elderly and the rest of society. In circumstances such as this, it is understandable that the experience of ageing has become problematized. Very real moral and socio-economic issues have converged to place on the agenda the question of the elderly. Sadly society cannot resist the temptation of evading these issues and is drawn towards recasting them as a demographic crisis facing society.

The component parts of demographic alarmism

Phil Mullan's study offers a closely argued critique of contemporary demographic alarmism. His study situates this discussion within the wider historical debate about the problem of ageing in order to explain what is similar and also what is very different about the debate today. His is a multilayered and subtle approach. Mullan suggests that there are a number of influences which have emerged independently from one another, which have converged to reinforce one another and create the problem of ageing.

Mullan convincingly argues demographic alarmism is very much an offspring of the contemporary climate of anxiety and insecurity. Clearly, we live in an age where insecurity concerning the labour market coexists with uncertainties about personal and family life. Sociologists have consistently pointed to the way in which taken for granted relationships and expectations have been undermined by contemporary social forces. Consequently society is continually subject to an ever-growing variety of panics. In recent years, panics about food, children, medicine and health and technology have followed one another. Fears about existential security have expressed themselves in the inflation of problems. One of the most overused words in our time is that of crisis. Whether it is the crisis facing the environment or the crisis of the family, the socio-political language of our time indicates a profound fear of the future. And predictably, demography provides one of the most obvious means through which these apprehensions about the future can be expressed.

Terms like the 'Global Aging Crisis' reflect the tendency to interpret future outcomes in the worst possible light. This pessimistic perspective often informs the deliberation on growing global life expectancy. Reports have argued that by 2050, the number of people aged 65 to 84 world-wide will grow from 400 million to 1.3 billion, while those aged 85 and over will grow from 26 million to 175 million — and the number aged 100 and over will increase from 135,000 to 2.2 million. One would have thought that this marvellous increase in life expectancy of human beings would be interpreted as a positive benefit of development. In the past, early death was usually interpreted as a misfortune whilst ripe old age was seen as something to aspire to. Today, however, the increase in life expectancy is either presented as a mixed blessing or worse still as a grave burden to society. As Mullan argues, this response is not so much the product of cool demographic calculation but of a much wider crisis-oriented perspective that prevails today.

The second influence that Mullan isolates is what he sees as a retreat from economics to a more anti-social and naturalistic interpretation of the problems facing society. The focus on demographic problems is illustrative of the broader tendency to represent economic issues in a naturalistic mode. In recent decades pessimism about economic development has given way to anti-growth and anti-productivity perspectives. Natural obstacles, particularly those linked to environmental concerns have encouraged the emergence of the relatively new concept of sustainability. These models continually emphasise the issue of inter-generational transfer of resources and the difficulty that economic activity today may pose for the survival of future generations. From this standpoint, an ageing society represents a troublesome claim on the resources of the productive generations of the future. And the problem of ageing is just one more burden that contemporary society hands over to those who will take over the helm in years to come.

It is the shift from the social to the natural, which explains the intellectual plausibility of the problematization of ageing. According to this outlook, the elderly become just one more burden imposed on future generations by a society which continually feels ill at ease with nature. Typically, the elderly are seldom understood as a product of a social construction. Instead they are presented as biologically very mature. The emphasis on the elderly as a burden is also very unconvincing. Why the elderly in particular should represent a uniquely special burden is seldom explored. Yet there are interesting arguments which suggest that a growth in the proportion of elderly might lower a country's investment needs and increase its living standards because new entrants into the labour force would require less capital.[7] It is far from clear whether this is a realistic scenario. However, the relative absence of debate on the economic opportunities provided by the growth in the elderly population indicates how the naturalistic worldview dominates thinking on this subject.

Finally, Mullan explains how the anti-welfarist agenda has helped to define the contemporary problem of ageing. Scapegoated for the financial difficulties faced by state budgets, the elderly have been cast into the role of a drain on society's resources. These arguments have acquired widespread currency in relation to the controversy that surrounds the provision of pensions. The new emphasis on the personal responsibility of people for ensuring their security in old age is not surprisingly linked to governments' attempt to contain spending on the elderly. The crisis of ageing is therefore not a million miles from the project of narrowing the foundation of the welfare state.

Mullan's historical analysis permits the reader to grasp the tactical use of the problem of ageing within a wider social and cultural setting. Indeed, it is the convergence of this tactic with the wider cultural and intellectual trends discussed above that allows for the author's multidimensional exploration of this issue. There is little doubt that this offers a brave and original approach towards an issue that is typically so often mystified. It has the force of argument for influencing the public agenda on the issue of ageing and will no doubt become a point of reference on this subject.

Frank Furedi
University of Kent in Canterbury

Notes

1.   See PG Peterson, 'Gray Dawn: the Global Aging Crisis', *Foreign Affairs*, January/February 1999, p43.
2.   See Hamish McRae, 'The strange case of falling birth rates in the West', *The Independent*, 11 June 1997.
3.   For a discussion of competitive fertility, see F Furedi, *Population and Development*, Polity Press, London, chapter 3.
4.   *ibid.*
5.   R Jack, 'Social services and the ageing population 1970–1990', *Social Policy and Administration*, vol 25, no 4, 1991.
6.   See *The Guardian*, 8 February 1999.
7.   See for example N Eberstadt, 'Too Few People?', *Prospect*, December 1997, p 53.

Preface

In a Channel 4 television programme in 1994 Will Hutton, former editor of the Observer and now Chief Executive of the Industrial Society, predicted that pensions would be *the* issue of the 1990s. This is proving too modest a timescale. Not only were the cost and adequacy of pensions growing concerns in many industrialized and ageing countries through the last decade of the twentieth century but it looks as if the pensions issue will run well into the new millennium.

By the end of his first 100 days in the White House President George Bush had announced the establishment of a high level task force to report on how to deal with the feared bankruptcy of the US Social Security fund. At the same time pension reform remains high on the political agenda in most European capitals, fueled by a series of European Union and UN reports highlighting the financial and social dangers of ageing populations. Meanwhile in Britain competing pension promises from the main political parties was one of the hotter issues of the 2001 General Election.

As a result the arguments in this book that ageing populations are neither an economic nor a social problem but are a positive sign of human progress remain both relevant and pressing. Also the need remains as urgent for a rational public debate on the real impact of ageing populations in order to dispel the more invidious myths.

One welcome change since the book was written are the signs that such a debate may be opening. The BBC, for example, chose 'The End of Age' as the theme for the 2001 Reith Lectures. Tom Kirkwood, Professor of Medicine and Head of Gerontology at the University of Newcastle, gave the series of stimulating talks and challenged the normal gloom mongering on the topic. He explained that science tells us that there is no set age at which particular morbid symptoms begin to arise. As a consequence given the rise in living standards experienced over the past half-century it is likely, he argued, that the positive trend towards living longer, healthier and fitter lives will continue. We encourage other institutions to follow the lead of the BBC in giving openings to such counter-stereotypical perspectives.

Some other motives for the increasing profile of the ageing issue are, however, suspect and reinforce many of the negative assumptions and sentiments against which this book argues. For example in national elections in both the US, in 2000, and Britain, in 2001, an explicit play was made for the elderly vote. Doubtless this will be replicated in forthcoming elections in other industrialized countries. Demographic ageing alone means that the elderly are becoming a bigger part of the potential electorate. In Britain, for example, there are already 11 million pensioners and this number grows by the year.

Many social commentators, marketing people and politicians assume 'grey power' is in the ascendant. Especially at elections there is much more to this than simply the numerical increase in the numbers of elderly voters. The obsession with the 'grey vote' also reflects a sense of resignation to the scale of political disengagement, and the consequent desire to court the people still most likely to vote. With surveys and the outcome of recent elections all showing that the under 30s today express voting intentions and practices well below average the focus on older voters is not surprising.

As with all stereotypes associated with the elderly, the ideas of grey power and the grey voting bloc are misleading. It is wrong, as well as patronizing, to view the elderly as a common fraternity who live, think, act and vote the same. In fact the old are probably more heterogeneous than any other age group.

As Debra Street, a researcher at the American Pepper Institute on Ageing and Public Policy, explained in the Wall Street Journal, 11 September 2000: 'The older we get, the more diverse we become as individuals, simply because life experiences have led us down different pathways'. Age is probably the least significant 'group' indicator of how people vote. Gender, colour, income and wealth are all much more important.

Such courting of the grey vote is unhelpful to the interests of the elderly, and not just because, as the charity Age Concern noted with regard to the 2001 British general election, 'No party has pledged to increase the basic state pension to an adequate level'. Moreover reducing the political message to such a narrowly financial one as pensions is scornful of the elderly as living people. Genuine humane concern for the dependent elderly is not measured by a few quid here or there, but by how society behaves towards them more generally.

A better life for the elderly requires as a starting point challenging, not reinforcing, the negative ways in which the ramifications of ageing are viewed. Too few yet take on those common arguments that demographic trends are against us. This is the way the discussion is usually framed. Longevity is increasing. Fertility has fallen since the birth boom years of the 1950s and 1960s. The support ratio, measuring the number of people of working age for each pensioner, is estimated to fall from about 4.2 today to 2.6 in 2031, once the baby boomers have all retired. So with more older people above retirement age, and fewer younger people of working age, society will just have to accept that resources are limited. These are the conventional facts that are believed to underpin the spectre of the ageing time bomb.

But, as this book argues, there is no time bomb. There is no ageing 'problem'. Greater longevity and falling early age mortality is a cause for celebration, not concern. Populations have been ageing and support ratios falling at pretty much the same rate for over 100 years, without generating the sort of financial and social crises being predicted today. The number of working people 'supporting' each pensioner has fallen from 14 to 1 in 1900 to 4 to 1 in 1990, and hardly anybody noticed. This book shows why.

People over the designated retirement age do not become worthless dependents in need of support overnight and should no longer be treated as such. Ageing is not an illness. And with people living not just longer lives, but longer, healthier and fitter lives, this myth of automatic dependence has less and less credence to it. Surely the time has come to scrap the fixed retirement age which helps institutionalize this false presumption.

Moreover, compared even to the misleading statistical 'support ratio', national wealth has increased at a much faster rate – by about seven-fold – over the century. Contrary to a widespread opinion, wealth generation has nothing to do with either the average age of the population nor with demographic ratios. Rather, it is a function of both the size and the productivity of the labour force.

Employment rates vary for all sorts of social and economic reasons between countries, regions and times. The vast majority of these have nothing to do with population ageing. These labour market changes have much more of an impact on national wealth creation than the net movement in the numbers of people of below and above the official retirement age.

Historically, outside periods of severe economic crisis, the active workforce in industrialized countries tends to grow. Even without an increase in the size of the workforce, productivity – output per worker – growth at the long-run trend of about two per cent a year keeps national wealth doubling every 35 years. This is much faster than the growth in real elderly dependence on social wealth.

So the elderly neither represent an 'unsupportable burden' nor could they be the cause of weakened economic growth rates. The ageing 'problem' does not exist.

These arguments need more public debate. If you wish to discuss them or help to promote them please get in touch: philmullan@easynet.co.uk

1· Introduction

Foreign Affairs – the prestigious international relations journal – ran an article in May 1997 that discussed the prospects for Japan, its economy and its role in the world. One might think that such an article would address the state of Japan's productive economic capacity, the state of its manufacturing base, or perhaps the implications of coping with its long running financial crisis. But no – the article's main concern was the implications of its ageing population for Japan itself and for the rest of the world. The article was titled 'Japan's Aging Economics', and began, 'Japan's demographic crisis. Japan's population is aging faster than that of any other country in the world... These seemingly innocent demographic changes will force Japan to shrink its famously high savings rate, reverse its proud trade surplus, send more industry overseas, liberalise its tightly controlled markets, and take on a more active, high-profile foreign policy. Ultimately, these changes will shift the balance of power in East Asia'.[1]

So the future of Japan – notwithstanding being the second largest economy in the world, the world leader in many areas of new technology, with one of the fastest rates of productivity growth among the advanced industrialised countries – is apparently determined by an increase in the average age of its population. This is an example of a trend that has become prevalent over the past ten years: the naturalising of economic and political discussions, and specifically giving a political economic discussion a demographic form.

Issues, and especially problems, that used to be understood by looking at how mankind operates and organises itself tend instead to be given explanations rooted in natural phenomena. The population structure is generally assumed to be such a natural phenomenon. This approach represents a retreat to a fatalist perspective. Man-made problems are susceptible intrinsically to man-made solutions. However, problems that are represented as deriving from natural factors are more inexorable. They have a dynamic of their own that is difficult for man to change and influence, at least in the short term. Instead man must adjust his behaviour and lower his expectations of the future. The discussion of the problems of an ageing population is a strong example of this tendency in late twentieth century thought.

I first became aware of this tendency when I was investigating changes in the British labour market during the 1980s. I began to research the trend of early retirement, and its greater prominence in all the major industrial economies. The pattern in many countries in the early 1980s was similar. Earlier retirement was being officially sanctioned as a fairly 'bloodless' way of coping with redundancies and unemployment.

Then, from about the start of the second half of the decade, I noted signs of a sea change in thinking. The same countries that had encouraged early retirement were now worrying about how to pay pensions and benefits to all these non-productive workers in the future. Increasingly the spectre of a demographic time bomb, of an ageing population, was brought into the discussion, to emphasise that these non-working people were becoming an intolerable burden. There were soon going to be too many elderly dependents for society to cope with because of the demographic trend. Early retirement, it was said, had to be resisted because it would aggravate this difficulty.

Why had the issue of ageing not been considered a few years earlier when the promotion of early retirement had been the fashion? Could the rise and fall of the early retirement strategy, and therefore ageing's late entry into the equation, be something to do with the stage of the business cycle? In the deep recession of the early 1980s, earlier retirement was favoured. Later, when the pace of redundancies slowed, other economic problems such as the level of government borrowing took higher prominence. The impact of population ageing appeared to justify this shift in emphasis.

The more I looked, the more I saw the issue of ageing being introduced into other economic discussions. Also the more my interest was aroused. There was something odd about this newly discovered prominence of ageing. The preoccupation was rarely thrown in as another interesting influence among many. Invariably ageing was regarded negatively, as a problem, as a threat and an unaffordable burden. Over the course of the 1990s I have noticed the wider spread of this concern. Today there is little left in political economy into which the ageing problem does not intrude. Glaring through all the commentary about ageing's impact are the negative implications – the dangers that this trend represents for the future of society. Discussion of ageing and its implications always seems to have a downbeat tone.

It is assumed that the most serious problems associated with ageing will occur some time in the second quarter of the twenty-first century, when the proportion of over 64s in Britain will exceed one-fifth of the population. But more immediately, we are told there are problems already which society must not delay in addressing.

For example, the secular economic slowdown across the advanced industrialised countries is explained by some as the result of older population structures. Hamish McRae, author of *The World in 2020*, believes growth prospects for North America, Japan and Europe are limited because 'the age profile of these regions... simply will not generate rapid growth'.[2]

Others claim the absence of the feelgood factor in many Western societies is due to ageing. An older population is said to be more cautious, worries more about the future, and has less to spend. This plays upon the classic stereotype of the elderly as grumpy and spendthrift – films such as *Grumpy Old Men* starring Jack Lemmon and Walter Matthau, or Richard Wilson's Victor Meldrew character from television's *One Foot in the Grave* series, come to mind. The implication is that an older population, even an affluent one, is bound to make society feel bad.

The failure of the housing market to pick up is also attributed by some to the phenomenon of ageing. The market has slowed and the supply of housing is increasingly outpacing demand. Old people are less likely to move, or when they do, it is often a move out of the private housing market into the old person's home or the cemetery. This adds to the available housing stock without any balancing demand. Meanwhile, at the other end of the age spectrum there are too few twenty-somethings to make a significant difference and kickstart a housing market recovery as they did in the late 1970s and 1980s.

The real worry expressed is where this is all heading next century when the baby boom generation gets into its sixties and seventies. Slower growth rates, higher taxes and inter-generational conflict have all been predicted. And there is something distinctive about these predictions, which seems to give them greater weight than many other forecasts of impending disaster.

Fears for the future that are based on demographic change are thought to have firmer foundations than other long term disaster scenarios – such as nuclear holocaust, global warming or energy depletion – because it is inevitable.[3] The post-Second World War baby boom is not a prediction. The babies have been born, and in the absence of major war, disease or other disaster, they will be retiring and joining the ranks of the elderly during the first three decades of the new millennium. There is nothing that can be done about them. They cannot be unborn. The baby boom generation is with us. So too is the succeeding 'baby bust' generation of the 1970s and 1980s when in most advanced countries birth rates fell below replacement levels. Nothing can stop these two generations getting older.

Accordingly, sometime in the early half of the twenty-first century the age structure of Western societies will shift sharply in favour of the elderly post-retirement cohort relative to the younger groups still of working age. This inevitability gives weight to the pertinence and appeal of the 'time-bomb' metaphor. The fuse has been lit. It will take about 20 years to smoulder but the explosion seems inevitable. The demographic catastrophe is just waiting to happen.

All the problems supposedly associated with personal old age – dependence, conservatism, low productivity, and an absence of dynamism and innovation – will as a result become society's problems. Most concretely and assuredly of all these dangers the burden of providing for the larger numbers of elderly people will fall necessarily on a relatively diminishing working population.

Overarching much of the anxious discussion are the budgetary implications across the advanced industrialised countries. The ageing of the population is perceived as creating a steadily increasing burden upon society in general and upon state finances in particular. An older population is putting greater demands upon the public expenditure budgets across North America, Japan and most of Western Europe. As the International Monetary Fund (IMF) recorded in the May 1997 issue of its *World Economic Outlook*, 'fiscal imbalances are still excessive in a large number of countries, with the prospective ageing of populations and the attendant pressures on health and pension outlays adding to the urgency of fiscal reforms'.[4]

As a group it is true that older people make disproportionate demands upon welfare services but that is in the nature of modern welfarism. Its proponents intended the welfare state to focus on this section of society. Old people tend to need more health care, more personal social services, receive more sickness and invalidity benefits and, of course, by definition receive all state retirement pensions.

The consequence is that in most commentaries on the problems of welfarism, concern about public spending focuses upon the cost of the one item which is unequivocally related to the size of the elderly population – pensions. As Anthea Tinker argues: 'Rising numbers of elderly people combined with a lack of economic growth have turned attention to what is usually the largest element in social welfare – pensions'.[5]

It seems to stand to reason that Western governments are going to face a serious funding crisis unless action is taken soon. The welfare state will have to undergo a complete overhaul. With pensions taking about 30 per cent of all social spending the pensions system stands out as the most pressing case for treatment. A report produced early in 1995 by the Federal Trust – a think-tank set up, ironically, by William Beveridge, the architect of Britain's welfare state – warned that demographic trends make private funding of pensions essential; governments will simply be unable to afford to support the growing number of senior citizens. Dick Taverne, author of the report, *The Pension Time Bomb in Europe*, said: 'there will be a crisis if we do not act now. This issue cannot be left on the political shelf for ten years.'[6]

The same concern also stalks America. Debate about the difficulty of cutting back on the US budget deficit usually ends up focusing on the demands of the ageing population. Numerous studies conclude that the government budget cannot be balanced without serious cuts in entitlements.[7] Three programmes account for well over one third of all government spending – Social Security, Medicare and Medicaid – and the bulk of this goes on elderly people.

As a result of ageing, forecasts for the US show that if nothing is done, by 2003 these programmes will eat up nearly a half of federal spending. Soon after that the Medicare programme will run out of money and in about 20 years the public retirement system is predicted to start to collapse. By then health care and federal pensions alone would, according to these predictions, consume every dollar of government revenue.

And ageing is no longer seen just as a problem for the developed world. According to several recent World Bank and United Nations reports, ageing is threatening societies outside the North, in the former Eastern bloc and in the South. Recent work by the renowned Austrian demographer Wolfgang Lutz concludes that ageing will replace the problem of population growth as a focus for public, political and scientific concern.[8]

The assumption in all instances seems to be that an ageing society causes mounting strains.[9] The argument of this book is that this assumption is incorrect. This is not to deny that there are social and economic difficulties across the industrialised world. Nor is it to question the demographic fact that its population is ageing. It is the causal relationship between the two that this book challenges centrally.

The essential thesis advanced here is that this growing preoccupation with ageing has nothing to do with the direct impact of demographic changes. Instead demographic ageing began its newfound prominence about two decades ago as a scapegoat for changes in society and the economy that have non-demographic causes.

Problems that were ultimately rooted in the generalised slowdown in all the Western economies post-1973 instead acquired a demographic determinant. This applied especially to the perceived difficulty of financing government spending and to the sluggishness of economic growth. From this beginning the fact of population ageing has since served for some as a compelling and apparently non-ideological pretext for reducing the role of the state in the economy.

More recently in the 1990s the obsession with ageing that has developed far beyond the traditional discourse of economics is also not because of demographic developments. It is more a function and reflection of the current state of Western thought, which is widely perceived as dominated by a mood of nervousness, heightened risk awareness, and pessimism for the future.

All decades have their labels. Many commentators already dub the 1990s the 'nervous nineties'. The phrase 'age of anxiety' has been bandied about so much it is almost a cliché. In 1998 two *Guardian* journalists Dan Atkinson and Larry Elliott published *The Age of Insecurity*, a book which was generally recognised to catch the social mood well (even if some of its analysis was less endorsed). In similar vein newspaper columnist Paul Vallely is representative of those who explain the revival of spiritualism as a response to the uncertainty of our times.

As he explained: 'Ours is a time of collective apprehensiveness. Economic uncertainty, job instability and the dissolution of the family under the pressures of the market spread a sense of insecurity.'[10]

The conclusion of this book is that the contemporary mindset of uncertainty makes society susceptible to the notion of a population time bomb. The negative presumption of 'too many old people' has become a motif for many of Western societies' anxieties.

Chapter 2 assesses both the reality and the changing perceptions of ageing during the past two centuries. The aim is to put into perspective the recent discussions so as to highlight their peculiarities. The form of the current preoccupation and of its evolution over the past two decades is then addressed in chapter 3. Chapter 4 explains why it is incorrect to assume that an ageing population necessarily becomes an unsupportable burden on society. The next two chapters, 5 and 6, expand this argument in respect of two specific concerns arising from an older population: the provisions of pensions and of health care respectively. Chapter 7 moves on to challenge the more general assumption that an older population structure has adverse implications for the economy and the pace of economic growth. The concluding chapter 8 summarises the book's findings and thesis.

Society is ageing but it is wrong to attribute this as the source of all, or any, of society's contemporary problems. Throughout the twentieth century populations have been ageing. They have coped adequately, without incurring the apocalyptic demographically caused crises forecast for our own future owing to further ageing. The explanation for the current preoccupation with ageing demands that this book examines why it was not a major concern in the past. We need to identify the specifics of today's circumstances that have propelled ageing to such prominence.

A closer examination reveals that there are two demographic time bombs to lay bare. The two are conflated in many people's minds. Also, in many ways the first fed into the second. But this approach of two bombs, or two phases of the preoccupation, helps to understand the phenomena better.

The first time bomb was a creation of a group of policy makers and opinion formers who, during the course of the 1980s, used the threat of the ageing population to justify attempts to narrow the state's economic role and, especially, to reform and curb the welfare state. This does not imply that all these people artificially manipulated the bomb image.

Many sincerely believe it to be true. As Anthea Tinker wrote of the 1980s discussion, 'more than anything else it has been the continued growth in the number of very elderly people which has concentrated people's minds on finance since it is usually the care of this group which is the most costly'.[11] This is the way many that have warned about the problem of demography genuinely perceive the ageing trend.

These were the prophets of the demographic time bomb. For most of the 1980s, although they were listened to politely enough, and were rarely questioned, they did not pick up a mass following.

However, from the end of the 1980s and through the 1990s, concerns about ageing started to become pronounced. The second time bomb started to tick. It was as if the audience of the rest of society had become more receptive. The problem of ageing, and the bomb metaphor, is now more widely and deeply felt. It is still used as an anti-welfare and anti-state argument, but it has become more than that. It has become a major anxiety of our times. Understanding better this shift in sentiment was an important factor in inspiring me to lay bare the true significance of the ageing discussion. In many books and articles on ageing the specific existence of this 'second time bomb' appears not at all, or is only tangentially addressed, even in otherwise balanced and well argued texts. Hence this book.

The key practical argument employed here against the notion of a ticking time bomb is that society has coped with ageing populations before and can do so again. This is based on the recognition that no modern society ever stands still economically, but is always tending to expand in its potential and capacity to create wealth. Notwithstanding the ups and downs of the business cycle, and even temporary bouts of stagnation, over the longer term industrialised societies produce considerably more wealth from one generation to the next. On the basis of extrapolating recent rates of economic growth and wealth creation, societies will more than cope materially and financially with the ageing trends projected today for the twenty-first century. In my view it would be better for everyone if economies could grower faster than the experience of the past quarter century.[12] But even on the basis of those sluggish levels population ageing shades into insignificance as a 'burden'.

Every demographic theory – from the mildest to the most catastrophist variety – takes as given the rise in the elderly dependency ratio as the key trend. (This is the ratio of over 64-year-olds to the population of working age, usually taken as the 16 to 64 age range.) More people of over the retirement age have to depend upon relatively fewer from the working-age group. The inexorable rise in the ratio of the elderly to the working population is presented as the statistical proof of the demographic time bomb. This common assumption unites even those who disagree on whether it 'will go off with a whimper or a bang'[13]

But this narrow arithmetical relationship obscures the more fundamental determinant of society's ability to reproduce itself and to provide an adequate standard of living for all its members, of all ages. *This determinant is the scale of productive activity* – people working together to produce a greater abundance of goods and services for the well being of humanity with ever higher levels of technology. Historically modern societies double their wealth about every 25 years. This pace of expansion projected into the next half-century dwarfs the extra cost for society from more elderly dependents.[14] For the historic productive dynamic of human society to fail us in this respect we would need to be facing an unprecedented prolonged period of sustained economic stagnation. And if for some unanticipated reason the dawn of the millennium ushered in such a Dark Age an ageing population would be a minor affair in the midst of much graver difficulties for humanity.

Even if, as it is more realistic to imagine, economic growth were to slow down a little compared to the past couple of decades, ageing could also not be scapegoated legitimately for this dulling effect. Other factors that may prevent people realising their productive potential are much more influential in determining society's present state and future prospects than anything demography can offer. For example, on the jobless registers of the advanced industrial countries that make up the Organisation for Economic Co-operation and Development (OECD), there are over 30 million people, and millions more who do not appear in the official figures. This is a tremendous waste of potential wealth creation. Ageing does not explain that fact. Nor is it just the number of jobs that determines society's productive strength. It is also the types of jobs and the state of technology. Some jobs are more productive than others are. Compare a bond trader with a steelworker. Over time the deployment of, or failure to deploy, new technology can massively affect output per worker. The age structure of a country also does not determine either of these determinants.

To repudiate the idea that ageing is a major economic and social burden it is necessary to challenge several prevalent myths about population ageing. This box summarises the key myths that this book seeks to disprove and the reasons they are important to question:

Myth: Ageing is the consequence of falling death rates.
Implication of the myth: given the assumption that ageing is a problem then improving mortality rates would not necessarily be positive.
Reality: The strongest force behind demographic ageing is falling fertility rates.

Myth: Ageing happens because old people live longer.
Implication of the myth: It may not be socially useful to reduce elderly mortality rates.
Reality: Life expectancy for old people has changed much less than life expectancy at birth. The age structure of a society is more affected by fluctuations in the younger section of the population, including the effect of falling infant and youth mortality. Also the past couple of decades of falling elderly mortality rates may have been exceptional.

Myth: Ageing is a natural phenomenon.
Implication of the myth: Ageing is inexorable, immutable and impervious to human intervention.
Reality: Population ageing is the consequence of social developments and changes; even what it means to be 'old' is socially determined.

Myth: Ageing is a permanent trend.
Implication of the myth: Ageing is unending and the problems conventionally associated with ageing will therefore inevitably worsen.
Reality: Contemporary ageing is mainly the outcome of a specific phenomenon – the post-War baby boom and succeeding baby bust, whose influence on the population structure will work its way out before the middle of the next century.

Myth: Ageing populations are unaffordable and represent a significant burden for society, especially for the welfare states in

developed industrialised countries, and this burden will intensify.
Implication of the myth: Spending on social programmes for the
elderly and for other sections of the population must be reduced to
offset the costs of coping with an absolute rise in the numbers of
the old.
Reality: Industrialised societies are already productive enough to
produce sufficient wealth to provide for the present elderly
population and even quite low levels of growth will satisfy even the
most extreme projections for the future pace of ageing.
Supporting this last myth, are two specific myths about pensions
and about health costs:

Myth: Ageing populations will bankrupt state pension schemes.
Implication of the myth: Pension arrangements need to be
reformed away from public pay-as-you-go towards private funded
schemes.
Reality: This distinction is of no bearing upon the key issue to
determine affordability – the future rate of economic growth and
the level of wealth creation at any point of time in the future. In
their operation, private schemes tend to be less efficient than
public ones so for society as a whole there seem to be no financial
grounds for this reform.

Myth: More old people mean an exponential rise in ill health and
in dependency.
Implication of the myth: Exaggerates the health and social service
cost of treating and caring for old people, and reinforces the notion
that ageing is a burden for society.
Reality: Ageing is not an illness. Most old people are neither ill nor
disabled and do not need looking after. One of the reasons most
people are surviving to old age is the improvement in living
conditions from earlier this century. A continued improvement will
make contemporary and future generations of the elderly fitter and
healthier than their predecessors.

Myth: Ageing populations hinder economic growth.
Implication of the myth: We must learn to lower our expectations
of material well being as we live in an ageing society.
Reality: The dynamic of economic growth is determined by other
social factors upon which demographic trends have no influences.

Notes

1. Milton Ezrati, 'Japan's Aging Economics', *Foreign Affairs*, May/June 1997.
2. *The Independent*, 29 July 1997.
3. Johnson and Falkingham (1992), p 2.
4. IMF (1997).
5. Tinker (1992), p 242.
6. *The Independent*, 7 January 1995.
7. *Business Week*, 19 December 1994, p 17
8. *The Guardian*, 19 June 1997.
9. Johnson and Falkingham (1992), p 1.
10. *The Independent*, 3 November 1998.
11. Tinker (1992), p 235.
12. I am not a supporter of the ideology of limited, 'sustainable' growth that, I believe, has become a convenient apology for slower growth.
13. Johnson and Falkingham (1992), p 2.
14. The number of 'elderly dependents' is also only a subset of 'more elderly people', since to be over 64 is not the same as to be dependent. This further deflates the significance of the arithmetical dependency ratio. We will return to address this and other myths of the dependency ratio in chapter 4.

2· Ageing in Perspective

Ageing is a promiscuous term. It is used in many different contexts and can refer to diverse trends. For example, ageing can be used as a neutral term which means almost the same as 'living'. From the day one is born, one lives and one ages. On the other hand most everyday usage of the term applies to the elderly, or those close to being old. It is seen as a more marked feature of older people – of one's elderly relations or neighbours: 'Aunt Joan is looking older these days', or 'She is showing her age', or 'She's ageing fast'.

The use of the term 'ageing' in specialist studies is no less muddled. For example, there is a discussion about biological ageing. Why do people age biologically? Is biological ageing a form of disease? Is ageing therefore treatable? On the other hand there is the field of gerontology, and the study of entire populations ageing. This is much more to do with changing structures, or age group proportions, of a population than to do with the combined effect of lots of individuals growing old. General physicians, geriatricians, economists and sociologists also have their own, and overlapping, perspectives on ageing.

The subject of this book is not about individuals getting older but the distinct social process of the collective ageing of society. However, a problem to address is that the two are not usually perceived as distinct. More than this, many of the conventional fears about demographic ageing rest upon a confusion of the different types of ageing. As A Warnes expresses it: two 'burdens' tend to be confused in the discussion on ageing – that to society, including the fiscal cost on government budgets, and that to the individual, both to the old themselves and perhaps, to their relatives and carers.[1]

The usual stereotype of individual old age is 'a period of unavoidable retreat, in the face of both ill health and poverty, of gradual withdrawal into passivity and dependence'.[2] This popular imagery serves to legitimise the public policy response to a different type of ageing: demographic ageing. One of the objectives of this chapter is to challenge this perception in order to provide the foundation for questioning many of these public policies.

A big part of the hold that fear about population ageing (in the gerontological sense) exerts is that many commentators superimpose an everyday understanding of ageing, the worry about growing old as individuals, onto the demographic trend. This confusion inflates a sense of the dangerous implications of ageing populations. When specialists and politicians warn of the demographic time bomb, it strikes a chord, as our semi-consciousness flashes to our own personal ageing time bombs – most individuals fear retirement and dependence.

This chapter is about pulling apart this key conflation between the sense of getting old as individuals and the process of population ageing. It will show why it is not legitimate to transfer assumptions about ageing made in the one context to the other context. In doing this it will dispel many of the confusions which litter the discussion around the demographic time bomb.

A key purpose here is to de-naturalise demographic ageing and reveal its social determinants. The main mystifications arise when the biological assumptions about individual ageing falsely extend into the realm of ageing populations. The chapter aims to de-naturalise the ageing discussion also by showing that the socio-economic implications of population ageing are not akin to some iron natural law. In reality the impact of ageing upon the fortunes of society depends upon other man-made factors. Demographic ageing is not natural. Nor are its consequences for society pre-determined.

Specifically it will point out a number of features of both population and individual ageing which tend to be obscured, covered up or ignored. Each of these should challenge one or more of the preconceptions which make demographic ageing such a concern:

• Neither population ageing, nor its implications for society, are natural. What humankind does in the future will impact upon both more than is usually assumed.
• Population ageing is not new, yet the preoccupation with it is. Why?

- Population ageing is not increasing steadily and inexorably, yet the belief is that the bomb expands until it can contain itself no longer and explodes.
- Old people are not all the same. They do not express the identical characteristics of a single homogenous group. Certainly it is widely misplaced to categorise all, or even most, old people as 'dependent'.
- Individual ageing is not a fixed process either but is also socially influenced. For example, since the older populations being forecast will contain more older people this will impact upon the social and economic roles of the elderly.

What is ageing?

Growing old seems like a natural process. The normal conception of ageing – defined in summary as the passing of life-years – is of a process of inexorable maturing and development. However, we should be sensitive to, and differentiate between, several different sorts of ageing: chronological, biological, and demographic.

As we pass along this list the natural component becomes less and less significant, and social factors exert greater influence. When we reach demographic ageing the social aspect is key. Conventionally, though, naturalistic conceptions are still believed to prevail even in this latter form of ageing – the one this book addresses most.

What is meant by chronological, biological or demographic ageing and how do they differ? The chronological is the most straightforward. It continues from birth until death. People age chronologically as they clock up their birthdays.

However, the pace of biological ageing is much less rigid or natural. It varies between societies, between different historical times, and between people. This is well recognised, but it is not always fully appreciated. For example, the predominant image of getting 'old' is of personal physiological and biological decline. It is usually accepted that this requires medical treatment. But even the recognition and acceptance of this possibility of medical intervention reveals that individual biological ageing is not as natural as it first appears. Health care can offset, stall or even reverse biological ageing.

Social intervention in this way can postpone 'old age'. Drugs and medical support can prolong active life. What a person can do at a particular age changes. It means individuals can become 'old' later. Being old can start at different ages.

Social development significantly extends both life expectancy and active life expectancy. Rising living standards and better public health measures, such as sanitation and cleaner water supplies, make it more likely people reach a mature age, in a healthier state, and hence experience 'ageing' for longer. The French demographer Patrice Bourdelais has usefully argued the need for a quantitative measure of 'equivalent-age' that is sensitive to improvements in health and life expectancy over time. He establishes that the reality of ageing has changed. A 60 year old in the 1990s is not the same as a 60 year old in the 1820s.[3]

Using this approach Bourdelais shows that since the age, in years, at which 'old age' begins increases over time, the percentage of old people in the population at any point can remain constant even while the age structure changes. More people above a certain age, say 64, does not equal the same increase in 'dependent' old persons. From this perspective a dynamic population can be said not to age at all. The steady, ascending lines on demographers' charts and their alarmist talk of the implications, find one answer in Bourdelais's horizontal measures of the aged in France.[4]

Also people of the same historical period can 'feel their years' at different ages. Social class and the type of working life one has endured are influential in this respect. Contrary to the usual presentation of everyone beyond the statutory retirement age as a homogenous group, with common age-related problems and for whom a monolithic response is required from the rest of society, people become 'old' at different ages.

One reason for the confusion about ageing being natural is this common blurring of the social component of biological ageing. But there is still (with the present state of technology at least) a natural component to biological ageing which appears to legitimise the narrowly naturalistic view. This is that life cannot be 'unnaturally' extended for ever.

Ultimately biological ageing cannot be resisted indefinitely. Individuals cannot be young for ever. The search for an elixir of everlasting youth has so far been one of the more futile of human endeavours ranking alongside the attempts to turn base metal into gold. There is no disputing the truth – if not the fatalist sentiment – of the bumper sticker: 'Life is a cabaret, old chum ... then you grow old and die.'[5]

Naturalistic notions of ageing are also encouraged by the association between old age and the act of dying – a transition from one state of nature, life, to another, death. This is an unsurprising view given that in many developed countries most people who die are old. In Britain, for example, over four-fifths of people who die are over 65. This link between old age and death seems further to confirm the common naturalistic perception of ageing.

This confusion between the natural and the social becomes much more problematic when it is extended to demographic, or population, ageing. Although population ageing and individual ageing are different phenomena, perceptions of the former tend to be influenced by everyday images of what ageing is assumed to mean for individuals. Most pertinent for this discussion, the notion of society being pulled down, or collapsing, under the weight of an ageing population seems only 'common sense', when it is considered that at a certain point chronological and biological ageing tends to be associated with a greater dependence and reliance on others, whether family, friends or public services.

Later chapters will show that with respect to economic participation and to health the conventional view of older people being a burden for others is much exaggerated. However, the more fundamental issue to be tackled is the illegitimate way the natural element of biological ageing becomes associated with demographic ageing. The fact that there would seem to be a big difference between societies and people, that populations, unlike individual people, do not die, has not lessened the confusion. On the contrary many social Darwinists have employed the image of shrinking or ageing populations as an expression or even cause of national decline, as if whole societies really could die out.

The danger which flows from the naturalistic outlook on population ageing is that its supposed social implications – such as the unsustainable burden upon the welfare state and for government budgets or pension funds – seem 'natural', too. The 'problems' of an ageing population appear as pre-ordained and as unalterable. Anthony Giddens, the British sociologist, draws out some of the consequences of the conventional naturalised notion of ageing: 'Ageing is treated as "external", as something that happens to one … . Against such a backdrop it isn't surprising that the population over age sixty-five is widely regarded as a medical and financial burden on the rest of the national community.'[6] Just as individual ageing appears out of personal control – at a certain time in their lives, individuals begin to feel old and maybe dependent upon others – so this is felt to be a characteristic of population ageing, a problem which is outside human control.

The commonsense assumption is that the ageing dynamic as well as its supposed implications are inevitable, unstoppable and unending. Hence the naturalisation of societal ageing sustains many of today's myths on this issue. For example, the need to cut state pension provision is depoliticised and appears plain common sense because of the inevitably relentless pace of increasing costs arising from the ageing population.

As John Vincent describes, 'Apocalyptic demographers have provided the new right financiers with ways in which to convince people that current pension arrangements are unsustainable.'[7] But one fact this perspective ignores is that population ageing has been going on for some time. Most developed industrialised countries are not in a demographically new situation. So the contemporary alarmism about the problem of ageing needs to be contrasted with the past.

In many circumstances and time-periods population ageing is an incidental matter which is rarely commented upon. In others it appears as a big threat or danger. How can this variation be explained? A clue is provided if we recognise that the higher profile ageing sometimes attains does not take the form of a neutral interest in the phenomenon. Ageing, in times when it is considered, is usually seen as a problem or a danger. In these conditions it provides both a metaphor for troubled times more generally, and can also play a role as alibi for other problems which have different non-demographic causes. In the 1980s, for instance, the widespread tendency emerged in Britain and other countries to blame population ageing for the wider economic malaise and the difficulties of sustaining social spending. In the 1990s, which many in the West have dubbed 'anxious times', there is receptivity for the naturalistic panic of the demographic time bomb.

The consequences of the confusing conflation of individual and demographic ageing is compounded by the way the naturalistic connotations reinforce the view that people can do little to overcome their problems, even though they are really social not natural difficulties. Ageing is understood as outside human control. Little can be done about its supposed economic and social consequences. The ageing fetish is more than an 'innocent', diversionary scapegoat. It becomes an apology for many social problems.

This is the big problem with much mainstream gerontology (the study of ageing). The social implications of ageing are both exaggerated and also erroneously presented as immutable, rigid natural laws.

Through the prism of demographic shifts, society's problems are interpreted in a fatalistic manner.

Specifically three inter-related, but false, assumptions are often made about population ageing – that it is natural, steadily inexorable and unending. In contrast this chapter will show that ageing is predominantly social, modifiable by future fertility fluctuations, and that social and practical factors ensure that it will come to an end. The main argument is that nothing about the ageing discussion is as natural as it first seems. A demystification of the fetish starts with a grasp of what causes population ageing.

The social character of old age

The definition of an ageing society is that over time there is a rising proportion of old people within the whole population. That seems straightforward. But is it? Who precisely are 'old people'? Ask elderly people themselves and one can get results different from the stereotype. Surveys of elderly people about how 'old' they feel, confirm the social element of ageing. Paul Thompson summarised the results of one as running 'completely counter to the stereotypes of old age'.[8] You can always find 65 year olds, and even 75 years olds who deny they are 'old'. And by the active lives they lead that is a fair statement. There are always some people *older* than others, but when and how do people become legitimately characterised as *old*? We therefore need to establish first what we mean by old people. We can look at this in two ways: at what age does a person first become 'old', and, when does 'the old' become a meaningful category? Both are socially determined. In answering these questions there are insights offered by critical gerontologists, such as Alan Walker and Chris Phillipson, who have argued that the experience of old age is determined more by economic and social factors and less by biological or individual ones.[9]

When does old age begin?

In Britain today the usual assumption is that old age begins at 65. But why 65? Think of some 65 year olds you know personally or in the public eye – they do not all seem equally 'old'. The arbitrary year 65 as the date of the onset of old age alerts us that it is a socially constructed year.[10] It is not that something biological or physiological or psychological always happens to people at age 65. Rather, society organises itself so that the year 65 becomes the dividing line between young and old for everyone in that society.

This tends to be forgotten. Instead most views of when old age begins just assume implicitly that it is naturally and biologically determined. But the age when 'old age' starts is heavily influenced by certain social, man-made influences and practices.

In particular the existence of 'old age' as a recognisable category, and, therefore, of ageing beyond a certain number of years, is a result of human progress. It is a function of human success in improving health standards so that some people can live longer. Contrary to all the contemporary negative notions of ageing as decay and burden, the fact that ageing is discussed as a significant phenomenon is the positive product of mankind's relative triumph over death.

Bourdelais' search for an equivalent-age measure takes him to chart how the threshold of old age changes over time. He defines his measure of old age as the age at which there is a certain common expectation of future life expectancy, say ten years of life left.

His results show that on average French males reached old age at 59.6 years in 1825, rising hardly at all to 60.6 years in 1937, but increasing more sharply through the Second World War and the post-War period to 67.4 years in 1984. This increase over the past half century is the result of declining mortality rates.

The determination of when old age begins is more than just a product of human progress in extending active life expectancy. It is also a social convention. The defining age of when one becomes old has not been common between historical periods and between countries.

The determining age for old age even varies between countries of a similar level of social and economic development. Throughout this century, and across different advanced countries, to be old could mean to be above 50 or above 60 or above 65 or above 70; these and even more ages have all been used. The convention changes over time.

Many factors play a role in establishing this convention. For example, the development of early geriatric medicine as a distinct discipline – itself a human achievement, and the product of previous progress in extending life expectancy – is doubtless one of the influences in establishing a sense of when old age begins. Geriatricians for a start need to be able to categorise and identify their subjects – the elderly.

H Kirk locates the first categorisation of old age at about the middle of the nineteenth century: reviewing 'nineteenth century medical works on old age there is much evidence to suggest that credit should be given to the Belgian mathematician A Quetelet ... for defining the start of "old age" ... "From 60 to 65 years of age, viability loses much of its energy, that is to say, the probability of life then becomes small.' (*Sur L'Homme et le Developpement de ses Facultés*, Bruxelles: L Hauman, 1836, p178).'[11]

Laslett recalls that it was a little later, 'in 1906, that Professor William Osler, later Sir William Osler, Bart., the most eminent physician of his generation in both Britain and America, made his notorious allusions to "the comparative uselessness" of people over 40 and the entire dispensability of people over 60.'[12]

The assumption is that this is a consequence of some physical defect or deterioration which is part of the association of old age with biological ageing. The classification of the medical study of the ageing condition as an epidemiology, as an illness, at the end of the nineteenth century contributed to this stereotype.

Kirk indicates the way the medical conception of old age extended into other areas. 'Medicalised' models of biological ageing began to develop extensively and attain wider currency.[13] This contributed to naturalistic explanations for equating retirement from work at an elderly age with the onset of bad health as a biological inevitability. This notion flourished despite the importance of other social factors in explaining the poor health of many of those forced to stop work. For example, for many working class people, especially manual workers, ill-health for the retired was simply a fact of life. It was not a natural fact of life, but one which was the product of years of debilitating work in bad conditions.[14]

Reviewing developments in late nineteenth century Germany, Kirk went on to argue the link between the medicalisation of ageing with pensions too:

'The developing biomedical images of old age were given much space in encyclopaedias, dictionaries and popular health literature after 1870. Therefore, the defined existence of old-age limits must also have influenced the legislators responsible for the first National Acts on old-age pensions'.[15]

Retirement and pensions – these were the key social factors which stand out above all others in determining the customary view of the threshold of old age: the normal age of retirement from work, and the closely-linked age of entitlement to pensions. The introduction of generalised pension and retirement schemes from the late nineteenth century developed in tandem with a consensus concept of old age and of when it begins. The common retirement age became seen as the time old age set in.

Janet Roebuck describes how, as a result of these innovations, 'twentieth century society in general (has tended) to accept the government's "pension age" or "retirement age" as the convenient dividing line between mature adulthood and old age'.[16] In order to emphasise this conclusion she contrasts the more fluid view of old age in earlier periods. An enquiry into the 1832 Poor Law, for example, indicated that there were a wide range of ages from the late 40s to the 80s at which the qualifying label, 'aged and infirm', might be applied.[17]

Pratt, too, perceives that 'elderly consciousness' emerged out of, rather than contributed to, the introduction of pensions.[18] Therborn endorses the significance of pensions in defining old age. He writes that 'the social prerequisite of old age as the third age of human activity, rather than as one of decay and waiting for death, was the establishment of pensions as a sufficient source of income for a decent standard of living'.[19] Although pensions were designed to allow people to withdraw from employment before physiological decline set in, the handing over of a retirement pension signified entering a new age of dependency which in thought usually retained its negative physical connotations.

The equation between pension age and old age did not get established immediately pensions were introduced. The relationship took time to embed itself in customary thinking. Internationally, the first state pensions were introduced in Bismarck's Germany in 1889. At this early stage there was still no direct relationship between pension age and standard notions of old age, not least because relatively so few lived long enough to draw them. Life expectancy was then about 50 years in Germany though the qualifying age for receipt of pension was 70.

In Britain discussions around state pensions for the old began at about the same time. Those involved had little definite to go on in establishing an appropriate age for commencement. Sufficient conflicting evidence was available to support almost any age past 40 as a suitable one for the start of old age as the entitlement for pension. Ironically it took the setting of a pension/retirement age to create a consensus of when old age begins.

The 1898 Old Age Pensions Committee eventually plumped for 65 as the pension age, justifying its decision as the age 'to which there is most concurrence of opinion'.[20] Lloyd George, the government minister responsible, had different ideas when introducing the 1908 Old Age Pensions Act. Setting the age requirement five years higher he 'made it clear that the main reason why the government had chosen the age limit of 70 was economy'.[21] Saving the Exchequer money was behind the setting of a high pension age – an approach which many industrialised countries, including Britain, have revisited in recent years in raising the official state pension/retirement age.

Neville Chamberlain's 1925 Pension Act reduced the male pension age to today's level of 65 years. Chamberlain's justification for lowering the age was linked not to narrow government financial considerations but to the state of the wider economy and the labour market. He claimed the lowering of the pension age would encourage people to stop working earlier and thus help bring about a reduction in the high, inter-war levels of unemployment.

The other innovation in 1925 was the explicit link Chamberlain floated between pension entitlement and retirement from work. This helped to reinforce the customary notion of when old age begins. A fixed age of retirement, more than pensions alone, fosters the stereotype than people above a certain elderly age have moved onto a new stage in life. As John Myles writes, 'the social character of old age is very much a product of the welfare state ... "old age became retirement" '.[22]

The phenomenon of retirement is of relatively recent origin, going back even less time than the history of pensions. At the turn of this century it was still unusual for older workers to retire. In 1901 two-thirds of males aged 65 and over were in full-time work. This compares with today when less than 8 per cent of over 64s do any type of formal paid work.

In Britain, Germany and America a fixed age for retirement only began to be introduced around the turn of the century. For example, in the British Civil Service compulsory retirement at 65 was introduced for some in 1890 and extended to more employees in 1898. With this development, retirement started to become seen as a significant event in the process of individual ageing.

The spread of an inflexible retirement age contributed also to the creation of a particular stereotype of the elderly, of the retired, as useless. Compulsory retirement implied people over a certain age could not be expected to be productive. Retirement brings the stigma for the individual retiree of being past it, of no longer being able to contribute to society, of being a drain on the working section of the population.

The age of retirement has never been determined by natural, biological factors but always by social circumstances. Most importantly it is linked to the provision of a public pension. This extends to the existence of other formal support mechanisms for the elderly.

For example, Kasturi Sen makes the point that in many Third World countries there is still no formal retirement age. In the absence of formal support mechanisms, economic participation rates for older people are high by comparison to those of their ageing Western counterparts. The differences in labour force participation rates between older men in developed and developing countries are considerable. They range from less than 2 per cent in Austria to 85 per cent in Malawi.[23]

In specific circumstances narrower labour market considerations can also be influential. To return to the developed countries it is, in particular, when the labour market is slack and unemployment rises that earlier retirement is often encouraged. In fact, retirement as a phenomenon only really took off as common practice during the 1930s. In the conditions of economic slump its use was accelerated as a means of reducing unemployment. Its limited significance before then explains why it took until the negotiations leading up to the Beveridge Report during 1941 and 1942 for retirement to be seriously discussed as the official condition for receipt of a state pension (despite what Chamberlain had floated in 1925).[24] In the end the state pension only became a retirement, as opposed to an old age entitlement with the 1946 National Insurance Act. This act introduced universal pensions for all those who had been in full time employment.

Retirement at 65 became the norm for the 1950s and 1960s, making this the conventional birthday for 'old age' to begin. With some justification Giddens answers his own question: what is old age?, writing: 'Old age at 65 is a creation, pure and simple, of the welfare state'.[25]

Since the 1970s the trend towards earlier retirement in most countries of the industrialised world has once more clouded the picture of when old age starts. This has extended the possibility for older people to withdraw from productive activity well before any significant physiological decline. Earlier retirement, in advance of the statutory pension age, has been widespread as a response to the sluggish economic conditions of the past two decades. It has provided many governments with a politically acceptable means for disguising the level of redundancies and the reduced availability of employment possibilities. The effect though is to lower further the everyday conception of when old age begins. Retirement at any age – 50, 55, 60, 65+ – still has the connotation of being 'too old', and moving into the 'dependent' period of life.

As a result differing, and younger, conceptions of old age have started to emerge. Referring to this trend the French gerontologist Guillemard has argued: 'the new social definition of old age that has emerged is ... a function of the labour market and its needs'.[26] It appears that with earlier retirement people grow 'old' earlier.

The emergence of old people

For convenience the rest of this book will use the 65 year old threshold of 'old age' (unless otherwise stated) as it is the one most widely used in Britain – being the statutory age of male retirement – and this text engages primarily with the British discussion and literature on ageing.

When does 'the old' as a term gain wide currency? In contrast to what is fatuously said about the poor, the old have most definitely *not* always been with us. Of course, throughout human history a minority of people have always survived into the older age groups but the over-64s were an insignificant proportion of the population in all countries much prior to the nineteenth century.

In a world where infectious disease was rampant and not yet possible to control few survived beyond 'three score year' and five, never mind the 'and ten' of the bible. Even by 1900 the percentage of over-64s in Britain was less than 5 per cent.

The use of the terms 'elderly', 'the old', or 'old people', to refer to a distinct segment of society is therefore almost meaningless much before the twentieth century. It is only as a consequence of mainly nineteenth century social advances that survival to higher ages has become more frequent this century. Progress in curbing premature death has allowed both the numbers of old to grow and the category 'old age' to take off.

A scientific or academic interest in old age, and therefore in ageing, is even more recent. Eric Midwinter, the director of the Centre for Policy on Ageing, remarked at the turn of the 1990s that 'the touchstone of old age as some form of specific discipline or subject has barely existed for half a century in the so-called 'developed' societies, let alone in the vast remainder of the world'.[27]

Take one obvious example to which we have already referred: the branch of health care dealing with the illnesses of older people. Nothing akin to geriatric medicine existed much before the middle of the nineteenth century. Before then old age was such a limited concept that it was even difficult to make generalisations regarding the views of different epochs about the medical aspects of ageing.[28] The term 'geriatrics', in fact, was only introduced into the English language in 1914, when used for the first time in print by an American doctor I Nascher.[29]

More significantly, it was not until the end of the 1940s that geriatric medicine began to emerge as a substantive medical specialism.[30] This was not the result of neglect or oversight but mainly because older people did not constitute a weighty social grouping much before that time.

What causes demographic ageing?

So far this chapter has emphasised highlighting the relative newness of 'the old' as a category. It is predominantly a phenomenon of the twentieth century. This section will expand on what seems like the opposite point – already touched upon – that there is nothing new about demographic ageing. It will explain that population ageing is not qualitatively distinctive as a process to account for today's peculiar preoccupation with it.

While demographic ageing is new in historical terms – in comparison to feudal or classical times – it is not sufficiently novel to explain the current pessimism about the unsustainable burden of the elderly. This raises the question of why there is a contemporary panic.

One can answer this in one of two ways. Either, mankind has been ignorant of the real demographic ageing process under way until some recent discovery has provided enlightenment. Or, this concern has little to do with the changing age structure of the population, in which case another contemporary non-population related factor, or factors, must underlie current anxieties, which for some reason have become focused upon 'ageing'.

As population trends have been an issue of some scientific interest at least since the publication of Thomas Malthus's *Essay on the Principle of Population* in 1798, the former explanation lacks conviction. Instead the latter approach is much more valid. Other developments are manifesting themselves today as worries about population ageing. First, though, we need to establish what is the same and what is different about demographic ageing today.

An ageing population, in summary, is one where the average age is rising. An increasing proportion of the population belongs to higher age groups. In most contemporary discussion the focus is on the greater portion of over-64s. An ageing population is therefore usually illustrated by the increase in the percentage of people in the 65 and over age group. (See Charts 1 and 2.)

Ageing populations are a feature of all industrialising societies. The process goes back at the earliest to the late eighteenth century in France and, more widely, in many other economically advanced countries, to the second half of the nineteenth century. One point always to remember, especially when the fashionable apocalyptic and gloomy prognoses about ageing are considered later, is that demographic ageing is almost always a positive expression of human development and progress.

This happens in two ways which are explored further below. First, ageing arises in response to winning the battle against premature death at all ages. Elderly people themselves tend to live longer. However, this has been a small influence on ageing historically. A greater influence on ageing comes from younger people living longer as a result of the curbing of widescale fatal disease and illness. For example, in Britain as in many developed countries, diseases such as cholera and typhoid are now virtually non-existent. As these 'escapees from death' grow old, the age structure shifts upwards, taking most effect one or two generations later. (Though if mortality continues to fall even faster among young people this will offset this influence on the trend towards an older population.)

Second, and even more influential, has been the fall in fertility rates. As Emily Grundy, from the Age Concern Institute of Gerontology, states 'in most populations fertility is the most important determinant of age structure'.[17] Fertility rates tend to decline in rough parallel with the influence of advancing economic and social development. Falling fertility brings ageing in its wake because with fewer young people the average age of the population rises; society ages.

Therefore, despite all the conventional negative connotations, the progress of both biological and demographic ageing, though distinct as explained above, has one thing in common. Though through differing mechanisms, each are expressions of human success stories.

The demographic transition

There is much mainstream discussion of the 'demographic transition' as underlying the ageing process today. In summary, this transition

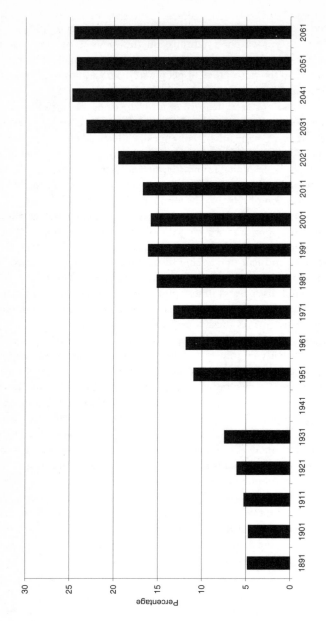

Chart 1: Britain's Ageing Population: the proportion of over 64 year olds
Source: OPCS (1993) and (1995)

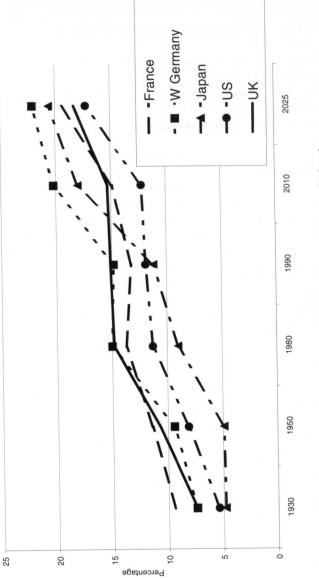

Chart 2: Proportion of the total population aged 65 and over

Source: Davis (1987), p275.

expresses the move in age structure as societies change from high mortality, high fertility levels to low mortality, low fertility ones. This shift is the combined product of economic development, industrialisation and urbanisation in today's developed countries.

The demographic transition is one of the most influential ideas of the twentieth century demography.[32] For example, the United Nations (UN) special 1993 *Demographic Yearbook* on the topic of ageing, puts the transition centre-stage.[33] In fact, such emphasis is misplaced for understanding the ageing process today in industrialised countries. The interest in this phenomenon is worth exploring.

For a start the idea of demographic transition has become fetishised by many users of the term. What could only at best be a reflection of reality has assumed an unjustified significance as representing the essence of the real process of population change. With the frequent assumption of its general applicability the term implies a rigid common historical process. The theory is often put forward as of relevance, not just to the historical ageing patterns in the advanced industrial countries, but also to population trends in the rest of the world. While adequate as an approximation to past population trends in some parts of the world it is not helpful in the way it is more widely used, either as applicable to the Third World today, or as a predictor of future trends universally.

The argument is generally based on a faulty premise because there are no natural abstract laws for human population growth. The causes and influences of population trends should always be examined in the context of a given society. Hence the danger of any population model – the demographic transition one, or any other. Models tend to blinker their users from identifying historically and socially specific understandings of demographic reality.

Also, to the extent to which the model had some validity, it is as a description of the past. The transition has already happened in the advanced industrial countries. It is no longer a significant determinant of ageing in the industrial world. Therefore, the catastrophist discussion of current ageing patterns in the West cannot be based upon transition effects. Before these contemporary factors are explained it is necessary to demystify the demographic transition process so that its historical relevance can be identified and, then, on the basis that it has little role today, it can be eliminated from current enquiries.

It is true that the initial, secular, trend towards ageing is associated with the demographic transition. It does approximate to what happened in the past in many earlier industrialising countries.[34] For example, elements of the demographic transition can easily be observed in Britain, the rest of Europe, the United States, Canada, Australia, New Zealand and Japan.

This argument is useful in highlighting a significant counter-intuitive point about ageing. It is commonly believed that the main factor behind ageing is rising life expectancy: people, especially older people, are living longer.[35] This is not the case. Ageing's main determinant is the secular fall in fertility rates, not people living longer old-ages. Changing fertility rates are more important than changing mortality rates in fuelling ageing. The historical shift from the relatively young age structure of a century ago to the relatively old one of today is largely a consequence of the transition from relatively high to low fertility which was set in motion in most developed countries in the last third of the nineteenth century. (See chart 3.)

Richard Smith explains the way this process works: 'A fall in fertility reduces those in the lower age groups and correspondingly increases the percentage of the population in the upper age groups'.[36] The average age of any population is more affected by the relative numbers of people in all the different age groups than by a change in the absolute numbers in one particular age-group. With respect to population ageing this means that a relative shift in the proportions from young to old is more important than the absolute numbers of elderly people.

Among professional demographers this is not a new discovery. One of the world's foremost authorities on demographic ageing, Nathan Keyfitz, recounted in 1975 that 'demographers know that a population that is increasing slowly has a higher proportion of old people than one that is increasing rapidly, and that differences in birth rates have a larger influence on the age distribution than do differences in death rates'.[37]

Historically then, ageing is a product not of changes in death rates, but of what happens at the opposite end of the life cycle – at the point of birth. The trend-fall in fertility rates, not mortality rates, was for a long time the most important factor driving ageing. This is sometimes described as 'fertility-dominated' ageing.[38] With each successive generation smaller than its predecessor the average age of the population had to rise. As a result the proportion, and not necessarily the numbers, of old people tended to rise.

The demographic transition thesis is a way of illustrating this trend. For ease of exposition the demographic transition is usually broken

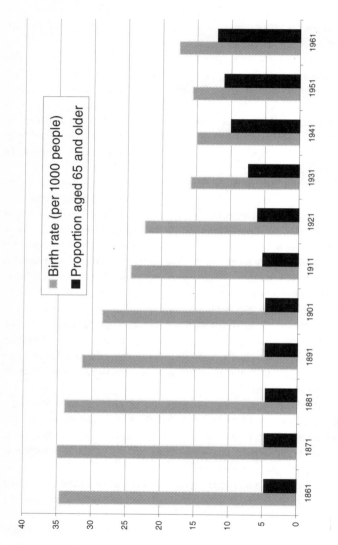

Chart 3: Falling fertility and ageing in England and Wales
Source: Keyfitz and Flieger (1968)

down into four stages. In different countries stages were more or less concentrated and operated over varying time spans.

Stage 1	High fertility, high mortality	Stationary population
Stage 2	High fertility, falling mortality	Younger, larger population
Stage 3	Falling fertility, low mortality	Ageing population
Stage 4	Low fertility, low mortality	In time a stationary population, with a higher average age than stage 1

Stage one is the stationary state before the transition. The usual picture is of a backward, non-industrialised, agrarian economy experiencing high death rates paralleled by high birth rates. The high birth and death rates tend to balance each other out to produce a broadly stable population size. As a result society has a youthful complexion. The age structure picture has a pyramid shape. (See diagram 1(a).)

Stage two shows the impact of industrialisation, higher agricultural production and the better control of famine and disease. It is marked by a fairly sharp fall in the mortality rate which is the positive by-product of economic development. Falling death rates are socially influenced by the cumulative fruits of economic progress.

A higher standard of living, better diet and improvements in sanitation and sewage, public health, hygiene and some medical knowledge mean fewer people die from poverty, disease and malnutrition.[39] Life expectancy tends to rise. Initially, the high birth rates of the earlier age persist.

Even though during stage two individuals are starting to live longer to a greater age, the paradoxical impact on the age structure of the population is, in the first instance, for it to get even younger, not older. This happens regardless of any assumption about which age group is affected most by falling mortality rates.

This is because the main determinant of the age distribution of the population is still the course of fertility. And at this point fertility remains high, meaning a large young population. In practice, mortality rate falls are also first concentrated among children, which further emphasises the youth bias in the population.

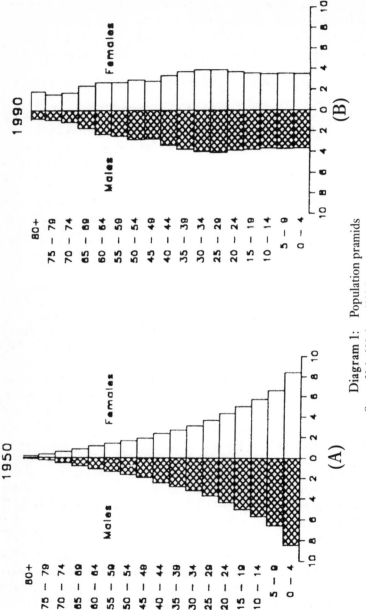

Diagram 1:   Population pramids
Source: United Nations, *1993 Demographic Yearbook*

The foremost influence on the demographic shift in stage two is not what is happening to mortality rates but what is happening, or rather not happening, to the fertility rate. High fertility is not at first affected by the broader economic and social developments. A large number of people continue to be born and with the lower mortality rate, fewer of these youngsters die creating a youth 'bulge' which weights the entire population downwards in age.

Not only will this first generation be larger as a result of declining infant and youth mortality but there will be a supplementary 'echo' effect when 20 to 30 years later this generation comes to child-bearing age and starts to produce its own offspring. Lower mortality levels also mean that there will be more women of child bearing age and fewer of them will be widows.

In contrast to the effect on population *structure*, the course of mortality levels have the greater impact upon population *size*. As the population becomes younger it also grows. This can be quite rapid depending upon the pace of divergence between the falling mortality rate and the constant high fertility rate.

Stage three starts when the fertility rate begins to fall, mirroring the earlier declines in the mortality rate. Ageing begins. Keyfitz explains that although the correlation is far from perfect, 'history seems to be saying that with more or less lag, industrialisation has led to reduced family size'.[40]

The slower response of the birth rate than the death rate to economic change is often attributed to the view that fertility decline depends more strongly on the alteration of established customs and practice. To put it crudely the mortality rate has a stronger objective social-technical determinant, while the fertility rate is to a greater extent subjectively influenced as a social-cultural process. Kuznets makes this point as follows:

> 'The reduction in mortality was accompanied, but not simultaneously, by a decline in fertility … . Modern economic growth has provided opportunities for a great reduction in death rates and inducements and requirements for a marked reduction in birth rates.'[41]

Among the socio-economic factors linked with the rate of fertility earlier this century were: rates of mortality for people of child rearing age (both women and men), marriage rates, the normal age of marriage, and the cultural role of the family. In the more recent period the proportion of women at work, the availability of childcare facilities, and developments in contraceptive and abortion technology have all played a part.[42] Overall some of these factors embody a causal element; others are co-factors brought about by other determinants.

Social class also has a bearing on the matter of birth rates. In most case fertility decline began in the middle classes and spread much later to the working class. (This contributed to the particular fears from the established élite in the early part of this century about the decline of 'their' class and of being swamped by the masses.[43])

At different times different factors predominated in the shift to smaller family size. In economically backward, mainly agrarian societies, a large number of children was often necessary for economic survival. For example, before the intensive use of technology, agricultural production is dependent on the extensive cultivation of the soil by large numbers of labourers. The progression to industrialisation and intensive production on the other hand begins to limit this incentive for having large numbers of children.

Urbanisation, especially, introduces pressures in the same direction. The introduction of even rudimentary social welfare systems from the end of the nineteenth century offsets the need for large extended families to look after the ill and the elderly.

Once fertility begins to decline the average age of the population will immediately start to rise, as each cohort born is smaller than the preceding one. The rate of population growth slows too. However, the ageing of the population structure tends to show itself in a marked way only after about a 30 to 50 year period of falling fertility.

The population is ageing overwhelmingly 'from below'. The population gets older not because of what is happening to the lives of elderly people but because of the fall in the relative numbers of babies joining the human stock. It has always been the case historically that a population ages more rapidly by reason of a reduced birth rate than as a result of a decreased death rate.[44]

When the fertility rate has fallen to around the replacement level – the level at which births balance deaths, maintaining a stationary population – we reach stage four. (In Britain today the replacement rate is about 2.1 children per woman.) The demographic ageing of a population continues for approximately another three generations after fertility has ended its decline and reached replacement levels. This is how long it takes the successively smaller birth cohorts to grow old. Thereafter, mortality decline *can* replace fertility decline as the main factor affecting the age structure. Once low mortality levels have been attained there is little scope for further significant reductions in mortality for infants, children and younger adults. Any further fall in mortality will tend disproportionately to affect older people and so can enhance the ageing tendency.

This is both because older people are already a larger proportion of the population and also because once mortality is low the vast majority of deaths occur among older people. Therefore improvements in mortality rates, for either social or medical reasons, will tend to predominate among already older people. This has been the trend in most industrialised countries since the 1960s. The United Nations *Demographic Yearbook* in 1993 confirmed that in low mortality countries the 'overwhelming majority of all deaths' is among the existing elderly.[45] It went on to report that since 1960 the expectation of life at age 60 had increased significantly in especially Japan, France, Germany, Spain, Switzerland and Austria.

When old age mortality falls in this way the population will tend to age further, but now 'from above'. On its own, though, this influence on the pace of ageing will be much weaker than the previous fertility-driven ageing. Eric Midwinter succinctly summarises the opinion of most demographers: 'When all the points about decreasing mortality and morbidity have been made, the main feature marking the rising proportion of older people is the dramatic fall in the fraction of younger people.'[46] One supporting argument, which has significant medical support, is that further declines in old age mortality will be much slower than over the past 20-30 years. This is an expression of the obvious point that there is a finite limit to the trend of falling old age mortality as elderly people have to die at some time. At this point, if fertility were in the region of the replacement rate, population numbers and the age structure would tend to stabilise. The age structure pictured by the model now looks rectangular. (See diagram 1(b).) By the end of the demographic transition the population may be static again, as at the start, but the average age is much higher.

To summarise: contrary to intuition derived from individual ageing, demographic ageing is much more influenced by changes in fertility levels than it is to do with reduced mortality levels. The dominant influence on the pace of ageing is the change in population structure resulting mainly from birth rate movements, which shifts the average age of the population. These cohort effects from differing fertility rates upon population structure are much more significant than the aggregate effects of many individuals ageing and living longer. To the extent that the latter is significant the main trend is that more young people survive to become elderly, not that elderly people live a lot longer. Summarising the influences in Britain in the 1970s an early report from the Department of Health and Social Security (DHSS) provided the sort of balanced assessment which has become less common in more recent years:

> 'Between 1966 and 1976, the number of people aged 65 and over increased by 20 per cent ... . This change in the age structure of our population is partly due to changes in birth rates this century, partly to improvements in the expectation of life for old people, but to a much greater extent to a marked improvement in the expectation of life at younger ages.'[47]

Although the main determinants of shifts in fertility rates have changed over the past 100 years, it will be shown that the importance of 'ageing from below' remains paramount in understanding demographic ageing today. The demographic transition may no longer apply but some of its insights still do. R Smith, for example, explains that the recent rises in the percentage, rather than the number, of over 60s are primarily the result of the sharp falls in fertility after the baby boom ended in 1964. This baby 'boom and bust' phenomenon of the post-War years is the major force behind the recent experience of ageing and of the projections for this continuing into the next century.

The British experience of ageing

In common with most of the Western world Britain's population has been ageing for over a hundred years. How does the real British experience stand in comparison to the transition model? At different times different factors dominated but what has been consistent is that ageing from below has usually been more important than ageing from above. As Clark and Spengler confirm in their respected study: population ageing is 'traceable mainly and essentially to a decline in fertility or gross reproduction.'[48]

In brief, it can be argued that in the nineteenth and early twentieth century Britain some positive comparisons can be made with the demographic transition model. The British historical experience does exhibit aspects of its features. But of more relevance for our discussion about the preoccupation with ageing today, the impact of the classical 'transition' upon ageing is nearly complete and is outweighed by other contemporary influences. As Peter Laslett wrote in 1984: 'The demographic transition, where fertility and mortality fall in concert with each other and so cause the secular shift in ageing, now virtually complete in both western and eastern Europe, is nearing its end in the US ... and ... other industrial countries.'[49]

Stage four of the model would have been reached in Britain some time in the inter-war years. That was when fertility levels first stabilised. C Fraser Brockington dates the end of the third phase at around the second half of the 1930s.[50] Hence as the twentieth century draws to an end the British population would be very close to the end of an 80-90 year stage four, final period of 'transition' ageing.

Yet ageing, commentators are always advising, is a major problem for the present – and future. Therefore, if this is true, it must be by reason not of the demographic transition but of 'non-transition' considerations. The real picture is that ageing from below does remain significant in Britain today, but for different reasons than outlined by the demographic transition model.

It is primarily a result of a specific episode: the post-Second World War baby boom and succeeding baby bust. This phenomenon, of course, distorts any contemporary trend effect of the classic stage four influence on the population structure. More importantly, it has a direct impact on the population structure that far exceeds any lingering influence of the 'transition'. Meanwhile, the projections for further ageing into the twenty-first century are influenced by an additional consideration as well: the wave cohort effect of the ageing of the baby boomers. The cohort effect in demography refers to what happens as a specific generation of people ages. The baby boomers are in their early middle ages now and will start to become 'the old' in 15 to 30 years time.

The British 'transition'

Now, in more detail, the British experience of the demographic transition. The ageing of the British population today is only to a small extent caused by the lingering 'demographic transition' effects. However, these factors will be examined first, since some commentators continue to give them undue importance. This review of them, however, is designed to show that they no longer have much bearing on the population structure.

Britain's population structure was fairly constant until the nineteenth century.[51] Death rates fell first, followed later by declining fertility. In Britain – the most accessible statistics are, in fact, for England and Wales – mortality rates began to fall consistently and increasingly during the nineteenth century. This can be interpreted as expressing the 'stage two' effects of industrialisation. (See chart 4.)

In the first half of the nineteenth century the pace of mortality change was quite slow. The improvement that did take place was mostly the result of progress in social circumstances and public health measures rather than medical advances. The medical breakthrough in dealing with smallpox was an early nineteenth century exception. In general the broad social impact of economic development on living conditions held much greater importance than specific technological medical innovations.

From about the 1850s mortality levels began to fall more steeply and life expectancy at birth started to rise appreciably. In England and Wales a secular decline in fertility began in the 1870s, a bit later than in the frontrunners of France and the United States. This can be seen as marking the start of 'stage three'. An ageing population was the inevitable consequence as successive birth cohorts fell in size, shifting the whole population's 'centre of gravity' upwards.

Although the fertility rate was declining, it was still well above the replacement level. Hence the size of the whole population was still growing, with a greater bearing on the shape of the population than the ageing trend. The fall in fertility rates only began to make itself felt on the numbers of over-64s two generations later when the last 'pre-stage three' birth cohort had passed their 65th birthdays to coincide with a more stable population size.

Chart 3 earlier in this chapter shows that the proportion of elderly people in the population was constant until the start of the twentieth century and only showed a marked increase after the 1920s. At the start of the century less than 5 per cent of the population was 65 or over. By 1921 the figure was still only 6 per cent. This rose to 11 per cent by 1951 and was touching 16 per cent by the early 1990s.[52]

In Britain, as in many other developed countries, the classic 'transition' process of demographic ageing is in its final stages. After the fertility decline slows and stops, it takes about three generations for the

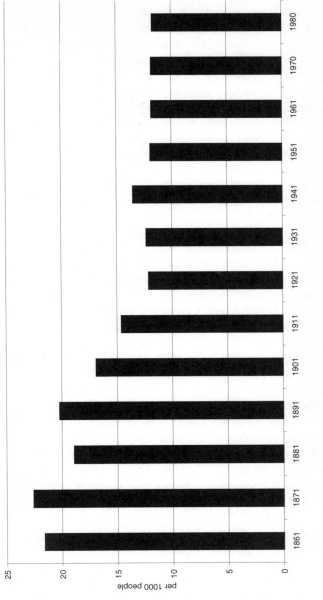

Chart 4: Falling death rate in England and Wales (per 1000 people)
Source: Keyfitz and Flieger (1968) and (1990)

ageing from below effects to work through. In many industrial countries the rapid fertility decline came to a halt in the inter-war years. This represented the end of phase three. A combination of new social conventions, greater female workplace participation levels, and the wider availability of new birth control measures, interacted to stabilise the birth rate.

Today, three-quarters of a century later, the consequences for the average age of the population have nearly dissipated. The generation born in the 1930s was the last one (until recent times) to be significantly smaller than its predecessor. As this cohort reaches old age this particular ageing from below factor disappears.

So why is the population still ageing? Some argue it is the result of the decline of elderly mortality rates. This is given too much significance. Ironically, the change in mortality that matters more to the age structure is the steady progress in reducing the mortality of young people. This is partly through the indirect 'stage three' factor as fertility rates tend to fall in the wake of declining death rates. But there is also a moderate cohort effect on ageing as the relatively larger population groups of young people resulting from fewer deaths themselves reach old age. This phenomenon is not of as great importance for understanding ageing as the others described, but needs to be understood in relation to addressing the appearance of 'too many old people'.

The improvement in life expectancy noted earlier has continued steadily through the twentieth century too. Progress has become smoother in recent years because with further medical and economic advance, epidemics and the effects of severe winters became less significant after about 1950.[53]

Throughout this century social progress in general continued to play the main causal role. The key factor in the first half was the decline in deaths from infectious diseases such as typhus, cholera, scarlet fever, smallpox, and tuberculosis. By the turn of the century the first two were virtually eliminated, with most of the rest curbed by the aftermath of the Second World War. As D Glass and E Grebenak emphasise this was not mainly the result of medical progress but of better living circumstances: 'The great reduction in deaths from infectious diseases was in the main due to sanitary or public health action.'[54]

With the development of immunology and advances in surgical technique, including anaesthesia, medical science began to have a bigger impact on mortality over the past 100 years. But even during the twentieth century the importance of the general rise in living standards in reducing mortality levels should not be underestimated. Improvements in general health care, health awareness, housing and nutrition levels have collectively played the biggest role in extending life expectancy.

Young people in the five to 25 years age range benefited most from the late nineteenth century progress in reducing mortality rates. The main cause of the saving of life in the young has been the conquest of infection. Death rates for other parts of the population did not fall until later. Infant mortality – children under one year old – did not begin to decline consistently until the start of this century and the spread of health visiting and ante-natal clinics.[55] Since 1910 there has been a considerable extension in life prospects for infants and young children.[56] (See chart 5.) (This timing was not universal; in Scandinavia infant death rates began to turn down from the 1820s).

In the inter-war years child death rates from infectious, parasitic and respiratory causes fell rapidly. The total number of male child deaths fell from 14 000 in 1921 to 8200 in 1933 (or 6.88 per thousand) to 3500 in 1945 (2.78 per thousand).[57] This represented a marked fall of a half in the 1940s.[58] Immunisation was the big factor in the early post-Second World War years. Improvements in infant mortality continue today with another marked reduction since the 1960s owing to the more widespread use of antibiotics. (See chart 6.)

This recent progress has been impressive. From 1961 to 1991 infant mortality fell by two-thirds, while neonatal (less than four weeks) and perinatal (less than one week and stillbirths) both fell by three-quarters.[59] Linked to this, falls in maternal mortality were also primarily a twentieth century phenomenon, benefiting from the better nutrition levels of pregnant women and the development of ante-natal services.[60] For most of the past 200 years, therefore, increasing life expectancy has mainly resulted from a reduction in the mortality of the younger population rather than an increase in the further lifetime of the relatively old.

Falling youth mortality has its own demographic ageing effect many years later as these relatively larger groups age. Ironically, this consequence of more old people at a later time reinforces the false idea that ageing is the result primarily of something which happens to the old.

To expand on this phenomenon, the past, steady fall in infant mortality from earlier this century is now contributing markedly to

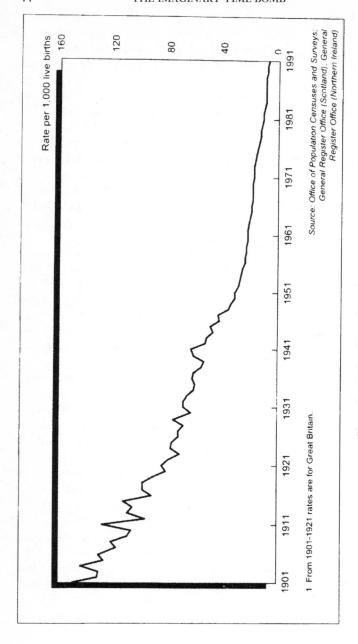

1 From 1901-1921 rates are for Great Britain.

Source: *Office of Population Censuses and Surveys;*
General Register Office (Scotland); General
Register Office (Northern Ireland)

Chart 5:   Infant Mortality / United Kingdom
Source: Social Trends 23, © Crown copyright 1993

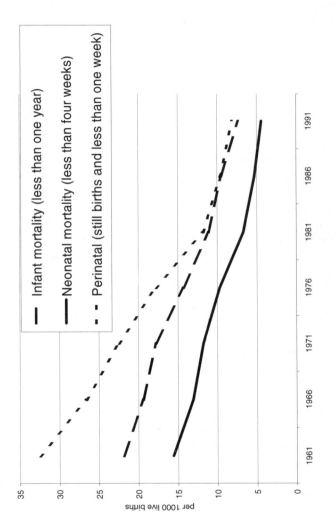

Legend:
— Infant mortality (less than one year)
— Neonatal mortality (less than four weeks)
-- Perinatal (still births and less than one week)

per 1000 live births

1961 1966 1971 1976 1981 1986 1991

Chart 6: Falling infant mortality (in Britain, per 1000 live births)
Source: OPCS (1975) and (1994)

population ageing through the cohort effect. It will continue to do so well into the next century. This happens because after a lapse of time, during which the greater proportions and numbers of young survivors get older, there is a boost to the numbers of elderly people. Youth this century enjoyed greater life expectancy so many more of them reach 65 at which time they boost the numbers of elderly. The impact has been most noticeable since the 1950s in the absolute rise of the number of over 64s. (See chart 7.)

However, some have mistakenly identified this recent jump in the *numbers* of elderly as evidence of a big improvement in life-enhancing drugs and the result of modern medical treatment of older people. From a medical practitioner's perspective J Williamson dismisses the popular myth that this expression of ageing is predominantly the result of modern medical technology. Until recent times, he writes: 'the general prolongation of life was almost entirely attributable to the dramatic reduction in infant and child mortality brought about by the control or elimination of previously lethal epidemic and pandemic infectious diseases.'[61]

Laslett concurs with this emphasis. Writing in the mid-1980s he showed that the big change in British mortality rates since the 1850s was the fall in infant mortality. As evidence he illustrates that life expectancy at birth has risen much faster than life expectancy from the age of 65.[62] With life expectancy rising for these reasons the life table has become more rectangular in shape. Ninety per cent of women and three-quarters of men now reach the age 65.[63]

Recently, however, the balance of which age group gains from falling mortality has begun to alter. This is partly because mortality rates for each age group cannot keep falling at the same pace for ever. Once infant and youth mortality is down to low levels it becomes more difficult to lower them further. The rate of decrease tends to flatten out.

This is why since the 1950s expectation of the length of life at birth, though still increasing, has slowed down a great deal in its rate of growth. Life expectancy for men at birth rose by about 25 years from 1891-1951, or by about four years a decade; since 1951 the increase has more than halved to less than two years per decade. Also for the first time, over the past 30 years only, there has begun to be some noticeable reduction in death rates for the elderly.

Glass and Grebenak conclude their 1960s historical study of mortality by predicting:

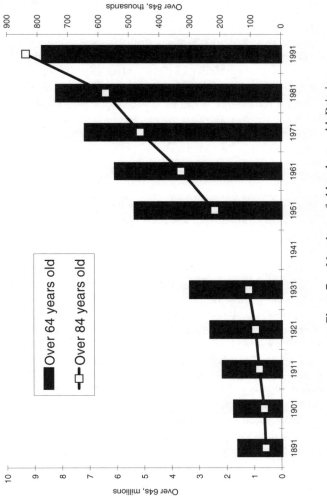

Chart 7: Numbers of old and very old, Britain
Source: OPCS (1993)

'What has happened during the past 100 years is in many respects unrepeatable. Any major increase in the expectation of life in the future must, in the main, come about by a reduction in the mortality of persons aged 60 years or over.'[64]

This is a statistical inevitability. There are more old people and a higher proportion of deaths – and, therefore, more potentially postponable deaths – occur among the elderly. In the UK the percentage of male deaths in different age groups has changed as follows[65]

	Percentage of male deaths by age group	
	Under 15	Over 65
1960	5	62
1970	4	64
1980	2	71
1990	2	75

Among this older constituency death rates from heart disease and strokes have fallen (though this has been offset by an increase in lung cancer deaths).

The unusual feature of the recent falls in old age mortality is shown by contrasting figures for the change in male life expectancy at birth, and at 65, over the 100 years 1861 to 1961. By the start of the 1960s on the basis of the average conditions of the time a new born baby could expect to live 68 years. This is more than 27 years longer than the 40.5 years of a century earlier. However, over the same period expectancy of the age of death for men who had reached their 65th birthday rose by only 1.4 years from 75.4 to 77 years.[66] So on average people lived a lot longer, but once they reached old age their probable remaining life span changed little. (See chart 8.)

Old age mortality levels only started to fall in the 1960s, with life expectancy at 65 growing by over two years since then. The statistical contrast with the previous century is therefore striking. Life expectancy after 65 grew more in the 25 years after 1961, from 77 to almost 79 years for men, than it did in the whole preceding century.

Falling elderly mortality is also expressing itself as the 'old old', or 'very old', group – the over 85s – being the fastest growing sector of the

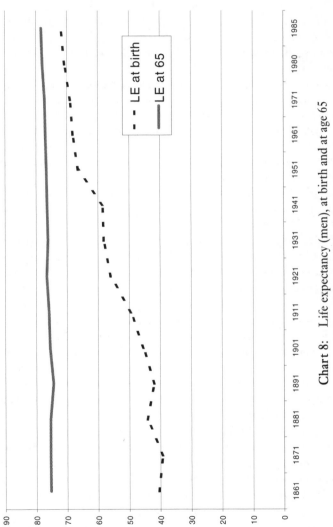

Chart 8: Life expectancy (men), at birth and at age 65
Source: Keyfitz and Flieger (1968) and (1990)

population recently. Some see the substantial growth in the numbers of the very old as the result of a cohort effect. Emily Grundy writes that the 'old old' are the survivors of the larger cohorts born in the first decades of the twentieth century.[67] The UN, however, doubts this argument and explains the high growth rates of the over 75s in the industrialised countries between 1950 and 1990 as 'probably attributable to mortality decline, because the growth rates are too high to be explained by cohort movements'.[68] A reasonable conclusion is that both factors are present.

While the fall in elderly mortality is a significant change it is not automatic that the impact upon the age structure of society will be all that influential, especially when the other, ageing 'from below', factors are included. For example, the very old represents less than 2 per cent of the population, so a high rate of growth of this small group is less impressive when viewed in absolute numbers. (See chart 7.) Also the rate of elderly increase is now slowing. Heller et al show that in the Group of 7 (G7) countries from 1980 to 2025 the rate of increase is likely to be at about half the rate from 1960 to 1980 – a fall from 2.4 per cent growth per year to 1.3 per cent.[69]

The real significance of falling elderly mortality for population ageing is conventionally exaggerated. The United Nations, for example, asserts that for more advanced countries old age 'mortality decline gradually replaces fertility decline as the major driving force of further population ageing'.

Some use this development in a way that reinforces the perception that old people are to 'blame' for living longer. Even the fall that has occurred, though, is nothing to bemoan in the way demographic alarmists do. It is another welcome sign of human progress. Christina Victor's investigation comes to the reasonable conclusion that the fall in elderly mortality probably reflects 'better health care and improvements in nutrition and other aspects of living conditions, as well as improvements in the availability and quality in medical care'.[70]

This experience of ageing 'from above' has undoubtedly reinforced perceptions of an ageing population today. The knowledge that there are more old, and especially, very old people around, corresponds to the orthodox notion of ageing. In reality, and even in crude statistical terms, societal ageing from below, and cohort ageing, still remain much more significant in the recent past and will be into the future.

The most significant contemporary boost to ageing arises from the contrast between the post-Second World War baby boom and the succeeding bust. The extrapolations used today to highlight the demographic time bomb are not a continuation of some long-term transition, but are mainly to do with the consequences of the specific 15 year post-war baby boom and its aftermath.

Baby boom and bust

Birth rates rose during the 1950s in comparison to the trough of the 1930s and late 1940s, peaking in 1964 at a fertility rate of almost three children, before falling away sharply again. This total fertility rate measures the average number of children born to women if they were to experience the age-specific fertility rates of that year throughout their childbearing years. (See chart 9.)

The 1964 fertility peak was 30 per cent above the 1955 level. In the 13 subsequent years of steady decline baby births fell by 35 per cent. However, in absolute terms even at its peak fertility never regained anything like pre-1920s levels when it was almost double the post-war average. Before the Second World War represented a different era in demographic terms that is unlikely ever to return.

Total fertility rate statistics overstate the pitch of the rise and scale of the subsequent fall because they obscure the linkage between these two shifts. Fertility change always has two main dimensions: 'quantum' and 'tempo'. Quantum refers to the ultimate number of children born – the completed family size, and tempo to the timing of these births, the age at which women give birth. The observed level of fertility in any year will be determined by both these factors.

It has been estimated that trends in post-war fertility in Britain and other advanced countries were only about one-third quantum caused, and two-thirds tempo. Most of the baby boom was as a result of women having children earlier. Benjamin and Pollard explain: 'The so-called "baby boom" was not a significant increase in fertility: it was not a "boom" at all but a change in the timing (that is, advancement) of births that would have occurred later.'[71] (See chart 10.)

Since the average family size did not change much over the 1950s and 1960s, this change in timing necessarily worked itself through in the following baby bust. The baby bust has itself been exaggerated statistically by a renewed delay in the timing of births since the 1980s. The mean age at childbirth has increased from 26.5 years in 1977 to 28.1 years in 1993. (See chart 10.)

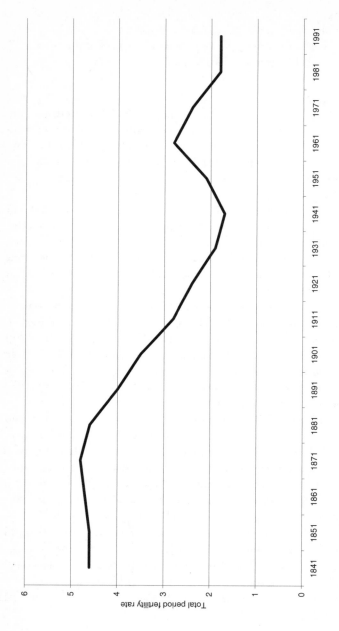

Chart 9: Fertility rates (TPFR) in England and Wales
Source: OPCS (Summer 1987) and (Summer 1997)

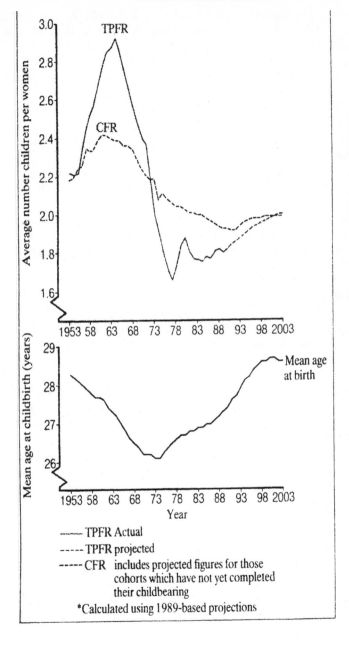

Chart 10: TPFR*, CFR*, and mean age of mother at childbirth*, 1953–2003
England and Wales

Source: Cooper (1991)

A number of conjunctural factors underlay the baby boom after the Second World War. These included the rise in living standards that accompanied the economic boom and the sense of secure full employment. People shared the sentiment of Harold Macmillan, the British prime minister from 1957 to 1963, of 'never having it so good', and felt they could afford larger families. Higher real wages can mean, in these more positive circumstances, that a couple feel they can afford more children sooner.[72] The broader post-war sense of stability encouraged reproduction, especially in contrast with the uncertainties of the 1930s slump.

Richard Easterlin writes that the main explanation for the baby boom was the 'relative affluence' of the 'depression cohort' in the post-war period.[73]

Medical advances contributed, too, with a drop in maternal mortality and in the numbers of still born. Demographic factors also played a role. A favourable change in the sex ratio of marriageable persons boosted fertility. This resulted from the ageing of the generation of men decimated by the First World War and the smaller number of British men who died during the Second World War compared to the First.

From the 1964 peak birth rates fell sharply below replacement level in 1973, to a trough in 1977 of 1.7 before stabilising in the late 1980s at 1.8, still a bit less than the replacement fertility rate. This baby bust was an international phenomenon within the advanced industrialised countries. (See table 1.)

The impetus for these falling fertility levels was again social rather than technical. The main innovation appears to be the increase in the numbers of working women, with the continuing relative inadequacy of proper childcare facilities discouraging pregnancy.

Later marriage and later childbearing were more symptoms of declining fertility, than its causes as is usually assumed. Women tended to marry later and get pregnant later because they wanted to postpone childbirth. Meanwhile, easier abortion and the availability of the contraceptive pill from the 1960s made it technically simpler for women to plan the smaller size of family they wanted.[74]

Easterlin argues that the changed economic climate contributed to the baby bust just as the different economic climate played a role in the previous baby boom. Just as economic prosperity helped bring forward childbirth and boosted family size, so the economic slowdown from the late 1960s, and a renewed sense of economic crisis and uncertainty, had

Table 1:   Total period fertility rates in selected countries, 1965–1983
Source: J Bourgeois–Pichat, 'The unprecedented shortage of births in Europe', in Davis et al (1987)

Country	1965	1970	1975	1980	1983
United Kingdom	2.83	2.44	1.82	1.92	1.77
England and Wales	2.85	2.42	1.78	1.88	1.76
United States	2.93	2.48	1.77	1.84	1.79
Japan	2.14	2.13	1.89	1.73	1.80
West Germany	2.50	2.01	1.45	1.45	1.33
France	2.84	2.47	1.93	1.95	1.79
Italy	2.55	2.37	2.19	1.66	1.53
Denmark	2.61	1.95	1.92	1.55	1.38
Ireland	4.03	3.87	3.41	3.23	2.74
Sweden	2.42	1.92	1.77	1.68	1.61
Holland	3.04	2.58	1.66	1.60	1.47
Australia	2.97	2.85	2.14	1.89	1.93
Canada	3.15	2.33	1.90	1.73	1.67

an opposite effect in delaying childbirth and reducing family size. Deteriorating economic conditions therefore helped drive the baby bust.[75] Easterlin, and others, have argued that more recently the downturn in the fortunes of young people has been a significant element in reduced fertility.[76]

This sharp fall in fertility during the late 1960s and 1970s accounts for the ageing from below phenomenon today. Whether as a result of quantum or tempo factors the fluctuations in birth rates have had, and will continue to have, a significant impact on the age structure of the population for many decades. Fewer children being born in these years – a form of ageing from below – raises the average age of the population again and makes the elderly a bigger proportion.

There is also in the late 1990s a one generation on, boom-bust echo effect, which is beginning to weigh in to reinforce ageing from below. Population cohorts tend to mirror the size of their parents' cohorts. The large group of women born in the baby boom, and now in their childbearing years will tend to produce a large generation of offspring, and with the succeeding smaller group of women, the opposite applies. Prior to this boom-bust echo effect reinforcing the pace of ageing, the rise in the number of children in the 1980s and 1990s is the echo effect of the earlier baby boom. This helped to slow and even temporarily reverse ageing in Britain, as shown in chart 1. (See chart 11.)

Today, though, some baby boom women are moving beyond their peak childbearing years. The smaller baby bust cohort starts to dominate in the childbirth stakes by the start of the next century, leading to a fall in the number of births. This will temporarily enhance the specific post-war process of ageing from below. There will be a second, shallower echo a generation later with a further rise and fall in the number of births from about 2010 to the 2030s.

Also at about this time the large baby boom generation will be reaching their 60s and beyond, reinforcing a larger over-64s section of the population. The baby boom-bust phenomena will therefore be influential until towards the middle of the twenty-first century. This explains the probability of a steadily ageing population through the first third of the twenty-first century. It also explains why the average age of the population is unlikely to keep rising beyond then. These specific boom-bust influences disappear.

To conclude, the ageing tendency that is such a source of concern today is primarily the product of a specific post-war period of volatility

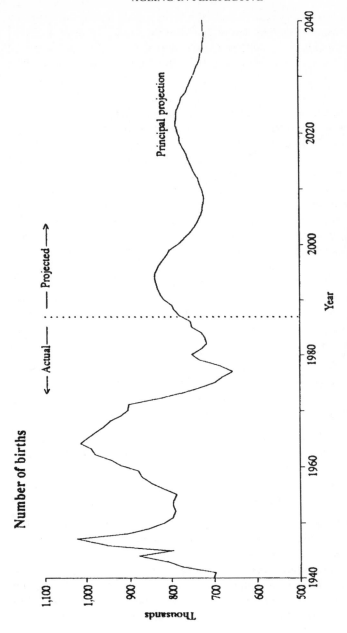

Chart 11:   Echo effect of baby boom and bust
Source: OPCS, *Population projections, 1987–2027*, p20

in fertility levels as a result of a range of socio-economic factors. Ageing today is therefore neither natural nor steadily inexorable into the distant future. Nor is it immutable even in the early decades of the millennium. Future changes to fertility rates could modify the picture significantly.

Population projections

Having established the dominant forces behind ageing today this chapter continues with a fuller exploration of the parameters for the future pace of ageing in Britain. The official population projections are that ageing will accelerate in the first third of the twenty-first century. (See chart 12.)

What weight should be given to the predictions of demographic malaise? The short answer is not too much. Projections are useful for all sorts of reasons. Not least they can provide the basis for taking action to change the future. However, there are big problems with assuming the standard projections provide a reasonably accurate picture of the future. Although these projections are widely employed to back up the case for a demographic time bomb it is rarely stressed that the government's own Actuary Department admits their deficiencies as forecasts.

Chris Shaw, a member of the Actuary Department, in an article 'Accuracy and uncertainty of the national population projections for the United Kingdom' explains that:

'The projections are made based on assumptions which seem most appropriate from the statistical evidence available at the time. However, the one certainty of making population projections is that these projections will, to a greater or lesser extent, turn out to be wrong as a forecast of future demographic behaviour.'[77]

In fact it is almost inevitable, except by a fluke, that the age structures projected will not happen. This is because there is a basic flaw in the way these figures are worked out with regard to their ability as forecasts: a projection based on the *present* state of affairs cannot forecast the future. Benjamin and Pollard clearly explain this distinction:

'In making forward, as distinct from current, estimates of the population of the country the term "projection" is used rather than "forecast". The reason is an important one. Demographers can do no more than analyse existing trends of births, deaths, migration, and throw them forward (extrapolate them) into the future. Hence the term "projection". This is a purely mechanical operation, carrying no expectation of fulfilment, as would be implied by the term "forecast".

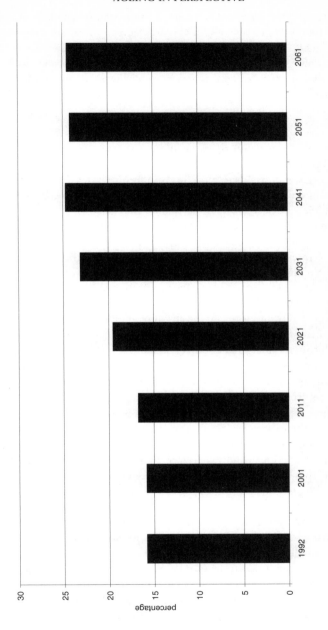

Chart 12: Over 64s in Britain (percentage of total population)
Source: OPCS, 1992 based National Population Projections (1995)

In projecting existing trends we are doing no more than spell out the implications in terms of what must happen if these trends are maintained. There is no implication that they *will* be maintained ... . Projections soon become out of date, therefore, and have to be regularly revised to take account of changes in the underlying trends.'[78]

Most concerns about future ageing trends rely upon these projections for their undoubted shock value. But these population projections are not guestimates of future population patterns. Instead they are extrapolations of what has already happened, with a few fairly fixed assumptions about trends in mortality and fertility rates. Hence they are bound primarily to highlight the consequences of the passage through life of cohorts already born. In particular, they abstract from the most important fluid influence upon future population structures – future levels of fertility.

This chapter has emphasised the dominant role of the 'ageing from below' phenomenon over 'ageing from above', and even over 'cohort ageing' in understanding the ageing process that has already occurred this century. Falls in birth rates, rather than the changing life expectancy of relatively old people, or even the absolute numbers of old people, have been the main factor behind population ageing. This historical emphasis on the fertility rate explanation for ageing is an instance of a more general conclusion. The main dynamic for any changes in the population age structure – upwards or downwards – have always been from below, from shifts in fertility rates.

What the demographic time bomb proponents ignore is that this is likely to be the case in the future too. This is because outside of major wars, the numbers of the newly-born are more volatile in size than any other age group. This cohort therefore always tends to have the biggest influence upon the population structure. For example, take the past two decades. The numbers of old have risen significantly during this time. Partly this is the ageing cohort effect of higher levels of fertility and of the falls in child mortality earlier in the century. Partly it is the result of higher living standards and better health care throughout their lives, in prolonging older people's lives.

But despite the coincidence of these pressures, fertility changes over the same two decades have been more influential upon the overall age structure. From 1971 to 1991 the under 15s age group fell by about two and two-thirds million. The over 65s grew by only one and a half million. This means that the average age of the population rose almost twice as much as a result of fewer youth than it did from more elderly. Ageing continued to be mainly from below even though ageing from above had become a significant factor for the first time.

Fertility rates are unlikely to drop secularly again over any extended period of time since they are already so low. However, fertility rates, since they are mainly socially determined, are more likely to oscillate than stay constant at some projected fixed rate. They are likely also to fluctuate sufficiently to affect the age structure, just as they have done in the post-war years. Sometimes this will make the population younger, sometimes older. It is more likely than not that, as in the past, this volatility will be the main influence on future population patterns.

Official projections of the future of ageing, of course, bear little resemblance to this pattern of fertility influenced demography. This is because official forecasts assume a stable fertility level. Rapid movements in fertility rates of the specific post-war boom–bust type are ruled out by the projection assumptions. Only the echo effect of the past baby boom is incorporated. By methodology, the official projections discount the sort of volatility of birth rates which could either reverse or rekindle ageing from below. (See chart 13.)

The projections for demographic ageing well into the next century, which so many people get worked up about, are mainly the result of one real, but specific, factor: the cohort effect of the baby-boomers growing old. As measured by the proportion of over-64s this influence upon ageing must peak some time around 2020-40. This has to happen, excluding the possibility of war or some other human catastrophe killing off a significant part of this cohort earlier.

The statement that ageing is bound to happen because the people who will do the ageing have already been born always sounds convincing common sense. These people certainly cannot be unborn. However, the problem with these population projections, and especially with basing public policy upon them, is that they exclude the reality of a changing world. They are wrong as forecasts not because of what they include, but of what they leave out. Their projections of how current generations age can be reasonably accurate. There is no doubt that the average age of the population will rise when the big baby boom cohort reaches age 65. The projections' main failing is that they ignore the prospect of other influential developments in the 'from below' sphere. This does not preclude their valuable use as a basis for taking certain policy initiatives

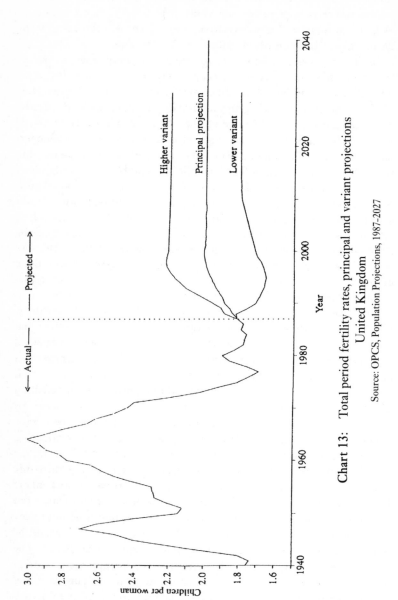

Chart 13: Total period fertility rates, principal and variant projections
United Kingdom
Source: OPCS, Population Projections, 1987–2027

which can modify the future. It does mean that they are mystifying as a snapshot of the future.

The ageing of the relatively large baby boom cohorts born in the Western world during the 1950s and early 1960s *will* influence age patterns up to the second quarter of the twenty-first century. That is incontestable. But by that time we can be certain of two other things.

First, the demographic impact of the baby boom will fade then too. The middle of the next century is also when the impact fades of the cohort ageing effects of the rapid post-war falls in infant mortality rates, which enhanced even more the size of the baby boom generation. The peak around 2040 in the proportion and numbers of over-64s expresses the working through of specific factors boosting ageing: the cohort effects of the post-war baby boom and the post-war fall in infant mortality. After this time, projections for ageing on the basis of current conditions level off and fall. The proportion of over-64s declines. It is telling that the familiar steadily ascending lines on the charts used by alarmist commentators do not extend much beyond 2040. Tables and charts of ageing projections ending at this time necessarily ignore these subsequent declines. (See chart 12 and table 2.)

Instead one-off ageing patterns can appear as secular and permanent. Cover the most rightward two decades in chart 12 to see this appearance. For advocates of the demographic time bomb thesis it is convenient that most visual presentations of population projections finish around 2040. The incorrect implication that ageing goes on and on enhances the explosive connotations of this ticking bomb.

The second aspect we can be sure about the future is that population patterns into the twenty-first century will be influenced by demographic events which have yet to happen. Just as the post-war baby boom was not anticipated by many only a few years before it began, so future birth trends cannot be predicted with certainty now.

As Chris Shaw reminds us, 'projections made shortly after the Second World War failed to anticipate the baby boom of the 1960s'.[79] Ironically, during the 1930s, in advance of the baby boom, there was a panic about the dangers of low fertility and expectation of future population decline.[80]

In line with the record of the past couple of centuries, we can be sure that economic, political and social factors will be the decisive influences upon future fertility levels. These forces in turn depend on future human activity and experience. A major international war, the

Table 2: Percentage of population over 60 years old in selected countries, 1990–2150
Source: World Bank (1994), p 349

Country	1990	2000	2010	2020	2030	2050	2075	2100	2125	2150
UK	20.8	20.7	23.0	25.5	29.6	29.5	29.7	30.3	30.7	30.9
US	16.6	16.5	19.2	24.5	28.2	28.9	29.7	30.3	30.7	30.9
Japan	17.3	22.7	29.0	31.4	33.0	34.4	31.0	30.7	30.9	31.0
Germany	20.3	23.7	26.5	30.3	35.3	32.5	30.4	30.5	30.8	31.0
France	18.9	20.2	23.1	26.8	30.1	31.2	30.3	30.5	30.8	31.0
Italy	20.6	24.2	27.4	30.6	35.9	36.5	30.9	30.5	30.8	31.0
Denmark	20.2	20.4	24.8	28.4	32.1	30.9	29.9	30.2	30.7	30.9
Ireland	15.2	15.7	17.8	20.1	22.9	28.2	29.4	30.1	30.6	30.9
Sweden	22.9	21.9	25.4	27.8	30.0	28.7	29.9	30.5	30.8	31.0
Holland	17.8	19.0	23.4	28.4	33.4	31.7	30.2	30.4	30.8	31.0
Australia	15.0	15.3	18.1	22.8	27.7	30.4	30.0	30.4	30.8	30.9
Canada	15.6	16.8	20.4	25.9	30.2	30.6	30.2	30.5	30.8	31.0
OECD Weighted average	18.2	19.9	23.1	27.0	30.7	31.2	30.1	30.4	30.8	31.0

protracted continuation of the past quarter century of sluggish economic activity, or the emergence of something like the post-1950 economic boom, would all bias future demographic happenings and produce a different age pattern in 2040 from that projected now.

Our criticism of official projections is not that they should predict a baby boom at some definite time. The point is more simple and less specific. Whatever does happen to births over the next 50 years will almost certainly be a more dominant influence on the age structure in the middle of the twenty-first century than the factors currently featured in the projections.

It is worth emphasising the views of the British government's own Office of Population Censuses and Surveys (OPCS), that 'despite increasing knowledge of demographic processes and the use of more sophisticated projection methods, projection errors remain inevitable due to the inherent uncertainty of demographic behaviour'.[81] As an example it reminded readers that its official 1971-based projection for the population in 1991 was 2.5 million too high. They had not anticipated the extent of the baby bust. Note that it is an unanticipated factor related to fertility that they highlight as having affected the population outcome. (See diagram 2.)

The pertinent point for us is that the from below and cohort influences on ageing of the post-war baby boom and bust will wane as the years pass. It can become swamped by other demographic trends that have not yet happened. As with many past population projections, forecasts based upon its exclusive importance are less than likely to have much proximity to reality. Yet the dire predictions of the demographic time bomb are often based upon this narrow and restricted assumption.

The peculiar mystifications of 'dependency ratios'
This probable distortion of the future population structure is taken to even more extreme and absurd lengths with the projection of dependency ratios. These ratios measure the number of over-64s, or the number of under-16s, or the total sum of the two, as a percentage of the 16 to 64s. The 16-64s are conventionally called the working age population, giving the implication that these people really are working and producing wealth for the whole of society. The dependency ratio – particularly the elderly dependency ratio – is probably the favourite device of demographic panic-mongers. It provides the mediating link

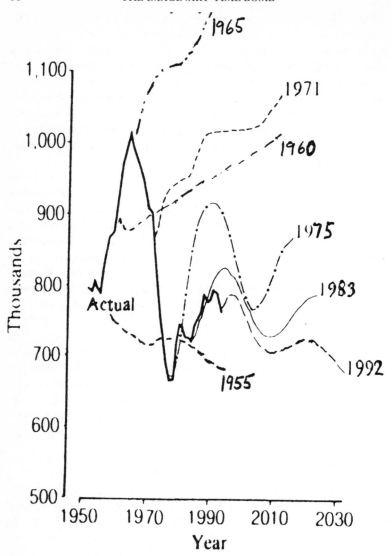

Diagram 2:   Actual and projected births
Source: OPCS, Population Trends, Autumn 1994 and earlier

between the sorts of population projections discussed above and the existing fears of the demographic time bomb.

The time bomb anticipates a relative rise in the numbers of elderly with a relative fall in the numbers of those of working age. This combination is supposed to wreck the economy and bankrupt the government exchequer because of the extra cost of pensions and health care for the elderly. Some predict it will provoke inter-generational warfare because of the greater tax burden on younger workers. All in all we are warned there is big trouble ahead, because of the rising dependency ratio. (See charts 14 & 15.)

The gloomy interpretations from the elderly dependency ratio are even more extreme than an objective look at chart 14 suggests. Contrary to what the chart reveals, much of the literature often downplays that the projected dependency ratio is pretty static until the second decade of the twenty-first century. Even the charts show that it is not until the third decade that either the elderly or the total dependency ratio rises much above today's level. This is when the ageing of the baby boomers born in the 1950s and 1960s starts to take effect on the measure of over-64s. The elderly ratio rises for 20 years, peaks in about 2038, then stabilises before falling away. Not a long period to give such weight to the demographic time bomb. Nevertheless, the belief of forever rising dependency ratios is what matters for the time bomb motif.

This book will return to assess the political agenda underlying the demographic time bomb in later chapters. The remainder of this chapter will limit itself to identifying a few of the statistical distortions of the dependency ratio. These are *in addition* to the problems with the population projections already outlined in the earlier section upon which these ratios are based.

First, the dependency ratio is an extremely crude device. The implication that everyone between the ages of 16 and 64 works is an absurdity. This fanciful idea ignores the unemployed, students, discouraged workers, the early retired, and vast numbers of other non-workers, including many women. Even for those with jobs it makes no allowance for the relative proportions of full-time versus part-time workers, who make a different contribution both to economic output and also to an economy's tax revenue.

Such shifts and changes *within* the 16-64 population are much more influential on the society's actual creation of wealth than a rising dependency ratio. Estimates for such changes will be provided in

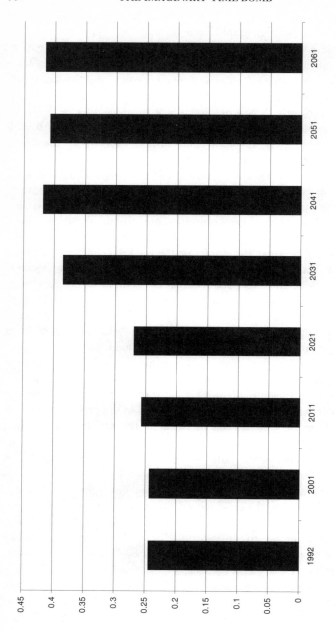

Chart 14:   Elderly dependency ratios
Source: OPCS, 1992 based National Population Projections (1995)

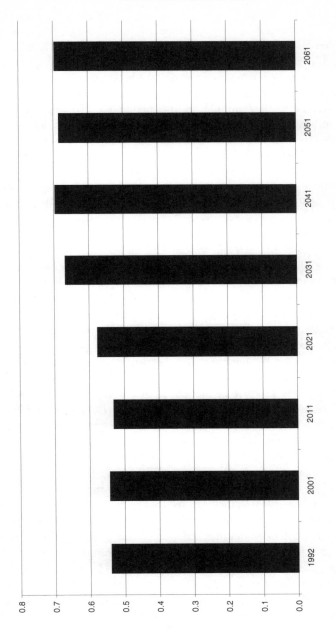

Chart 15: Total dependency ratios
Source: OPCS (1995)

chapter four, which will show the relative insignificance of an ageing population to society's productive capacity when compared to these other factors.

Second, the *elderly* dependency ratio will always exaggerate what is happening to the *total* dependency ratio, the latter comprising both the young and old. There tends to be an inverse relationship between the proportions of young and old in the population. By definition a population's age structure is either getting younger, or older, or is stationary. In the first two instances the youth and the elderly dependency ratios will move in opposite directions. In the stationary case all the dependency ratios will be static too.

As Midwinter shows: 'An odd sum may be calculated, for if the younger and older elements of the British population are tallied together for Victorian times and today, the total of about two-fifths is the same: it is the internal switch within what is often called the 'dependent' population which has been epic in scale.'[82]

More significantly still, this figure remains at about the same level until the population projections expire in 2061. Even at the 2038 peak the proportion of total dependents, young and old, would be about the same as it was in the early 1970s, although then it was children who comprised the majority of dependents. (See charts 16, 17 and 18.)

Therefore concerns about the costs of more elderly people should be at least partly neutralised by the reduced expenditures on fewer children in the projections. Robert Clark explains that 'the increased cost of maintaining the elderly will be moderated by cost reductions associated with having relatively fewer children to support'.[83] But the reduction of health costs as a result of fewer baby births (which tend to be expensive of health service resources) and less expenditure on child allowances and education rarely get mentioned as an offset in the discussions about the 'burden' of ageing.

Samuel Preston, the original American gloom-merchant of inter-generational war, drew attention to the ironic shift in focus for population concern from too many children to too many old people. He described that 'after decades of calculations showing the huge net public cost of children due to their consumption of public resources long before they start yielding the (heavily discounted) stream of tax payments, the new age bias in public expenditures has reversed the charges'.[84]

So on some occasions the worry is about the costs of youth dependency, on others about elderly dependency. Since the total

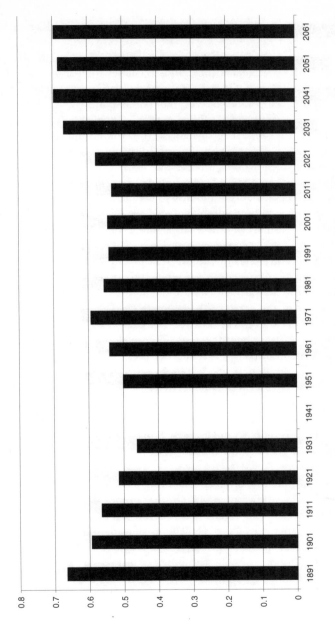

Chart 16: Total dependency ratios over the long term

Source: OPCS (1993) (1995)

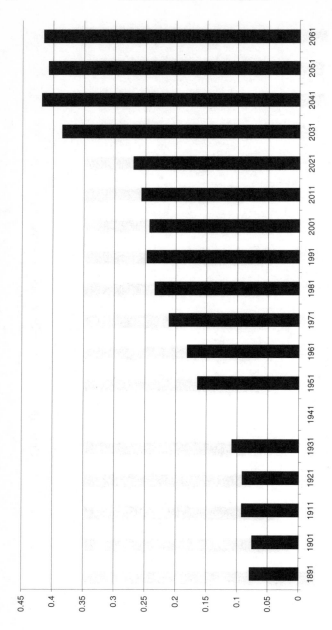

Chart 17:   Elderly dependency ratios over the long term
Source: OPCS (1993) and (1995)

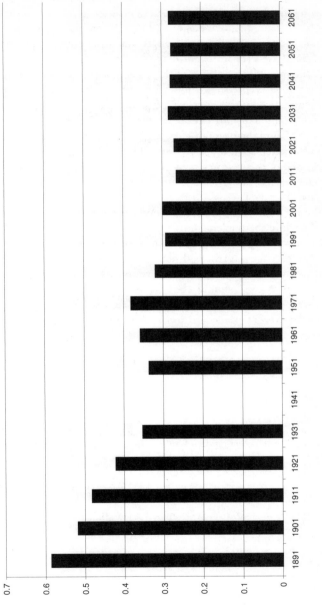

Chart 18: Youth dependency ratios over the long term
Source: OPCS (1993, 1995)

dependency ratio is relatively stable over long periods, including those during which public expenditure is seen to be affordable, it could be the case that particular one-sided demographic shifts emphasising either too many young or too many old are being blamed for public expenditure pressures that have a separate non-demographic source.

Third, the possibility, at least, of there being some non-demographic cause(s) for today's preoccupation with the burden of demographic ageing is emphasised if the elderly dependency patterns throughout this century are examined. Old age dependency ratios are today growing more slowly than in the past not more rapidly as might be assumed from the volumes written about them recently. They grew at a more rapid rate in the first half of this century than in the second, rising by 80 per cent from 1911 to 1951, but by less than that figure in the succeeding 40 years.[85] (See chart 17.)

So if the high period of the rising elderly dependency ratio is fading, why has the panic about ageing only recently started? British society has coped with a tripling in the proportion of over-64s between 1911 and 1991. In comparison a further 50 per cent rise over the next 50 years does not seem that onerous. The arguments from Johnson and Falkingham that we should be wary of 'simple demographic determinism' seem entirely justified.[86] The real non-demographic reasons for the recent preoccupation with ageing is the subject of the next chapter.

Notes

1.   Warnes (1993).
2.   Thompson (1992), p 26.
3.   Bourdelais (1993).
4.   See review of Bourdelais, 1993, in *Ageing and Society*, vol 14, 1994.
5.   For a statistical presentation of this truism see Gavrilov and Gavrilov (1991).
6.   Giddens (1994), p 170.
7.   Vincent (1996), p 9.
8.   Thompson (1992), p 26.
9.   Tinker (1992), p 250.
10. These themes are well covered in Phillipson (1982).
11. Kirk (1992), p 489.
12. Laslett (1987), p 154.
13. Blaikie (1990).
14. See Laslett (1987).
15. Kirk (1992), p 483.
16. Roebuck (1979), p 416.
17. Roebuck (1979), pp 417–8.

18. Pratt (1994), p 284.
19. Therborn (1995), p 94.
20. Therborn (1995), p 421.
21. Therborn (1995), p 422.
22. Myles (1983), p 470.
23. Sen (1996), p 107.
24. Blaikie (1990).
25. Giddens (1994), p 170.
26. Guillemard (1985), p 406.
27. Midwinter (1990), p 221.
28. Peterson and Rose (1983), pp 289–94.
29. Nascher (1914).
30. Andrew Blaikie (1990), p 18.
31. Grundy (1996), p 14.
32. See, for example, Coale and Demeny (1966).
33. UN (1993).
34. See Coale and Hoover, (1985); Singer (1949); Furedi (1997).
35. The assumption about the primacy of rising life expectancy ranges from prestigious studies such as the World Bank's *Averting the Old Age Crisis*, 1994: 'Rapid demographic transitions caused by rising life expectancy and declining fertility mean that the proportion of old people in the general population is growing rapidly' (p xiii), to newspaper reports, such as *The Guardian*, 27 January 1996: 'The pensions and welfare crisis thrown up by longer life expectancy and shrinking workforces is a challenge confronting the wealthy West generally'.
36. Smith (1984), p 413.
37. Keyfitz (1975), p 267.
38. See, for example, UN (1993).
39. See Kuznets (1979), chapter on 'Population trends and modern economic growth: notes towards an historical perspective.'.
40. Keyfitz (1975), p 279.
41. Kuznets (1979), pp 120 and 133.
42. Davis (1987), p 59.
43. See Lewis (1979).
44. Although counter-intuitive, this assessment has been recognised among demographers for some time. See, for example, the book produced by The Population Institute (1966), to coincide with the United Nation's first World Population Conference in Belgrade in 1965.
45. UN (1993), p 30.
46. Midwinter (1990), p 223.
47. DHSS (1978), p 7.
48. Clark and Spengler (1980), p 5.
49. Laslett (1984), p 383.
50. Brockington (1956), p 56.
51. See Wrigley and Schofield (1989).
52. For more detail of the historical picture see, for example, Carver and Liddiard (1978).
53. OPCS (1993), p 7.
54. Glass and Grebenak (1966), p 76.
55. Brockington (1956), p 113.
56. Smith (1984), p 413.
57. Royal Commission (1950a), p 68.

58. Social Trends (1993), p 96.
59. OPCS (Autumn 1994) and (Autumn 1975).
60. See Brockington (1956), pp 106–22.
61. Williamson (1990), p1.
62. Laslett (1984).
63. Ermisch (1990).
64. Glass and Grebenak (1966), p 79.
65. UN (1993).
66. Figures taken from Keyfitz and Flieger (1968).
67. Grundy (1996), p 15.
68. UN (1993), p 12.
69. Heller et al (1986), p 27.
70. C Victor (1991), p 30.
71. Benjamin and Pollard (1980), p 179.
72. See Ermisch (1988). Here, though, he also warns against a deterministic understanding of the impact of wage levels: 'There is strong evidence that higher women's wages raise the cost of an additional child by increasing earnings foregone, and the higher opportunity cost reduces the likelihood of another birth, but couples respond to higher men's earnings by having more children and having them sooner.' (p 77) One can go further and say the particular weight of these, and other 'economic' influences will depend upon the interaction with other wider social and cultural factors.
73. Easterlin (1976).
74. Ermisch (1990).
75. Easterlin (1976).
76. Easterlin, Wachter and Wachter (1978).
77. OPCS (1994), p 24.
78. Benjamin and Pollard (1980), pp 211–12.
79. OPCS (1994), p 31.
80. See Lewis (1979), pp 42–3, and chapter 3 below.
81. OPCS (1994), p 24.
82. Midwinter (1990), p 223.
83. Clark (1978), p 249.
84. Preston (1987), p 171.
85. Source: Keyfitz and Flieger (1968) and OPCS (1994).
86. Johnson and Falkingham (1992), p 47.

3. The Preoccupation with Ageing

The contemporary worries about ageing and the demographic time bomb have their origins in the 1970s. But a heightened interest in the topic has only moved into the mainstream even over the past decade. The emergence of the spectre of an ageing society has been fairly abrupt. It is also unprecedented. There had been outbursts of demographic fears before, from the social Darwinists in particular, but never has society held such a specific concern about the dire implications of ageing populations. This chapter explores the specific factors behind this peculiarly rapid flourishing of a popular concern.

Even specialist demographic literature on ageing is quite recent, reflecting this absence of social interest in the subject. In the first half of this century there was barely any. Writing in the mid-1960s Townsend and Wedderburn commented about the subject that: 'between 1901 and 1947 ... . There was a dearth of published information and, apparently, of interest too'.[1] Even in the period since the Second World War there was, until recently, only sparse research, discussion or writing on the subject. It is revealing given the narrow statistical reasoning with which some explain today's preoccupation - namely the rate of ageing – that there was such minimal interest earlier despite the proportion of elderly people roughly doubling in many developed countries over the first half of the century.[2] The rate of ageing earlier was clearly not sufficient grounds for generating much interest, never mind concern in the topic.

Although the pace of population ageing has been fairly constant over the whole twentieth century the awareness and fixation upon it is more recent. This chapter will both chart the evolution of the preoccupation and also explore the reasons for its emergence at this point in history. It will show that the main determinant for the rise of concern now is not population trends in themselves, but that the ageing preoccupation is a suitable manifestation for contemporary anxieties – fears with different, non-demographic roots. Non-demographic factors account for a changing perception of a fairly consistent demographic trend. Western societies that seem afflicted by a pervasive sense of uncertainty, insecurity and incoherence are prone to worry about the future. At an individual level people who feel isolated and vulnerable are disposed to inflate threats to their personal well being. The fear of population ageing is both a metaphor and one focus for these sentiments.

The evolution of a fixation

Beginning about 20 years ago the US led the way in giving greater consideration to ageing. As with many other social and cultural matters where the US led, other developed countries soon followed. Interest spread across the rest of the industrialised world during the 1980s.

The first official recognition of ageing came in 1976, designated as the first international Age Action Year. A survey of the quantity of literature produced on the subject of ageing confirms the greater interest building up as the 1970s unfolded. In their extensive American survey of 1978, Robert Clark, Juanita Kreps and Joseph Spengler described how low fertility and the fall in elderly mortality rates had only recently stimulated the interest of economists in examining the economic impact of ageing.[3] At that time the discussion on ageing was still primarily a derivative of the consideration of other demographic matters, rather than the area of central interest it has attained today.

In these early stages ageing was also different from the present in that it was not blamed for economic problems. It is worth noting the wider point that for most of the twentieth century demography as a whole had been studied as a subject in its own terms, rather than as a cause of economic movements. Today's linking up of the two disciplines is in some ways reminiscent of the nineteenth century. Simon Kuznets noted that for most of the twentieth century:

> 'The definition of "economic" has become progressively narrower. At one time populations' movement were an integral part of economic theory, but since the latter part of the nineteenth century, demography has been a separate field.'[4]

The shift away from demographic explanations for economic phenomena towards the end of the last century represented a step forward in scientific inquiry. It reflected the search for social instead of natural explanations for what was happening in the economy. The return by economists and other social commentators to be obsessed with demographic issues marks a reversion to the more primitive level of thinking of the nineteenth century. In some ways it is also an unwelcome return to the approach of some social Darwinists who used demographic trends to gauge the prospects of a country, race or class.

Demographic interest among economists re-emerged after the Second World War.[5] A new school of literature linking demography and economic development began to grow. Many of the main journals on population issues were even more recent, being launched in the 1960s and 1970s. These included *Demography* in 1963, and *Population and Development Review* in 1975.

The earlier reviews of demographic developments in the developed world were not unaware of ageing. However, in contrast to later writings, their forecasts were usually undramatic in tone. For example, the OECD's third study of projected demographic trends in 1966 - the previous two were in 1956 and 1961 - concluded soberly, 'on balance the global dependency rate increases over the years 1965-1980 … though only moderately'. It pointed mainly to the declining effect of First World War deaths within elderly cohorts to explain the increase.[6]

More often ageing would be introduced merely as one factor among several into the discussions that arose about the impact of the fall in fertility levels following the post-war baby boom. Because of Europe's shorter baby boom this concern with low fertility first resumed in Europe from the mid-1960s before spreading to America by the early 1970s.[7]

With the launching of the World Fertility Survey in the early 1970s a major effort got underway to try to understand fertility change both in the developing and the industrialised world.[8] The focus was mainly on the pace of population growth, rather than on population age, and especially on the consequences of slowing or even zero population growth.

In this demographic literature ageing was generally recognised to be the inevitable accompaniment to the historic trend of falling fertility. From this perspective the shift from fertility boom to bust was seen to cause further population ageing. However, this was usually stated neutrally. In the early contributions few writers expressed much specific concern about the consequences. This absence of alarmism is a notable feature of the earlier demographic literature and discussion, both about ageing itself, and also its possible economic and social implications.

On the contrary the new science of gerontology was devoted mainly to elaborating and promoting a new art of living for the elderly. The focus was on encouraging people to make the most of their 'third age' (see below), with an emphasis on activity and participation.[9] Old age was seen as an opportunity rather than a penance.

Most writings in the late 1960s and early 1970s were sanguine about the ramifications of low fertility, of ageing and of declining population growth. This probably reflected the positive mood of the times. Problems identified then were usually regarded as soluble challenges rather than the insurmountable difficulties of today. For many then, the demographic trends discussed were welcomed rather than regarded as a problem. William Serow and Thomas Espenshade reported about the early 1970s' literature, much of it American, that 'the overall consensus of opinion thus far would appear to be that the net impact of a decline in population growth would be positive, in terms of a per capita measure of economic well-being'.[10]

However, by the mid-1970s sentiments began to change. Some thinkers started to become gloomy about the implications for economic growth of slow growing, or stationary, populations. In line with this wider shift in outlook some writers began to focus more on the economic costs of the burden of maintaining greater numbers of older people. Robert Clark et al noted the emergence of a 'considerable literature', mainly originating in the US, on the economic impact of ageing on consumption, savings and accumulation in the second half of the 1970s.[11]

In this period of renewed economic slowdown following the golden years of the post-war boom discussion in many Western countries turned also to the labour market aspects of old age. Elderly people were considered from the perspective of being potential early retirees, justified by the claim that their economic contribution diminished with age. Early retirement became one of the more acceptable ways of moving people out of the jobs market to help to reduce the headline official unemployment figures. Gaullier says that in France by the early 1980s 'the policy of old age has ... become a policy of employment'. At this time interest in the issue of elderly people was often driven by considerations of the appropriate employment policies needed to cope with the economic slump.[12]

In Germany, too, ageing initially attained relevance at least partly as a result of labour market concerns. Kohli, Rosenow and Wolf argue that the pressures to encourage earlier retirement were a significant factor behind the rise in prominence of the ageing issue. They explained how in the conditions of higher unemployment the determined practice of promoting earlier retirement for older workers was 'however reluctantly - broadly accepted ... . The main factor behind this development, as well as the actual debate, is the pressure of the labour market.'[13]

From about this time also studies began to be conducted on the social security and pension implications of ageing populations.[14] Initially at that early stage of interest in the subject most research concluded that the costs would be manageable and rejected the opinion that there would be an unsustainable increase in the burden of old dependents.[15]

Even as late as 1984 in Britain the official OPCS discussions on ageing were far from alarmist. The OPCS's report on the 1981 census noted the rise in the numbers of elderly and forecast that this would continue through the 1980s. However, its main message was the reassurance that after 1991 the 'growth ceases so that, at least for a time, the overall numbers hardly change'.[16]

The British discussion tends to parallel trends elsewhere in the industrialised countries and lag just a few years behind the US. The 1970s discussion in Britain on population ageing began as a small, technical and often health-related sub-speciality within demographic studies. For example, one of the first British periodicals devoted to ageing was the medical journal *Age and Ageing* launched in the early 1970s.

By the 1980s interest in gerontology had grown and had established an independent niche for itself, initially in the academic milieu.[17] A separate school of social gerontology became recognised, incorporating a multi-disciplinary approach to identify the ways in which social and cultural factors entered into the ageing process. In 1981 the journal *Ageing and Society* began publication under the joint auspices of the newly established Centre for Policy on Ageing and the British Society of Gerontology. Its first editorial noted the recent emergence of 'a greater awareness of the ubiquitous nature of ageing and the value of studying it as a topic in itself'.[18]

With academics like Alan Walker from Sheffield University and Essex University's poverty expert Peter Townsend (who subsequently moved to Bristol University) at the helm, it sought to criticise and transcend the existing narrow approach to ageing. They aimed to go beyond the traditional emphasis on the biological and psychological changes brought on by individuals getting older. In the opening article of the inaugural issue Townsend set the critical tone. He argued for a new sociology which saw 'that the dependency of the elderly in the twentieth century is being manufactured socially and that its severity is unnecessary'.[19]

Labour market forces were also seen to be prominent in Britain. Alan Walker sympathetically endorsed the cornerstone of Chris Phillipson's instructive book *Capitalism and the Construction of Old Age* that 'the process of retirement is the major element in the social definition of old age'. Older workers, they believed, were made to operate as a reserve army of labour available to be sucked into the labour market when needed and quickly dispensed with when no longer required. At this time, they claimed, old people were viewed as significant only in narrow economic labour market terms.[20]

The 1980s saw the real birth of ageing as an intellectual area of interest in the West. The maturing process was quite concentrated and intense. It soon spread across several disciplines. In the sphere of economics the topic was formally recognised when the *Journal of Economic Literature* introduced the category 'economics of ageing' in 1982. A new school of population economics became established with its own publication, the *Journal of Population Economics*, launched in 1988. A year later American sociologists first published the *Journal of Aging and Social Policy*.

As the 1980s progressed concern with population ageing also became more extensive outside the universities. It spread from a still relatively specialist academic consideration to become a topic for discussion within many national and international institutions. The prestigious *Milbank Memorial Fund Quarterly* in America published a special issue on 'Ageing: demographic, health, and social prospects' in the summer of 1983, followed by another on 'The oldest old' in the spring of 1985. The implications of demographic ageing began to achieve a wider hearing.

The social secutiy and pension implications were becoming regarded as especially problematic by governments and their advisers. This represented a contradictory concern in light of their previous support for earlier retirement. The positive effect of older workers giving up work earlier in keeping down official unemployment levels was now seen as offset by the additional cost to the social welfare budget of more elderly non-workers.[21] A major OECD report on public pensions published in 1988 noted this international shift in the course of the 1980s. Governments moved from encouraging earlier retirement to reduce unemployment, to the recognition of a burgeoning concern that early retirement benefits can discourage work and boost the cost to state treasuries from retirement pension payments.[22]

In most countries in the early 1980s early retirees were encouraged with the incentive of receiving state pensions early too, but by the later 1980s this was seen by some governments to be proving too costly. Although in Britain state pensions were not paid early for those who retired from work before the statutory retirement age, there were similar pressures. There was a cost to the Exchequer in the level of sickness benefits often granted liberally to the early retired. These payments were higher than unemployment benefit and were tolerated for a long time as a financial encouragement for stopping work early.

As well as governments, international institutions increasingly began to take more interest in ageing. The UN started to address the issue of ageing regularly in its annual *World Economic Surveys*. Whereas in 1978 it had worried that the baby boom's contribution to the working age population was boosting unemployment, by its 1983 report it was expressing concern that an ageing population was one of the factors behind the elusiveness of the world recovery.

In 1987 the UN first extensively discussed the dilemmas of an ageing workforce and the early retirement trend. This growth of demographic consciousness was further expressed by the innovation in 1988 of including population figures amidst the economic data, a practice that has continued ever since.

A Special Issue on 'Selected demographic indicators' in the 1989 UN survey noted how the supply of demographic data had recently improved substantially. Assessing some of this data it highlighted its concern that:

'The world's population has entered a period of demographic aging (except Africa). Overall the ratio of persons in the dependent years to those in the more productive years is declining.'[23]

Without being too explicit, it reminded readers 'It is generally agreed that there is a significant but not necessarily simple or direct relationship between population changes and economic development.'[24]

Other international bodies were also expressing an interest. Earlier the World Health Organisation (WHO) had convened a major meeting on the 'Epidemiology of Aging' in January 1983. This was soon followed by a succession of reports on the social and economic implications of ageing from established bodies including the International Labour Office (ILO), the Council of Europe, the IMF and the OECD.[25]

By the late 1980s a flourishing area of academic and institutional concern was becoming more widely recognised in the rest of society. Peter Laslett brought the issue mainstream for many people with his book *A Fresh Map of Life: the Emergence of the Third Age* published in 1989. In it he drew attention to the opening up of a much more significant 'third age' after work – the second age – and before dependency and senility – the fourth age. This 'third age' was of variable and uncertain duration but could easily occupy over a quarter of the average life ranging from early retirement in the early or mid fifties to chronic ill health and dependency, from the late seventies or early eighties.

The phrase 'third age' originated from the French Universities du Troisième Age, which began to be instituted in the 1970s. It entered the Anglo-Saxon vocabulary when the first of the British Universities of the Third Age was founded in Cambridge in 1981. Laslett described the economic and demographic prerequisites of a third age as being a reasonable chance of reaching that age and there being enough people to qualify as a community. He confirmed that it 'only made an appearance in Britain during the 1950s and did not begin to establish itself as a settled feature until the 1980s'.[26]

Overall during the course of the 1980s the discussion about ageing was acquiring a significance quite distinct from its earlier beginnings. Ageing was moving from an area of specialised interest into an everyday assumption. Certainly interest in the issue was expanding quantitatively. There was a proliferation of books, articles and high-level conferences on the subject that continues to the present and shows no sign of abating.

But alongside this quantitative growth there has been a qualitative shift too, that has become even more noticeable in the 1990s. Ageing has crept into more and more areas of discussion as an assumed fact of life that must be taken into account. From economics to marketing, from politics to sociology, social trends are increasingly discussed from a demographic perspective.

At the same time the tone of the commentary has tended to become more pessimistic. In his earlier writings Laslett drew attention to the strengthening of this negative stereotyping of the third age, a phenomenon whose emergence he had viewed much more positively. In challenging the reasons for the unfavourable images of old age he had noted that, 'increases in length of life after 50, 60 or 70 are ... the grounds on which alarm has also been sounded as to the inevitable strain on our medical and other services, since it is these people who make the heaviest demands on them'.[27]

This negative view of ageing parallels the broader trend in intellectual thought this decade that tends towards the negative. Low expectations and caution have replaced vision and ambition. A cautious attitude that generally assumes the worst finds a strong echo in the problemitisation of an ageing population. For many commentators writing in the 1990s, the demographic trend has become more than a preoccupation. It has become a cause for panic. The image of the 'bomb' – the demographic time bomb – is so widespread that it has become a cliche within the discussion of population ageing.

In the 1990s coverage by international organisations has become more extensive. Almost every issue of the OECD's *World Economic Outlook* features concerns about the budgetary pressures.[28] Similar concerns are raised in the IMF's *World Economic Outlook*[29] and the UN's *World Economic and Social Survey* – especially the 1994 issue with a chapter on 'Economic and social implications of population dynamics'.

The worry about ageing provides a paradoxical complement to the longer established concern about population trends over much of the rest of the planet – too many babies. While the predominant concern about the South or the Third World is the population explosion, the specific anxiety for the North is population ageing.

Paul Kennedy, the British historian, links these two fears about population trends. Kennedy came to public attention in the late 1980s as a reluctant but influential forecaster of American imperial decline. He is now a pacesetter in the game of apocalyptic futurology. In a pessimistic and fatalist vision of the future published in 1993, demography occupies centre stage:

'While the demographic explosion (combined with reduced resources) is the greatest problem facing developing regions, many developed nations confront the opposite problem of stagnant or even negative population growth ... . Whereas developing nations have the burden of supporting millions younger than fifteen, developed nations have to look after fast-increasing millions older than sixty-five'.[30]

Kennedy is not alone in dressing 1990s angst in Malthusian clothes. Pierre Lellouche, an international relations specialist, and long-time adviser to the French president Jacques Chirac, also introduces ageing into his vision of the threat facing Western civilisation from an invasion of outside barbarians. He sees an apocalypse in the year 2000 with the unprecedented demographic growth of the population of the South contrasting with the ageing populations of the rich North that will remain stationary around the one billion mark.[31]

The racial connotations of such statements are not difficult to draw: too many of them (black), too few of us (white) and those there are, are too old. As Kennedy notes, without any self-criticism, discussion of ageing societies links with 'the further issue of deep-rooted cultural and racial anxieties, nicely described in one work as "the fear of population decline"'.[32] Kennedy is referring to the 1976 text by M Teitelbaum and J Winter of the same name.

Similar anxieties are explored in Ben Wattenberg's *The Birth Dearth* published towards the end of the 1980s.[33] He spelt out his worries about the cultural implications for Western civilisation of the main demographic trends:

'Western culture was dominant forty-odd years ago after the end of World War II, when the West made up about 22 per cent of the earth's population. Today the West comprises 15 per cent – and we are still dominant. Because of demographic echo-effects dealing with people already born, it is just about a sure thing that it will decline to under 9 per cent by 2025 and probably down to about 5 per cent by 2100 if present trends continue ... It is ... unreal to suggest that our values will remain untouched as our numbers go down, and down, and down, if our economic and military power go down, and down, and down. It will be difficult for tiny minorities, growing weaker, to set the tone or values of the world.'[34]

The metaphor all these commentators are employing is between a smaller, and, to make it worse, an ageing and physically deteriorating population, with an ageing and declining and less influential nation. This analogy is pertinent to understanding the process by which the preoccupation with ageing took off among some intellectuals, before spreading and deepening across most Western societies.

To summarise, over the past 20 years the demographic discussion has progressed from viewing ageing as a relevant population trend with some wider economic consequence to being a cipher for our anxious times. The conventional association of old age with decay and decline seems to make ageing an appropriate and attractive metaphor for societies that are themselves exhausted politically and intellectually, and lack positive visions for the future.

A population panic in the 1930s

Before exploring further the determinants of today's preoccupation with ageing, it is revealing to note that demographic fears are not entirely novel. We have described that the surge of interest in demographic ageing is predominantly a post-1970s phenomenon. However, there have been earlier incarnations this century of a concern with other aspects of demography, namely in the 1930s. These provide some historical precedent for non-demographic anxieties assuming a demographic form. Today's concern, though, stands out for being much more pervasive and powerfully felt.

To avoid any misunderstanding of the point in this section, it is important to stress that the current trend with respect to ageing is unprecedented. Making this following historical digression to the time before the Second World War is in no way seeking to establish a spurious continuity of today's concern with ageing, from earlier demographic worries. There is no eternal twentieth century interest in ageing, nor is it an issue that ebbs and flows. Today's intellectual mood, and the corresponding obsession with the problems of ageing, is historically specific to our times. For instance then, in the inter-war years, unlike today, demography remained a mainly specialist topic of interest. A big difference from today is that the concern at that time never took off as a wider social anxiety. Rather the sole purpose of this historical illustration is to indicate the way the highlighting of certain demographic trends can express different worries and sentiments.

During the inter-war years, several commentators expressed concern about the falling birth rate and the anticipated resulting effect of a shrinking population. It was a time of great social uncertainty, especially in Britain and most of Europe. The British optimism of the pre-First World War Edwardian years had drained away. In the economic sphere, it was around this time that the debate about the 'British disease' took off, i.e. the way Britain seemed to be losing out to its competitor countries. Even members of the ruling élite questioned what lay behind Britain's stagnation and relative economic decline. Was it government policy mistakes, obstinate trade unions, poor calibre managers, or the pernicious influence of the City? The range of suspects revealed an extensive loss of faith in formerly dependable social institutions.

Recognition that Britain was encountering new difficulties spread into other areas too: industrial strife, rivalry with other leading national powers, colonial unrest. All this spawned a new sense of malaise within the establishment classes. The onset of the slump in the 1930s reinforced the pessimistic feeling that nothing could be relied upon and that things were falling apart. In some quarters this gloomy mood stimulated a doom-mongering discussion of demographic trends.

The demographic focus then was falling fertility. In explicit language, which would appear out of place today, this was linked to a perception of national decline. The recognition of the secular decline in birth rates was adduced by some as underlying Britain's more tenuous position in the world. Sir James Marchant, secretary to the influential National Birth Rate Commission, had already concluded during the grim days of the First World War that, 'In the difference between the number of cradles and the number of coffins lies the existence and persistence of our Empire.'[35]

The Scottish doctor Halliday Sutherland, writing in 1922, pursued the same theme of the overriding importance of population matters for the future of society:

'Our declining birthrate is a fact of the utmost gravity, and a more serious position has never confronted the British people. Here in the midst of a great nation, at the end of a victorious war, the law of decline is working, and by that law the greatest empires in the world perished. In comparison with this single fact all other dangers, be they of war, of politics, or of disease are of little moment.'[36]

There was an explicit élitist element to this discussion. The worry about falling fertility often focused on the more specific concern that middle class birth rates were declining more rapidly than rates in the working class. Eugenicists, who still had considerable influence before the Nazi experience later discredited them, complained that this lowered the quality of the population and precipitated national decline.[37]

Neville Chamberlain, when Chancellor of the Exchequer in the mid-1920s, was also aware of demographic trends. Less controversially he focused more on the quantity, rather than the 'quality', of the population. In a budget speech he commented on the dangers of the declining birth rate for an imperial power.[38]

A few economists sought to theorise this fear by arguing that falling fertility would extend the slump. The dominant figure of inter-war economics, John Maynard Keynes, spelt out what he saw as the problems by linking it to his theory of effective demand. Declining fertility, he argued, would have an adverse effect on demand and result in even more unemployment.[39]

A concern about falling fertility continued until the Royal Commission on Population reported in 1949. The backdrop to the commission's work was the alarm caused by the steady fall in the birthrate since the 1870s. The Royal Commission in general endorsed this concern by warning that these demographic trends could make society 'dangerously unprogressive'.[40]

Its particular worry was that there were too many unproductive consumers in comparison to the number of productive workers. In the spirit of encouraging a reversal of falling fertility and the procreation of a sizeable generation of potential workers the commission recommended family allowances and social services for the benefit of children and mothers.[41]

However, these proposals were never discussed in full by Parliament. By the time the report was published this particular panic was nearly over. What accounted for this change? Some point to the fact that the birth rate was already climbing. Society was in the first stages of the post-war baby boom. However, since the early 1950s was too early to have known that this increase in fertility would have been sustained, other non-demographic factors must have played a role too in changing attitudes to population matters.

The main reason was that the end of military conflict and the first indications of renewed social stability and economic prosperity informed a more positive outlook in general. Demographic concerns, in general, tended to dissipate in the propitious conditions of political stability and a strengthening economic boom.

This historical digression indicates that in conditions of social uncertainty and anxiety - notwithstanding the many substantial differences between those decades and today - demographic concerns can take off.

A neutral view of ageing

Another historical comparison, this time with the post-war boom period, more sharply highlights what is different about demographic consciousness in current times. We noted earlier that there is evidence of sporadic interest in ageing since the Second World War. But this represents no continuum of concern. Today's focus upon ageing has contemporary roots. It is not the cumulative outcome of some gradual awakening of consciousness with respect to population ageing. Not only was interest in ageing infrequent in those times. More importantly, the striking difference is that ageing was viewed then in neutral terms, rather than as a problem as is the case increasingly during the past two decades.

On those rare occasions in the early post-war years when demographic ageing was discussed, it was done so in dispassionate, objective terms. For example, in the 1950s, Brockington's survey of relevant public health issues did mention the growth in the numbers of elderly people. He pointed to trends that are strikingly similar to those highlighted in our contemporary literature:

> 'The proportion of aged people is certain to increase still further during the next 30 years ... . The numbers living beyond 75 and particularly beyond 80, when the greatest difficulty arises, will advance sharply.'[42]

The same trends were recognised then as create such concern today. Population ageing was not some secret yet to be discovered. It was simply that then few saw reason to devote much attention to it. It was not regarded as a harbinger of apocalypse. Ageing populations in the industrialised countries were regarded as pretty incidental, unrelated to the prospects for economic prosperity and the provision of better social welfare. Brockington, for example, was explicit that, 'Despite the great numbers of old there is no cause for alarm. It is well within the capacity of a highly developed country to meet their requirements.'[43]

Of course, he was proved right. Not only were his forecasts for population ageing over the next three decades substantially correct, so was his confidence in the ability of an industrialised country to cope with this change. As was predicted in his time, by the mid-1980s Western society was considerably older than in the 1950s. Yet despite the grim warnings issued by a few lone individuals in the early post-war years, the economy and society had not collapsed under the weight of the increased numbers of elderly people.

This shows that knowledge of the same demographic ageing trend can evoke different reactions in different times, in the 1950s compared to the 1980s-90s. In the former period the discussion, albeit limited, tended to be neutral or even benign; in the latter it is increasingly catastrophist.

In the compilation of papers presented at the Hoover Institution seminar in 1985 on low fertility, the editors also noted this inconsistent approach. They concluded that 'depending on mood and temperament, as much as analysis, a declining population may be seen under different lights'.[44]

The French population historian Patrice Bourdelais came to the same result from his studies into demographic ageing, concluding that the discussion of ageing is not value-neutral. He noted that in the far past ageing has often been an indicator and metaphor of national weakness, degeneration or senescence. In nineteenth century France, he illustrates, ageing only began to be seen negatively as a problem after the trauma of defeat in the Franco-Prussian war. Earlier, in contrast, ageing had been regarded optimistically as the consequence of triumph over death.[45] This record alerts us that concern about ageing tells us more about the state of thought in society at any time than it does about objective demographic trends. Today's panic over the demographic time bomb is a sign of a society that feels itself to be in trouble – a sense of danger that is the outcome of social and political rather than demographic factors.

Building a time bomb
In understanding the hold of the demographic time bomb fear it is helpful to distinguish two trends, even though in reality they have been closely intertwined. The first is the creation of an agenda by various individuals and institutions, which identifies ageing as 'a major problem'. In most respects this is an agenda which scapegoats ageing as a primary source of contemporary economic difficulties. This has been fuelled by the consciousness of crisis that exists. Generally, this takes the form of a renewed concern about the amount of resources available. Too much is being wasted, too much is being consumed, and more production only creates more problems, especially for the environment. The notion of too many old people burdening the rest of society and consuming our inadequate quantities of resources is especially appealing.

Secondly, the conditions that make people susceptible to concern about this particular problem must be identified. Concern about ageing has during the 1990s extended across the whole of society. Today there is a ubiquitous sense of an impending disaster arising from the economic burden of demographic ageing. Ageing has become regarded as another of those inexorable phenomena, such as global warming, which we can probably do little about and which will force us all, sooner or later, to lower our sights with respect to our expectations of the future.

Another way of looking at this duality is that over the past 20 years there have been two mutually reinforcing phases to the entrenchment of the ageing concern. In the 1970s and for much of the 1980s the dynamic was predominantly economic and financial. It was about government cost cutting, or, as it worked out in practice, cost increase limiting. Most Western governments adopted the rhetoric of curbing state expenditure. Then from the late 1980s and through the 1990s ageing has become one manifestation of the wider generalised sense of unease and malaise that has taken hold. These two influences will be examined in their own terms and in their interaction.

First, how did the problematisation of ageing come about during the 1970s and 1980s? Institutional concern about the financial consequences of population ageing had its origins in these decades. This has been specifically evident on the part of national governments, beginning in the US and spreading to Europe and Britain. Alan Walker describes how:

> 'Population projections to the middle of the next century have aroused considerable fears among national governments and international agencies about the rising public expenditure costs associated with an ageing society. Thus most Western governments have either taken, or are contemplating taking, measures to restrain public spending on older people.'[46]

What has driven the emergence and spread of concern by institutions and economists about ageing populations? As shown earlier the phenomenon of population ageing is not new. Nor is it uniquely rapid today. In fact only a selective use of statistics allows one to anticipate anything extraordinary for the future pattern of ageing. Even then it is a fairly short-term phenomenon to about 2040. There is nothing specific in empirical terms to fuel the contemporary preoccupation that demographic ageing is an issue of our particular times. So, if there is nothing specific within the ageing phenomenon itself, what other factors are responsible?

In a recent weighty publication the UN claimed credit for its own role in fuelling the interest in ageing. It asserted that 'the topic of ageing began to receive increasing attention with the adoption of the International Plan of Action on Ageing in 1982 by the United Nations'.[47] That is one answer but, leaving aside the narcissistic aspect, it is also rather circular. It begs the question why was this plan adopted *then*.

The UN generally launches grandiose plans from international conferences as an expression of existing concerns rather than as the original initiator. Why did the UN convene this, its first World Assembly on Ageing in Vienna in the July of 1982, attracting delegates from 121 nations? More broadly why did the UN and other national and international institutions start to get involved with studying the social, economic and health situation of the elderly at the start of the 1980s?

As noted previously the early manifestations of the ageing discussion emerged a few years after the end of the post-war boom in the early 1970s. Through that decade, and for much of the 1980s, the ageing issue arose mainly within the context of the ideological and financial case for cutting back on the welfare state. This was itself an aspect of the emerging orthodoxy that public spending had to be restrained.

In response to the worldwide economic slowdown in the 1970s, state spending began to be perceived as the problem across most industrialised economies. The British political columnist Simon Jenkins summarised the new mood: 'To economists in the 1970s, (public spending) growth came to seem no longer a passive beneficiary of prosperity but a potential saboteur'.[48] Today pretty much everyone holds this anti-state sentiment.

Ageing is used as a neutral, non-ideological, apolitical pretext for legitimising reductions in public and especially, welfare spending. The assumption of 'too many old people' impresses the need and urgency for welfare reform. It is presented as self-evident that what society could afford in one demographic case can no longer be funded in a different one. In a paper presented in 1985 Carolyn Weaver bluntly summed up the case:

> 'If sustained, low fertility and the consequent aging of the population will strike at the heart of social security systems as we know them today. This concern was voiced clearly by Stanford Ross, then US Commissioner of Social Security, when he said, "We are confronting a worldwide issue which goes to the very viability of the institution."'[49]

Demographic ageing's key role in the 1980s was as a politically respectable way of legitimising the anti-welfarist cost-cutting mood. It has contributed to the project of discrediting the welfare state. Alan Walker locates the growth of the ageing panic in the 1980s as closely linked to this wider anti-state agenda. 'Political ideology', he argues, 'has distorted and amplified the macroeconomic consequences of population ageing to legitimate anti-welfare state policies.'[50]

Expanding on this thesis he writes:

> 'Political concern about the cost of ageing has been amplified artificially in order to legitimate policies aimed at diminishing the state's role in financial and social support for older people ... . Official unease is not about the cost of ageing *per se*, but rather the public expenditure cost.'[51]

Jay Ginn has also speculated that myths about older people are deliberately manipulated for definite ends. Specifically she believes that those who wish to justify cuts in public pensions depict older people as threatening the viability of welfare states through their demands on resources.[52]

Minkler and Robertson explain how the ageing discussion allows welfare changes and cuts, not just directed at the elderly, to become politically 'invisible'. The cuts appear to be merely the limits of the possible.[53] The justification for welfare reform becomes technical, rather than political or ideological. Opponents of the welfare state used the ageing panic to help naturalise and legitimise their objectives, to give these a supposedly objective basis in an unfortunate but unyielding natural trend of an ageing population.

Demographic ageing became presented as a legitimate explanation for why resources are tight and for why there cannot be enough for all social welfare needs. Warnes summarises the tendency to use the 'ageing burden' in this way:

> 'It is in the career interest of international civil servants to discover, exaggerate and project an imminent fiscal "crisis" with seemingly irrefutable presentations of statistical evidence. During the 1980s, vested professional interests have coincided with the dominant neo-liberal economic orthodoxy to reduce public expenditure.'[54]

In this vein the World Bank asserted that 'because health and pension spending rise together, pressure on a country's resources and government budgets increases exponentially as populations age ... . High government spending on old age security crowds out other important public goods and services'.[55] And when, as a result, 'belts must be tightened', it is reasonable to review commitments made in the area where the pressures have mounted, or use these pressures as a pretext for reductions in other budgets.

Through assisting the consolidation of a pro-cuts mood, the notions of old age and ageing as big problems for society helped both delegitimise the elderly and legitimise the cuts. The change in demography – perceived as an objective phenomenon – was highlighted as a significant danger making it possible to cast the necessity for proposed cutbacks as 'non-political'.[56] This helped to hide, or at least relativise, other more significant social factors pushing up public spending, including unemployment, and early retirement as a result of the lack of jobs.[57] Blame is attributed to a 'natural' phenomenon like ageing, not to any social or economic factors.

Raymond Jack spelt out, in a thoughtful review of social policy developments during the 1970s and 1980s, that the 'tactical' role played by demography in welfare discussions is not entirely new. There is a history to demography being introduced into the welfare debate to serve other ends. He relates:

> 'In the politics of welfare the "problem" of the ageing population has frequently played a tactical role, and in this sense the post-war development of social policy and social services is inextricably bound up with the growth of the aged population. This is because approximately half of all expenditure on social security, health and social services is devoted to people over 60 who constitute less than 17 per cent of the population.'[58]

The use of ageing as a component in the consolidation of the anti-welfarist consensus advanced at slightly different times, and in slightly different forms in different Western countries. John Myles describes the initial expressions of this outlook in America. He writes that by the mid-1970s:

> 'The "crisis" of old age security had been discovered. In the usual formulation, the roots of the crisis are attributed to demography: the system of old age security entitlements currently in place in the capitalist democracies cannot withstand the rise in the number of old people projected for the decades ahead.'[59]

American economists' particular interest in the social security implications of ageing had first been aroused for many of them by an article from Martin Feldstein in 1974.[60] This set the scene for the beginnings of a new consensus that ageing would put pressure on government spending, especially for the Old Age, Survivors, Disability Insurance (OASDI) programme.

It was in 1975 that the Advisory Council on Social Security first forecast a future deficit on the social security fund as a result of ageing. It proposed a rise in the retirement age to 68 to offset the growth in benefit costs. The next year this prospect was highlighted in the OASDI Board of Trustees report.[61] In 1977 Clark reported to a Center for Population Research conference that ageing was becoming an important item on the congressional agenda and anticipated that it would continue to rise in importance.[62]

Estes describes that as conditions in the US economy worsened in the late 1970s and early 1980s 'increasingly strong political and economic interests became invested in defining Social Security as a system facing crisis'.[63] At the end of the 1970s President Carter broke with the tradition of short term analysis in his 1980 federal budget report and took the initiative of incorporating the long term warnings of the burden which the rise in old age dependency would mean for the pension programme. He forecast that resultant pension costs alone could raise the US tax burden from 33 per cent of Gross Domestic Product (GDP) in 1980 to almost 50 per cent by 2030, assuming the ratio of retirement benefits to average wages were maintained.

With the authority of the most powerful man in the world behind it, this report gave official credence to the problem of ageing. It described how an increasingly elderly population, rising life expectancy, and the distinct trend toward declining labour force participation by older people, could combine to create a retirement and medical system funding problem in the twenty-first century. The alternatives presented were stark: either higher taxes, or lower benefits and later retirement ages.[64] By 1981 a crisis in social security was declared by the president, joined by politicians, economists and policy analysts of many persuasions, paving the way for the Social Security Amendment Act of 1983. As Estes highlights, 'The crisis designation provides an impetus to "do something", while preparing the public for the idea that sacrifices will have to be made.'[65]

By the mid-1980s Boserup could reflect that 'public budgets are already burdened by increasing expenditure due to the longer lifespans of the elderly and the high cost of life-prolonging health expenditure for old people'.[66] By then this type of statement was common currency in American policy circles. The problem of ageing was well established as a pretext for state expenditure spending cuts.

This use of ageing within the US state/welfare debate has been followed elsewhere. Baldock and Evers report the ubiquitous use of the 'demographic pressures' argument in their study of the common shift away from public welfare care systems evident in Sweden, the Netherlands and Britain since the early 1990s.[67] They show how cuts in many of the post-war European welfare states were justified 'because of demographic, economic and ideological pressures common to all European nations'.[68]

Daatland also describes how since this time all the Scandinavian countries have become increasingly concerned with the public spending implications of ageing for their relatively generous welfare systems, and that this has provided one reason for curtailing them.[69] Similarly Anne-Marie Guillemard has said of the French discussion of welfare: old-age policies are 'the trouble-spot of the Welfare State'.[70]

Reviewing the European situation Hamish McRae, columnist for *The Independent*, sums up the perception in the second half of the1990s:

'The social security network created by European governments has become extremely expensive to operate, and will become more so as the European population gets older and a diminishing proportion of people of working age have to support a larger number of dependants … . As the European population ages, health care for the old will place a still greater burden on the smaller cohort of people of working age. To this should be added the cost of state pensions … . (Most) European countries do not have substantial funded pension schemes, where each generation of workers saves for its own pension. Instead these countries rely on the next generation of taxpayers to pay for the pensions of the previous one. As the ratio of worker to dependant deteriorates, all European countries will find their government budgets or social security funds under increasing pressure.'[71]

Focusing on Britain for a moment, the negative assumption about the burden of ageing has helped underpin the cut backs in public welfare provisions for almost two decades. Even as far back as the 1970s the Labour government's pronouncements gave a flavour of what was to come by raising the prospect that population ageing could become more costly for the welfare state, and on all our pockets. A 1978 document from the DHSS, titled 'A Happier Old Age', summarised the argument:

'Helped by improved health services, better housing, and other social conditions, more people are living longer. But the rise in the number of very old people puts a great strain on health and social services. And on all our pockets – because more pensioners living longer means more to pay in tax and national insurance.'[72]

During the 1980s this potential crisis resulting from ageing populations was deployed frequently to justify constraints on public expenditure. Responsibility for the crisis of state spending was at least partly placed upon the existence of too many old people.

It was no accident that in February 1980 it was to a gathering of the charity for older people, Age Concern, that the social services minister Patrick Jenkin spelt out the new Tory government's approach to welfare. In language, which was to become familiar, Jenkin criticised a welfare state based on universalist principles for undermining independence, the family and individual responsibility, and for fostering a damaging dependency culture. The minister claimed:

'Over the last couple of decades we have tended to get the perspectives wrong ... . We should put the responsibility for day to day help back where it belongs – into the communities where people live. The statutory services have of course an important role as a back up to this informal and voluntary effort ... . But ... the primary responsibility rests with the community.'[73]

The role of the community in this speech, as the place 'where problems arose and were often solved',[74] appeared to some at the time as a concession to post-war liberal thinking. In fact it heralded that state support for old people was no longer sacrosanct. This theme was made more explicit in a White Paper *Growing Older* the following year, 1981. Drawing attention to the increasing proportions of elderly people the DHSS explained:

'The government's overall priority is to reduce and contain inflation ... . We have to hold back public spending and concentrate on the revival of the economy ... . Money may be limited, but there is no lack of goodwill. An immense contribution is already being made to the support and care of elderly people by families, friends and neighbours, and by a wide range of private, voluntary and religious organisations. We want to develop these activities so as to develop the broadest possible base of service.'[75]

The White Paper kept reiterating that the ageing trend simply made it impracticable to think the existing systems could continue. Other methods must be found. The merits of 'care in the community' were espoused as the necessary way forward. Responsibility for the elderly was to be taken by individuals, by families, by neighbours, by volunteers, in fact by any means except by reliance on collective public provision:

'Public authorities simply will not command the resources to deal with (an ageing population) alone; nor, even if they did, would it be right or possible for official help to meet all individual needs ... . It is the role of public authorities to sustain and, where necessary, develop – but never to displace – (personal) support and care. Care *in* the community must increasingly mean care *by* the community ... .

Whatever level of public expenditure proves practicable, and however it is distributed, the primary sources of support and care for elderly people are informal and voluntary ... .

There should be a wider appreciation of the limits to public provision and finance. Public authorities or public finance simply cannot meet wholly – or even predominantly – the increasing needs of the increasing numbers of old people. This will be a task for the whole community ... .

Improving the lives of elderly people must involve the whole of society.'[76]

It was at this time too that old people began to be used as the scapegoat for other harsh spending decisions in Britain. The trend towards more old people was deployed as the pretext for cuts elsewhere in the state budget or for the imposition of tax rises. With the elderly then taking around one third of social spending costs the White Paper argued that more old people would mean a still greater burden: 'For the time being, therefore, any additional resources devoted to elderly people can only come from other spending areas, or from taxpayers as a whole.'[77]

Since those early warnings, public sector cost cutting and the promotion of personal responsibility have been linked with the growing numbers of elderly on many more occasions.

For example, in 1984, prime minister Margaret Thatcher for the first time explicitly used the 'demographic time bomb' image to justify spending cuts. To an American audience – a traditional venue for her to try out her new arguments – she claimed that as a result of the rising elderly population 'Britain faced a "time bomb" over social security spending ...' and she said she would not sit by and 'do nothing' about the cost of pensions and the National Health Service. At the same time she also 'criticised the effect on personal responsibility of public spending on health and pensions. "You are redistributing responsibility and you are taking quite a bit of a man's independence by taking away so much of his income." ' [78]

Later that year, in the Green Paper *The Next Ten Years*, the government went so far as to argue that 'the main factor affecting the social security programme is the provision which has to be made for the elderly'.

Deploying the argument that demographic trends left them little choice, government ministers began the shift towards the privatisation of pensions and the encouragement of occupational and private pension schemes in place of an adequate state pension. The mid-1980s reform of pensions, overseen by social security minister Norman Fowler, was rhetorically driven by the government's concern about the level of spending on pensions required in the future to maintain the ageing population. Ratios of national insurance contributors to pensioners were presented to support the argument that the cost of maintaining the full State Earnings Related Pension Scheme (SERPS) would be prohibitive.

The government's policy pushed further down the road of individual responsibility, arguing the need: 'to distinguish what can and should be organised by individuals and their employers, and what can and should be organised by government'.[79] In this spirit SERPS was substantially modified by the 1986 Social Security Act.

Two years later the 1988 report, *Community Care: Agenda for Action* from Sir Roy Griffiths, used 'common sense' arguments about the demographic necessity to curtail social provision of long term care in order to legitimise a financially driven objective. Later this approach became much more general in the welfare debate. Baldock and Evers describe how changes in the care of the dependent elderly in the 1980s were a particular precursor to a broader redefinition of the role of government and wider changes in the welfare state.[80]

The Griffiths' inquiry terms of reference made explicit the primacy of cost cutting. The terms were 'to review the way in which public funds are used to support community care policy and to advise ... on the options for action that would improve the use of these funds as a contribution to more effective community care'.[81]

The subsequent 1989 White Paper, *Caring for People: Community care in the Next Decade and Beyond*, adopted Griffiths' recommendations for extending 'care in the community' for the elderly and other dependent groups. It again highlighted the demographic urgency for the changes, warning that:

'Most people needing community care are elderly and there is an increasing tendency of elderly people to live alone ... . (Population) growth will be greatest amongst the very elderly (over 85s) who are also most likely to be disabled and in greater need of community care.'[82]

Its solution to this dilemma was presented in empowering tones:

'Helping people to lead, as far as possible, full and independent lives is at the heart of the government's approach to community care. Improving the services that enable them to do that is a continuing commitment shared by all concerned ... . Promoting choice and independence underlies all the government's proposals.'[83]

Pursuing this perspective the 1990 National Health Service and Community Care Act for the first time gave legislative endorsement to care in the community for the elderly. The legislation retained Griffiths' use of the rapid pace of ageing as necessitating the reforms. Tinker et al's assessment of the development of policy towards the elderly was certain that 'the objective of cost containment has undoubtedly influenced policy towards the care of elderly people'.[84] They point out the not-so-subtle change in the meaning of community care that had taken place during the 1980s: from 'care in the community' to the concept of 'caring by the whole community'.[85] As Arber and Ginn noted in 1990, even the idea of a 'carer', who looked after old people 'in the community', was still quite novel at the time: 'Ten years ago,' they wrote, 'the term "carer" did not exist.'[86] The ageing pretext made easier and faster this transformation that in the end has facilitated welfare cost cutting.

One does not need to be an irredeemable cynic to recognise cost cutting, not merely cost efficiency, as underlying the official implementation of 'care in the community' for the elderly. Baldock and Evers claim that 'In the UK ... the primacy of cost containment in the debate about the care of the elderly is very explicit.'[87] Jack, too, makes a convincing case that 'central to this (community care) agenda has been the cost of providing health and social services to a growing population of retired people and the alleged implications of this for the future of the welfare state'.[88] The cuts process becomes excused by 'natural' demographic shifts.

In this way the ageing concern served the authorities the dual role of making old people acquiescent to welfare cuts and younger people cognizant of the need to turn to private provision and not look to the state for help. The old as a distinct grouping in society was made to occupy two roles. First, they were scapegoats for financial problems (excessive and unsustainable levels of public spending). Secondly, they were either a remedial target (cutting welfare provision for the elderly became a means of central cost cutting), or a justification for other cuts owing to the supposed mounting and unsustainable burden of providing for the old.

Today this sort of response is a conventional wisdom that no longer needs to be substantiated. International institutions ritualistically incorporate the financial burden of ageing populations into their equally ritualistic calls for fiscal consolidation by the industrialised countries. In its clamour for the reduction of state budget imbalances in 1995 the International Monetary Fund claimed 'user fees for some types of public services and better targeted support programmes' need to be considered and 'reforms will also be needed to alleviate future budgetary strains resulting from aging populations'.[89]

At the same time the OECD made a similar demand from its member states. It emphasised the need to reduce public sector deficits and debt-to-GDP ratios 'particularly in view of the expected increase in fiscal burdens associated with ageing populations ... . In view of medium-term pressures from pension commitments and health care programmes, which will rise as populations age, it is all the more critical to address fiscal imbalances as soon as possible'.[90]

Overall then, ageing populations have become an accepted scapegoat for cutting back on state spending in Britain and across the industrialised countries. In this vein Johnson and Falkingham concluded their study, *Ageing and Economic Welfare*, with the prediction that as a result of population ageing 'it is ... unlikely that existing policy regimes will be able to live on into the third or fourth decades of the next century without fundamental restructuring'.[91] After only a few years this prediction is close to fulfilment.

Concern about ageing has proved influential in helping to forge this anti-welfarist consensus within key strata of elite opinion formers. The ageing population became a convenient pretext to justify tightening up on state expenditure and on welfare spending in particular.

Carroll Estes sums up this function. Noting how 'ideologies of individualism, self-help, privatisation, and pro-competition are being used to delegitimate public programmes and reduce expectations about what governments can and should do to ameliorate social problems', she explained how there was a subjective basis to this justification for austerity. It 'lies in the socially constructed notion that federal spending on the elderly and the poor is the cause of the problems of the US economy. Blaming ageing obscures the origins stemming from the capitalist social system'.[92]

Developing the personal responsibility aspect of this argument, she described how in the US, 'Social Security's problems have been portrayed as the product of "mistaken" generosity in domestic programmes, of demographic ageing, and the fault of those *choosing* to retire early - ignoring health status, age discrimination, and structural unemployment problems that significantly contribute to early retirement.'[93]

To summarise, population ageing in the 1980s became a convenient scapegoat to justify welfare provision cuts. Underlying concerns about the development of the welfare state as too expensive and poorly run were made more specific by highlighting the welfare costs of ageing. Ageing became seen as a cause of financial problems, and, in particular, welfare spending troubles and a justification for welfare cuts, both for the elderly and for other parts of society.

An age of anxiety
Before the 1990s the argument about the financial burden of ageing usually remained reasonably dispassionate. It was also restricted to relatively narrow circles of specialists, politicians and social commentators. However, over the past decade what began as mainly a pragmatic pretext for government cost cutting has become transformed into a more pervasive worry about the future. The ageing discussion has moved beyond, though still incorporates, its original cost-cutting agenda.

At the same time, over the course of the 1990s the concern about demographic ageing has gained a much wider social purchase. This has come about mainly because of a changing mood that has, in different forms, influenced those in authority, opinion formers and the wider public outlook. The new mindset can be summarised as one of generalised anxiety and is based upon the view that society has moved into uncharted territory. In the sphere of economics this is generally attributed to the twin effects of globalisation and the pace of technological change.

More widely it has become commonplace in the nineties to talk about 'malaise'. Many contemporary writers including Anthony Giddens, Christopher Lasch, William Rees-Mogg, John Gray, Ulrich Beck have articulated or described the new mood of unease, a heightened perception of risk and a generalised erosion of certainty.[94]

The UN *World Economic Surveys*, for example, provide one barometer of the change in sentiment. During the 1980s the UN would often describe its reports on the world economic recovery as merely 'tinged with uncertainty'. By 1988 it was becoming less sure about the future and pointed to an environment with more downside risks. It reviewed the 1987 stock market crash as instilling 'fears of similar turbulence to come', and warned that exchange rate and interest rate instability 'might again lead to major financial disruption'.[95]

By the next year it was even less sanguine in pointing to the greater risks and climate of unpredictability occasioned by the extension of internationalisation. Specifically it spelt out its 'worries that the US might have to raise interest rates to attract funds and that eventually the confidence of foreign investors might erode, with a consequence of a great upheaval in the international economy'.[96]

The UN's 1990 review of 'The Year 1989' incorporated even more fears of economic and political trouble on the horizon. The end of the Eastern bloc was seen as opening up an era of great uncertainty and apprehension alongside new opportunities.

One consequence of this shift in outlook has been to exacerbate the negative connotations of population ageing. This spread of concern about population ageing in the last decade of the century is especially ironic given that the ageing phenomenon is not just slow at present, but it is even slower this decade than in the last one.

Ageing has become one of those phenomena that manifest the sense of social malaise afflicting most Western countries. The assumption that ageing is a problem is now one of those 'facts of life' that illustrate the angst characteristic of the 1990s. Concerns about societies growing older both reflect and appear to provide evidence for a perturbed social mindset. The initial financial motivation behind the highlighting of the difficulties caused by an ageing society has been built upon by this prevailing sense of economic and political uncertainty.

This change in attitude derives from two main mutually reinforcing factors. The first is a broader sense of crisis, not so much in the economy as narrowly perceived, but a wider feeling that things are not working as they are supposed to, a sense that society is out of control. The inflated anticipation of a global financial meltdown and of a return to 1930s-style slump in the summer of 1998 was indicative of this mindset.

Secondly, this coincides with the uncertainties brought on by the termination of many post-war political arrangements. This has both international and domestic dimensions. The changes that have swept the world over the past decade have fostered a sense of unease. The end of the Cold War at the end of the 1980s was initially welcomed as a triumph of Western values. However, this triumphalism soon dissipated when it was seen to have removed a vital raison d'être for many Western institutions. Being against the East provided coherence for the West. Now a more difficult question was posed: what is the West positively for? Once revered institutions lost both self-confidence and authority. Starting with the most directly affected, the military alliance of NATO, this malaise soon spread to other international institutions, and then to domestic ones. Most institutions now seem affected by this new mood, as they stumble from crisis to crisis. Governments, parliaments, the judiciary, traditional Western churches and in Britain the monarchy, have all fallen sharply in public esteem.

Previous ideological agendas have also lost their relevance and purchase. Beginning with socialism, this trend spread to the mixed economy ideas of Keynesianism, corporatism and welfarism. More recently the neo-liberal doctrine of free market capitalism has succumbed to the same fate. This extensive crumbling of the competing ideals and institutions of the post-war order has undermined many of the ruling élite's certainties of the past. As a result the powers that be across the industrialised world feel they have lost their bearings.

These new uncertainties about how to operate are paralleled by a growing sense of social fragmentation. Commentators worry about the end of the age of deference. Others emphasise the breakdown of the previous moral order. Fears about crime, the breakdown of the family, disaffected youth and the erosion of trust or social capital are widespread.

This feeling of uncertainty and insecurity influences discussion and debate in all spheres of life. Politicians have lost popular authority and have tended to limit their objectives. The main idea coming out of political think tanks on both sides of the Atlantic seems to be that there are no more 'big ideas'. Most Western governments have adopted a narrower agenda of managing what exists rather than seeking to intervene in society in pursuance of more ambitious aims. In Pat Kane's words, nudging pragmatism has overtaken strict planning.[97]

In business, conditions are felt to be tougher and more out of control partly as a result of operating in the new global market. The pace of technology change, especially in Information Technology, adds to the sense of working in a new business environment with the past no longer valid as a guide for action. Three forces – connectivity, speed and intangibles – are said to be blurring the rules and redefining our businesses and our lives.[98] As Stuart Crainer wrote about the business world at the end of the 1990s:

> 'This is the era of questions. Questioning is in vogue – Charles Handy has carved a lucrative niche as the working world's question master. Insecurity is the awkward new reality.'[99]

For individuals, jobs are seen to be less secure. The frequency of downsizing announcements throughout the ups and downs of the economic cycle reinforces the loss of belief in security of employment. For individuals uncertainty at work has extended into the home, reinforcing the notion that the once reassuring institution of the family is in decline.

Interacting with the élite's loss of nerve, the erosion of previous collectivities is a major source for this popular mood. The demise during the 1980s of trade unions and of less formal mechanisms of support, solidarity and community have left people more on their own than ever to face the problems of everyday life. The social fragmentation and individuation that has ensued has made life seem more insecure. There is a sense that there is no one you can trust, sometimes not even yourself. This has spawned a much greater popular consciousness of risk and of fear for the future. Social surveys in the 1990s, for example, report the sea change that parents now assume that their children will be worse off, rather than better off, than themselves.

Risk today is not mainly seen as a general problem facing society. The most pervasive and debilitating form of risk consciousness is that risk is seen in a more individualised way. Paul Hershey, senior financial analyst at Mintel the retail analysts, noted this important trend in a report in 1996: 'the public is slowly recognising that economic risk is shifting away from the state and company to the individual.'[100]

The sense that life is riskier in general fosters a terrain where problems are exaggerated and popular panics can emerge. These social trends of the past period generate the general climate for the inflated concern of population ageing. But what explains the specific concern about ageing? Several of the common assumptions about ageing outlined in chapter 2 help give population ageing particular purchase in a period of general uncertainties.

First, because of the process of individuation, concern about personal ageing is especially strong today. As a result of the frequent conflation of different types of ageing these intensified apprehensions about the individual ageing process easily transpose onto the phenomenon of demographic ageing. The particular hold of the demographic time bomb is therefore partly a function of the individuated sense of anxiety that is so widespread today.

Individuation turns people in on themselves, to what is closest to them, to their own lives and those closest to them. It accentuates one of the strongest fears people feel for themselves and loved ones – growing old and dependent. At a personal level uncertainty about what life has in store can quickly focus upon such fears. The life assurance and pensions company Allied Dunbar struck a chord with many with its advertising slogan: 'For the life you don't yet know.'

In this respect the ageing panic is most powerful in its impact on the young and middle aged rather than those who are already old. Younger generations do not just have their own old age to worry about and plan for, but also concern about who will provide for old people in general, and for their ageing parents, in particular.

At a time when state provision for the elderly is well known to be under the axe this worry has clear substance, even if it is often exaggerated. Economic changes have contributed to this greater fear about old age. Labour market reorganisation and especially the onset of the practice of early retirement have exacerbated a feeling of uncertainty about one's older years. In Britain it will soon be the case that only half of 55 to 64-year-old men are in paid employment. This means many can expect a 'third age' after work of at least 20 years, which appears daunting in anticipation. People are unclear about what they will be doing during these years. Will they stay healthy? Have they made sufficient, or any, financial provision for these non-salaried years? Will they have any positive role to play?

The fear of living too long, and of the health and financial problems that may accompany you on your elderly way, is exacerbated by change in one particular support organisation – the family. The idea that the family is dead is itself an exaggerated concern of our times, peddled initially by some social scientists and other opinion formers. Nevertheless, while the family survives, the family structure is changing in ways that appear to reinforce our own fears of old age.

There is greater independence between generations that tend to be more mobile geographically. They are more likely to work and live apart. This contributes to the breakdown of the extended family structure and helps exacerbate the concern about who is going to be there to look after you in your older, dependent years. An irony of this contributor to the concern about ageing is that the greater independence of over-64s, who are fitter and healthier than their predecessors, and pursue much more active lives, means most elderly people do not fit the stereotype of burdensome dependents. Nevertheless a change in the family structure that results from greater elderly independence, becomes a source of additional fear of elderly dependence.

The worry about inter-generational conflict is another overstated concern that reinforces the negative connotations of ageing. But to say it is exaggerated is not to doubt the reality of the perception of such tensions between generations and the existence of genuine worries between people of different generations. Opinion surveys, for example, confirm that many old people are scared of youth. There may not be a sound basis to this outlook but it exists nevertheless. The sense of social breakdown and fragmentation is inflamed, and everyone's susceptibility to the concern about ageing is magnified.

A second factor behind ageing's strong hold is that it seems to be a natural problem. This is relevant to another feature of the new sense of anxiety: the strengthening of an acceptance of limits to growth. The 1990 UN *World Economic Survey*, referred to above, endorsed the more modest view of what should be expected in the way of growth in the future that has become common:

'Throughout the world there was an important awakening to both local and global environmental threats to future development and the need for joint action. There was also a readiness, which had been growing throughout the 1980s, to re-examine fundamental assumptions about the nature and the objective of economic and social progress, and a reaction against the neglect of the human condition.'[101]

The sluggishness of the capitalist economy has tended to become accepted. Moreover, the limitations to future growth are often presented as the result of natural barriers. The economic impasse becomes accepted as the inevitable and natural consequence of a world of limits.

This is symptomatic of the way ideas of progress and human improvement have given way to a fatalistic feeling that less can be done to improve conditions in the future. For example, the notion that governments can do anything significant to address major economic problems is generally considered naive and outdated. Especially since the end of the 1980s there has been a growing disbelief in the effectiveness of state action. Current fatalist attitudes to the state reflect the perception that traditional state institutions and practices are inappropriate to contemporary problems and tasks.

The diminished significance attached to the role of the state is symptomatic of a general mood of lowering of expectations which pervades society. The earlier belief that state action could solve most problems has been abandoned. The combination of economic depression and the exhaustion of the past politics of left and right has created a unique type of consensus which accepts that nothing much can be done.

The loss of faith in the state is paralleled by a more popular crisis of belief in politics and of directed human action. If state intervention or political activity is seen to be doomed from the start, then any broader attempt to solve the problems of society also has to be abandoned. From this view there is little point in even trying to alleviate the difficulties we face. The possibility of effective human action in social affairs recedes.

This increase in an acceptance of impervious limits gives supposedly natural issues like demography a particular attraction. Ageing, viewed as a natural constraint, becomes one justification for the acceptance of lower horizons of what is possible. As McRae concludes in his book outlining his predictions for the next 30 years: 'Demography alone will tend to curb the rise in living standards.'[102]

This is more than a problem of justifying lower economic expectations. A preoccupation with limits amounts to a loss of faith in human capabilities and in the potential to learn and adapt. In these myopic conditions, perceived problems – such as ageing – tend to be exaggerated or inflated. With challenges built up to be bigger than they really are, this further exacerbates the tendency to dismiss any possibility of society's coming up with solutions to its problems. Rather than seeking to resolve social problems there is a tendency instead to attribute them to external factors.

When society is troubled, scapegoats tend to become more popular. Ageing is presented today as such a scapegoat for many genuine economic problems. It is a different type of scapegoat from those employed in the quite recent past with respect to economic concerns.

It is widely recognised that since 1973 the Western world has experienced a marked economic slowdown, compared to the rest of the post-war period. This period has been broken into a series of recessions, with the recovery phases each being less dynamic. Growth levels and productivity rates have both slowed. Earlier in the past quarter century there were other scapegoats, other attempts to find exogenous, non-endogenous causes for this slowdown. For example, Middle Eastern oil sheikhs, and the trade union barons. What is significant today is that as these specific scapegoats have faded into the background, or been removed effectively from the scene, there has been a tendency to replace them not with new troublesome social groups but with non-economic, non-social, more natural explanations. Ageing fits this bill. The difference with the new scapegoat of ageing is that this is not a replacement of like for like. There has been a shift from specific problems which can potentially be controlled or dealt with, to non-specific, almost supra human, natural explanations, which by their character are even more difficult to tackle.

Thirdly, the way that ageing seems inevitable and inexorable adds to its purchase as a contemporary concern. As Johnson and Falkingham recognise, the idea of a demographic time bomb appears to rest on firmer foundations 'than other catastrophe predictions such as global warming and energy depletion. This is because the baby boom generation will be retiring between 2010 and 2025, and nothing can be done to change that.'[103] Ageing will happen, it cannot be stopped and all mankind can do is take a few compensating measures such as privatising pensions schemes.

This appeal of inevitability is reinforced because it pertains to the medium term future, and so cannot be proved or disproved with any assurance. The time bomb will explode not so early that there would already be indisputable evidence of its harmful effects, nor too far in the future that it will not affect our own lives and even more those of our children.

To summarise, perceiving the world in an increasingly individualised way people tend to inflate or exaggerate problems in general. The dominance of the individual perspective especially enhances the focus on the personal risks we face through our lives. Accordingly the many risks associated, or even believed to be associated, with old age – illness, immobility, dependence, violence, abuse, senility, and death – all assume a higher profile and focus. This enhanced sense of fearing one's own old age creates a particular receptivity to the concern about population ageing.

The conventional image of personal deterioration linked with individual ageing makes the image of personal senility a ready metaphor for social decay. A society worried about an uncertain and possibly decaying future becomes susceptible to apocalyptic panics in general. The individuated outlook makes concerns about personal ageing and, by association, demographic ageing particularly appropriate. The belief that ageing is a natural and inexorable process reinforces its hold on popular consciousness. What better symbol for a society that has lost faith in its own future than to be haunted by the spectre of old age, decay and senile dementia.

The outcome of all this panic contains a genuine worry. The fear of ageing further helps propel the sense of individuated anxiety. The danger is that this tends to paralyse people and encourage passivity in the face of confronting genuine social problems and challenges. The worries about demographic ageing are spurious. But the genuine hold these fears have is problematic when it reinforces the existing mood of fatalism. It encourages a lowering of expectations of the future and undermines the belief that it is worth working together to overcome perceived problems in pursuit of a better world.

Notes

1. Townsend and Wedderburn (1965), p 10.
2. See Tinker (1992), chapter 3.
3. Clark, Kreps, and Spengler (1978).
4. Kuznets (1965), p 121.
5. See Furedi (1997).
6. OECD (1966).
7. Espenshade and Serow (1978).
8. Davis et al (1987), p 345.
9. Gaullier (1982), p 178.
10. Serow and Espenshade (1978), p 18.
11. Clark et al (1978), p 949.
12. Gaullier (1982), p 178.
13. Kohli, Rosenow, and Wolf (1983), p 25.

14. See Rejda and Shepler (1973); Hogan (1974); Turchi (1975); Clark (1977); Reddaway (1977).
15. Serow and Espenshade (1978), p 65.
16. OPCS (1984).
17. See Tinker (1992).
18. Editorial, *Ageing and Society*, vol 1, no 1,1981, p 2.
19. Townsend (1981), p 5.
20. Walker (1983), pp 390–91.
21. See Parker (1982).
22. OECD (1988b), p 58.
23. UN (1989), p 211.
24. UN (1989), p 211.
25. See ILO (1984); Council of Europe (1984); Heller, Hemming and Kolmert (1986); OECD (1988a); OECD (1988b); OECD (1988c).
26. Laslett (1987), p 137.
27. Laslett (1987), pp 143–44.
28. See, for example, the October 1992 and October 1993 issues of OECD, *Economic Outlook*.
29. See, for example, IMF (1994), p 41.
30. Kennedy (1993), p 35–6.
31. Lellouche (1993), p 34.
32. Kennedy (1993), p 39.
33. For a full exposition of the racial factor underlying much contemporary discussion of population issues see Furedi (1997).
34. Wattenberg (1987), pp 97–98.
35. Marchant (1916), p 17.
36. Sutherland (1922), p 155.
37. See Lewis (1979), pp 33–48.
38. *House of Commons Debates*, 300 (1934–35), col 1634.
39. Keynes (1937), pp 1–5.
40. Johnson and Falkingham (1992), p 2.
41. Royal Commission (1949).
42. Brockington (1956), p 202.
43. Brockington (1956), p 205.
44. Davis et al (1987b), p 352.
45. Bourdelais (1993).
46. Walker (1990), p 394.
47. UN (1993), p 5.
48. Jenkins (1995), p 11.
49. Weaver (1987), p 274.
50. Walker (1990), p 377.
51. Walker (1990), p 378.
52. Ginn (1993).
53. Minkler and Robertson (1991).
54. Warnes (1993), p 318.
55. World Bank (1994), p 2.
56. See Peterson (1982), for an alarmist view of the notion that the social security crisis had been created by a demographic explosion of older people.
57. Estes (1980).
58. Jack (1991), pp 286–87.
59. Myles (1983), pp 462–3.

60. Feldstein (1974).
61. Pitts (1978), p 163.
62. Clark (1978), p 259.
63. Estes (1983), p 447.
64. US President (1979), p 377.
65. Estes (1983), p 447.
66. Boserup (1987), p 240.
67. Baldock and Evers (1992), p 292.
68. Baldock and Evers (1992), p 292.
69. Daatland (1992), p 39.
70. Guillemard (1986).
71. McRae (1994), pp 54, 61.
72. DHSS (1978), p 4.
73. Jack (1991), p 285.
74. Central Health Services Council (1978), p 4.
75. DHSS (1981), p 2.
76. DHSS (1981), pp 3, 59, 64.
77. DHSS (1981), p 3.
78. *The Times*, 25 January 1984, p 5.
79. DHSS (1985).
80. Baldock and Evers (1992).
81. Griffiths (1988), p iii.
82. DHSS (1989), p 62.
83. DHSS (1989), introduction and p 4.
84. Tinker et al (1994), p 10.
85. Tinker et al (1994), p 10.
86. Arber and Ginn (1990), p 430.
87. Baldock and Evers (1992), p 309.
88. Jack (1991), p 284.
89. IMF (1995), p 5.
90. OECD (1995), pp xii, xiv.
91. Johnson and Falkingham (1992), p 188.
92. Estes (1986), pp 121-23.
93. Estes (1986), p 128.
94. See, for example, Davidson and Rees-Mogg (1992).
95. UN (1988), p 1.
96. UN (1989), p 3.
97. *The Independent*, 6 January 1999.
98. See Davis and Meyer (1998).
99. *Financial Times*, 12 December 1998.
100. *The Independent*, 16 May 1996.
101. UN (1990), p 1.
102. McRae (1995), p 266.
103. Johnson and Falkingham (1992), p 2.

4· Is Ageing a Burden?

The preoccupation with ageing is a preoccupation with the *problem* of an ageing population. The conventional assumption is that the elderly represent a bloc of similar people that collectively generates a significant burden and social problem for the whole of society.[1] In economic terms there are two common negative assumptions about the impact of demographic ageing. On the one hand it is presented as a drain or unaffordable burden on the economy. Secondly, it is viewed as a constraint on economic growth.

This chapter challenges the first notion that ageing represents an unsupportable burden for society. (The second point is addressed in chapter 7.) It will argue that it is well within the capacity of any industrialised country to meet the requirements of the numbers and proportions of old people forecast by even the most dramatic projections. It will seek to explode the myth that society will be unable to cope with an ageing population.

This approach runs directly counter to the conventional wisdom about ageing. Invariably more old people are assumed to mean greater problems. Ageing is believed to intensify the strain on health services, overwhelm the exchequer as a result of higher pension payments, and create enormous pressure for succeeding generations owing to the need to devote precious time and resources to provide care for the elderly.

For instance, the title of the World Bank's most substantial publication on the subject leaves no doubt where this key international institution stands: it is called *Averting the Old Age Crisis*. Ageing is regarded as a 'crisis', facing the old in particular, but affecting humanity in general. Michael Bruno, the World Bank's chief economist, summarised the predicament:

'Systems providing financial security for the old are under increasing strain throughout the world. Rapid demographic transitions causing rising life expectancy and declining fertility mean that the proportion of old people in the general population is growing rapidly ... . The result is a looming old age crisis that threatens not only the old but also their children and grandchildren, who must shoulder, directly or indirectly, much of the increasingly heavy burden of providing for the aged.'[2]

Such a presentation of the demographic time bomb is now commonplace and has extensive popular purchase. However, our survey of the more specialist literature on the burden represented by ageing throws up a significant anomaly. No one has come up with a compelling financial case why ageing is so burdensome. The only way the argument 'works' is to assume an overnight explosion in the numbers of old people while everything else, and in particular society's economic capacity, is assumed to stay fixed. This chapter will explain the illegitimacy of such use of the statistics.

A burden for the rest of society

The greater resources required to look after old people are posed as an 'unsustainable' burden on the rest of society. Old people are viewed as a great weight imposing itself upon and crippling the rest of the population. This is often explained as happening via the impact on social spending for which the rest of the population has to pay.

The most widespread argument employs a measure of the dependency ratio that was addressed in chapter 2. Sometimes its numerical inverse, the 'support ratio', is used, but the argument is exactly the same. A survey of the position in Germany illustrates this form of the 'burden' argument:

'At the moment there are roughly three Germans of working age for every senior citizen, in a pensions system where, as generally in the West, the working generation pays the pensions of the retired. By 2035, however, for every five people of working age there will be three retired. And in an era of soaring unemployment, the five refers to those of working age, not necessarily those in a job.

'The three retirees, meanwhile, can expect to live five years longer than they do now - another five years of drawing on pensions, plus the exponential rise in health care costs as people get older'.[3]

Does ageing really cause such an excessive, or 'unsustainable', burden? Before addressing this question let us quote one further prediction of demographic difficulties:

'There are two features of the trend of our vital statistics which have an important direct bearing on the problems of public finance. First ... the number of persons between 16 and 65 years of age is already approaching its maximum and must be expected to decrease rather than increase over the next thirty years. Second the number of persons over 65 or 60 years of age is increasing rapidly, and must be expected to be very much higher in thirty years time than it is today. The first of these facts will diminish the buoyancy of the revenue. The second will increase the charges falling on the budget from the relief of old age. In combination, they must aggravate the budgetary difficulties of the next generation, which in any case are likely to be formidable.'

The conclusion drawn from this assessment was definitive: these trends can lead to national extinction.[4]

This prediction sounds representative of many contemporary concerns about ageing. However, the 1949 Royal Commission on Population made it. It referred to a 30-year span of history that is now long past. It was anticipating the supposed formidable burdens of an ageing population through to 1980.[5]

With hindsight it is easy to see that the demographic funding problem identified in 1949 was seriously overestimated. Significantly it was not in their population forecasts that they were amiss. Their population forecasts for the numbers of elderly were reasonably accurate. Employing various combinations of assumptions about mortality, migration and fertility the statistics committee estimated that by 1992 there would be a total population of between 43 to 56 million, of which between 7 and 9 million would be over 65. The actual figures were 56 million and 9 million respectively – not bad guestimates. [6]

However, this 30-year period of demographic ageing did not create the anticipated budgetary problems. This suggests that non-demographic trends took precedence over the ageing tendency when it came to the affordability or otherwise of a particular number and proportion of old people. The key factor ignored was economic growth during the same period, which more than doubled the amount of economic wealth created annually.

With this unrealised 'demographic time bomb' in mind, this chapter explains why the future population structure based on today's ageing projections will not bring about an unaffordable burden. The next section begins by looking again at the famed 'dependency ratio', and extends the discussion of some of its statistical distortions identified in chapter 2.

To recap, dependency ratios are widely regarded as useful indices of the burden on society of the population ageing.[7] There are three commonly used ratios:

- the aged dependency ratio is conventionally defined as the population aged over 64 divided by the population aged 16 to 64;
- the youth dependency ratio of under 16s as a percentage of 16 to 64s;
- the total dependency ratio of under 16s and over 64s as a share of the 16 to 64 population.

Increasing aged ratios have become one of the most prevalent expressions for illustrating anxieties about the economic burdens of population ageing.

The dependency ratio is a crude and misleading ratio for several reasons:

(i) It is illegitimate to fetishise any particular elderly dependency ratio, or to give it any predictive power about the economic pressures and circumstances of the country to which it applies. However, in most of the literature about ageing, dependency and support ratios have acquired a centrality and economic significance that they do not deserve.

Dependency ratios in the advanced industrial countries vary widely. In 1990, for example, they ranged from 16 per cent in Australia to nearly 28 per cent in Sweden, with a weighted average of about 20 per cent. The UK came in the top half at 24 per cent.[8] This wide range raises a paradox. Why is that just about every developed country *including those at the bottom of the spread* worries about an increase in its present ratio? What is so limiting about the current ratios, especially for countries in the lower regions of the range, that any increase is a problem? On a statistical basis Australia could see a 50 per cent 'worsening' of its ratio and still be well below the current Swedish level. Sweden is coping with this level in the present, so why not Australia in the future? If Sweden can cope now with a higher level that many other countries will only reach in about 30 years' time, what is the problem for these other countries? The significance frequently attributed to the current ratios does not seem rational.

Also, empirically, there is no determinate connection between relative ratios between countries and their relative paces of economic growth. For example, take the world's three economic giants. In 1980, Germany's elderly support ratio was four. In the US it was nearly six and in Japan it was over seven. Yet Germany and Japan, with ratios above and below the US respectively, were both at that time regarded as the world's two economic locomotives, and the US was believed to be in economic decline. So the assumption that a particular population age structure has a particular implication for economic growth is not justified empirically.

(ii) As discussed in the last chapter a rising elderly dependency ratio is partly offset by a falling youngster dependency ratio. The same low fertility rates which bring about demographic ageing will result in fewer young people and, thus, in a declining youth dependency ratio.

Falling youth dependency ratios can easily offset and in some circumstances even reverse a rising elderly ratio. For example, in Britain between 1979 and 1994 the number of elderly people rose by 931 000 while the number of young people fell by 889 000, reducing the net rise in 'dependants' to only 42 000. When translated into dependency ratios, the consequence was that while the elderly ratio *rose* from 28.4 per cent to 29.9 per cent, the total ratio *fell* from 59.3 per cent to 57.1 per cent.[9]

David Thomson usefully puts the post-war fluctuations in the total dependency ratio in Britain into a longer historical perspective. Although rising from 71 per cent in 1951 to 85 per cent in 1971, before falling away again to 81 per cent in 1980, even the peak 1971 level was *below* the level recorded during the second half of the nineteenth century. (See chart 16 in chapter 2.)

Overall he concludes that 'late-twentieth century workers carry a burden of dependence which is by no means exceptional, given the experiences of Britain during the past 150 years'.[10] The real cost is unexceptional but, in contrast, the level of concern about it is unprecedented.

Looking at projections for the future the offsetting factor of falling youth dependency also gives sober results. For example, the US elderly dependency ratio is expected to double by 2040, invoking all the usual warnings of the dangers of social disaster. Yet, the aggregate dependency ratio in 2040 is forecast to be lower than the 1970 level. That is a falling young dependency ratio is projected to more than offset the increasing aged dependency ratio.[11]

Therefore, it is wrong to translate automatically an ageing population into a bigger call upon public finances. For America Thomas Gale Moore estimated that 'the rise in the cost of programs for the elderly is at least partly and may be totally offset by declines in the cost of supporting fewer children'.[12]

With respect to health service costs Sinclair and Williams argue that while old people are in general less healthy than the average adult, the increased number of elderly should be set against decreased expenditure on children's health care as a result of the decline in the birth rate.[13]

As a further example of this effect forecasts for Germany provide a striking counter-intuitive result. Among advanced industrial countries, as chart 2 illustrated, Germany is forecast to exhibit one of the sharpest, most dramatically ageing populations over the early twenty-first century. The elderly dependency ratio rises at one of the steepest rates.

However, an OECD study projects that Germany is one of the few countries where public social expenditures will be lower in 2040 than in 1980. Extra spending upon pensions is more than offset by reductions in public spending on education and family benefits, which result from the parallel fall in the youth dependency ratio.[14] Falling proportions of young people more than compensate for even rapidly rising proportions of the elderly.

The exact trade-off of the costs of young and old vary both historically and also between countries. Clark, Kreps and Spengler's survey of economic literature noted the difference of views over whether fewer younger dependants compensates fully for more older dependants. Interestingly as a reflection of the shift in mood, they reported that the earlier discussions on ageing tended to be more sanguine about the combined effects than more recent estimates.

For example, Serow and Espenshade used the German experience of the tripling of the elderly dependency ratio from 1925 to 1975 to show that negative assumptions of ageing first advanced in the 1930s were unjustified. Ageing, they wrote, 'has never led to an economic setback or a breakdown of the pension system, as was prophesied by many observers whenever birth rates turned down'.[15]

They explained that one reason was that in Germany 'it costs society about one-fourth to one-third more to bring up an average child from birth to the age of 20 than to support an average person of 60 years over the rest of his or her life.'[16]

Today, in contrast, it is generally argued that old people cost the public purse more per head than do young people. Pension and health care costs for the aged are usually calculated to exceed the education and health care costs of the young per person. In OECD countries overall it has been estimated recently that public spending per old person on social services and transfers is two to three times as great as public spending per child. In Britain the estimated ratio is about 2.1:1.[17]

Another estimate based upon the US system is that 'about three times as much public money is spent, on the average, per aged dependent than is spent on a younger one'.[18] Gibson and Fisher estimate that people over 65 use health care services at roughly 3.5 times the rate (in money) of those below 65.[19] Putting this another way Binstock estimated that in the mid-1980s in the US 'persons aged 65 and older, now about 11 per cent of the population, account for about a third of health care expenditures'.[20]

Whichever of these young versus old trade off estimates is most accurate, the point remains. While a falling number of young dependent people may not compensate on a one-for-one basis for a rise in elderly dependants, there is at a minimum *some* compensation that undermines the most apocalyptic predictions of the financial and social consequences of ageing.

(iii) An ostensibly strong argument from the demographic panic-mongers is that there is nothing you can do about these 'unsustainable' dependency ratios of the twenty-first century: the part of the population that will be old then has already been born. The generations that will be old next century have been born in this one. They cannot be unborn. This argument seems to give substance to the unpreventable character of the ageing phenomenon and of rising dependency ratios.

However, there is a inconsistency in this argument. It obscures the fact that their concern about the burden of ageing rests upon a measure of proportions, not of absolute numbers. They refer to measures of a dependency, or support, *ratio*, not a certain size of the elderly population. And while the people who will be 65 in the 2030s must have already been born, those who will be in their 20s at that time have still to be born.

Projections of the movement in dependency ratios tend to assume that after a few years a fixed fertility rate applies thereafter into the future. For a start it is worth noting that fertility projections have not had a great record for accuracy. Chapter 2 described how projections made shortly after the Second World War failed to anticipate the baby boom of the 1960s.[21]

This was one of the mistakes the 1949 Royal Commission made in warning of an emerging demographic crisis. It claimed that the problem of an absolute rise in the number of old people was unavoidable since 'these figures cannot be affected by any future changes in the birth rate'. This ageing population was deemed as increasing the burden upon the Treasury and 'it is out of the question that (future births) should increase to the extent that they would be required to prevent that proportion from rising substantially over the next thirty years'.[22]

But this is what did happen. The unanticipated baby boom helped slow down the pace of population ageing considerably. Other fertility projections than those of the 1950s have also proved to be poor forecasts. (See diagram 2 in chapter 2.)

In particular, today's forecasts preclude the possibility of any volatility in birth rates in the future. Yet such volatility is what has happened in the second half of the twentieth century. Relatively minor shifts in the fertility rate have played havoc with various projections of the pace of ageing in the closing decades of this century. Viewing together charts 10 and 17 shows how the rise in fertility in the 1950s and 1960s helped cause a decline in the elderly dependency ratio in the 1990s and first decade of the twenty-first century unanticipated in the early post-war years. Just as changing social and economic circumstances influenced these fertility fluctuations in the past, so it is myopic to exclude them from the picture in the future.

One far from slim possibility is for a return to the higher fertility rates of levels similar to the early 1960s. Following three or more decades of low fertility levels this would bring about a younger population structure. It would cause a substantial fall in the elderly dependency ratio about 20 years later once this bigger cohort attained working age.

Dependency ratios based on constant fertility (and fixed rates of change of mortality levels) necessarily emphasise only what has happened, and exclude the prospect for the dynamic of change in the future. Given the inaccuracy of past projections and the unlikely assumption of future constancy this must throw doubt on today's official projections for the population structure in the middle of the next century.

(iv) Trends in the old age dependency ratio do not give any guide to what will happen to the real 'burden' on future working populations. These ratios assume that all old people are 'dependent', a dubious assumption. As was shown in chapter 2 the category of dependence resulting from ill health or disability applies to only a small minority of the elderly. With the tendency for the health and fitness of elderly people to improve, this statistical assumption is likely to prove increasingly incorrect. Also the crude dependency ratio, as noted in chapter 2, does not give a real indication of the ability of one section of the population – that of 'working age' – to provide for the 'dependents'. This depends mainly on levels of unemployment, labour force participation rates, productivity and earnings levels.

The 'working population' in the crude dependency ratios is only an unrealisable potential of the size of the working population. There are already many that do not work and are unlikely to for physical or social reasons. These include, for example, the severely disabled, or those involved in full-time care of the young or of the elderly, which precludes the opportunity of working. There are far more such people of 'working' age who do not work for economic and social reasons, or because they are at school or college.

This has two main consequences. First, it means that the 'real' dependency ratio of actual non-working to actual working people is already much higher than the demographers assume. More importantly, it means that the increase in the dependency ratio as a result purely of ageing is much less pronounced than the forecasts assume, since it is diluted by other factors. The recent experience is that labour market trends have been *more* significant in influencing 'real' dependency ratios than demographic trends.[23]

Walker also makes this point in challenging the scientific legitimacy of crude dependency ratios. He notes that most demographic projections are bound to mislead because they ignore changes in unemployment and labour force participation rates over the period of projections, usually 50 years.[24] Jackson argues the same point in his critical review of the treatment of ageing in economic theory. He is especially sceptical of the use of crude dependency ratios at a time of high unemployment.[25]

It is revealing of the less gloomy atmosphere of the late 1940s compared to today that the 1949 Royal Commission accepted that the use of crude dependency ratios could over-dramatise the peril from ageing. At the time the government estimated that the straight pensioner to contributor dependency ratio would rise from 0.16 to 0.31 between 1945 and 1975. However, using a ratio of 'productive capacity' to 'consumers' needs' ratio, and including expected increases in productivity, the report stated soberly that 'the burden which the need to maintain an increasing number of retired persons will throw on a stationary or declining working population is not likely to prove very onerous'.[26]

To establish what this means for today this book has carried out a study of Britain over the years 1979 to 1994 to isolate the relative significance of various economic and labour market factors on the real dependency ratio. (See table 3.) The 'real' dependency ratio, in contrast to the 'crude' ratio, incorporates the impact of labour market changes on the real numbers of dependents and workers.

Apart from this period being recent, this time-span has the extra advantage that the actual civilian workforce in employment (excluding those on government training programmes) is fairly similar in the start-year and end-year, even though there are fluctuations in between. This makes comparisons over this period relatively easy to interpret.

To be compatible with the state retirement age over this period, the crude elderly dependency ratios are calculated as the number of men aged 65 and over and the number of women aged 60 and over as a proportion of the 16 to 64(male)/59(female) population. For the purposes of this illustration, the unreal assumption is used that all the elderly are dependent.

The index constructed of the 'real' dependency ratio measures the base as all those either in employment or self-employment. Three ratios are calculated over this base:

a)   population aged 65/60 and over;
b)   'real' dependents aged 16 and over. This includes the unemployed, the economically inactive (which includes unpaid full-time carers, the retired, the non-working sick and disabled, discouraged workers, students), and people on government training programmes;
c)   total 'real' dependents which also includes the population aged under 16.

The data are taken from two main official sources: the Department of Employment (DoE) workforce figures published in the *Employment Gazette*' and the OPCS population figures published in *Population Trends*. Although the figures from these two sources are not exactly compatible they are close enough to draw meaningful conclusions. For example, the workforce figures from the *Employment Gazette* assume a total population aged 16 and over of 41 146 000 in 1979 while the population figures from *Population Trends* give 42 779 000. In 1994 the respective figures are 44 277 000 and 45 097 000. In both years the OPCS figures are above the DoE figures, by 4 per cent in 1979 and 2 per cent in 1994.

The calculations for the real dependency ratio are done twice. The first time all workers are treated as equivalents. The second time, part-time workers are regarded as half a full-timer. The latter is called the adjusted real dependency ratio.

The main conclusions are:

a) The real elderly dependency ratio starts higher and rose faster than the crude elderly dependency ratio;

b) The total real dependency ratio, including young people, increases more in absolute terms than the real elderly ratio;

c) Labour market factors outweigh demographic ones in heightening the 'real' dependency ratio. Unemployment and the rise in economic inactivity among the working age population is alone almost twice as influential as the increase in the elderly population;

d) When the figures are adjusted to include the shift from full-time to part-time employment as reducing the working base in the real dependency ratio, the impact of ageing is exceeded even more by labour market trends. Table 4 presents this conclusion in a different way. Labour market changes, which increased the number of dependents and/or reduced the productive capacity of the working population, exceed the increase in old people by three times. (See table 4.)

Labour force employment rates have therefore been much more significant than the changing population structure in determining the productive capacity of the economy and the demands placed upon it by dependents. If crude dependency ratios have so deceived in the recent past, there is no reason to assume they will provide an accurate guide to the future.

Table 3:   Real and crude dependency ratios, Britain 1979-94
(Numbers in thousands)

	Mid-1979	mid-1994	change
Population:			
All ages	55324	55753	+1429
Under 16	12545	11656	-889
16-64/59	33323	34713	+1390
65/60 and over	9456	10384	+928
Dependent ages	20591	20633	+42
Crude dependency ratios:			
Elderly crude dependency ratio	28.4%	29.9%	+1.5%
Total crude dependency ratio	66.0%	63.5%	-2.5%
Workforce:			
Civilians in employment, including self-employed	24453	24199	-254
Of which:			
full-time	19751	17649	-2102
part-time	4702	6550	+1848
Full-time equivalents (using two p-t = one f-t)	22102	20924	-1178
Unemployed (ILO definition)	1466	2717	+1251
Economically inactive	15310	16424	+1114
Unemployed and inactive (all ages 16 and over)	16776	19141	+2365
Government training schemes	0	285	+285
Total dependents 16 and over	16776	19426	+2650
Population under 16	12545	11656	-889
Total dependents	29321	31082	+1761
'Real' dependency ratios:			
'16 and over dependency ratio'	69%	80%	+11%
'Above retirement age dependency ratio'	39%	43%	+4%
'Total dependency ratio'	120%	128%	+8%
Adjusted 'real' dependency ratios, using f-t equivalent workers as base			
16 and over	76%	93%	+17%
Above retirement age	43%	50%	+7%
Total	133%	143%	+16%

Source: DoE and OPCS

Table 4: Increase in various segments of the population between 1979 and 1994 (Thousands)

Population aged 65/60 and over	928
Unemployed	1 251
Inactive workers up to age 64/59	186
Fall in full-time equivalents	1 178
On government training programmes	285
Total labour market changes	2 900

Source: DoE and OPCS

There is one other labour market trend that is relevant to our discussion. Over the past quarter century female participation rates have been rising, contributing to the economy's productive output. Most would agree that some link exists between more working women and falling fertility.

Hence the same trend of falling birth rates which boosts the aged dependency ratio is also related to the increase in economic activity rates by women thereby boosting the size of the economic cake from which dependents share. If more employment was available, especially of an adequate quality and linked to childcare facilities, it is doubtless the case that even more women would work. Once again it is the case that economic and social factors play a more decisive role than demographic trends in determining the scale of national wealth, part of which provides for dependents.

(v) The most significant factor which the greatest number of preachers of demographic apocalypse ignore is that in 50 years' time the size of the economy which will exist to provide for its relatively older population will be much larger than today's. The size of the national wealth, from which provision for the elderly and other dependents is made, will be considerably larger than today. This larger amount of annual wealth produced will be well able to support even the most extreme forecasts of the future size of the elderly population.

The usual projections and apocalyptic predictions leave out of account changes in the productive capacity of the economy. These changes have nothing to do with demography. The key influences include the pace of technological innovation, the levels of productivity attained, and the number of workers productively employed.

Even over the past quarter century of relatively restrained economic conditions the British economy's trend economic growth rate has been about 2.25 per cent. For the purposes of illustration, assume this rate continues. (If the economy were not to continue to grow even at this relatively sluggish rate the problem would lie elsewhere, unrelated to demographic movements. See chapter 7.)

So what can be expected to happen for the 50 year span in Britain from 1992 to 2042? (See table 5.) Based on the official figures, in 1992 national output was valued (in 1992 money) at £615 billion. Welfare spending amounted to £160 billion, or 26 per cent of GDP, of which spending on the elderly 16 per cent of the population was £62 billion, or 10 per cent of GDP.

Table 5:   Growth of economic wealth and
           the burden of ageing

	1992		2042		
	£bn (1992)	% GDP (1992)	£bn (1992)	% GDP (1992)	% GDP (2042)
National output	615	100	1870	304	100
Welfare spending	160	26			
Welfare spending on 16% elderly	62	10			
Welfare spending on 24% elderly	93	15		15	5
Double real welfare spending on 24% elderly	186	30		30	10
Triple real welfare spending on 24% elderly	279	45		45	15

(Assumes 50 years, GDP growth at average of 2.25% pa)

Most projections put the elderly population in 2042 at 24 per cent of the population, a 50 per cent increase on 1992. If this increase were to have happened overnight in 1992 and welfare spending per elderly person was constant, spending on the 24 per cent elderly population would have jumped to £93 billion or 15 per cent of GDP.

Shoot forward 50 years: what percentage of GDP would the real equivalent of £93 billion represent in 2042? Starting from £615 billion in 1992, national output after compound growth of 2.25 per cent a year over 50 years would become £1870 billion in 2042. £93 billion is only 5 per cent of this amount. Therefore, allowing for average growth rates, the 'burden' on the national economy – and on taxpayers – of spending on the projected *greater* number of elderly, at the same standard of living as today, would be only *half* what it is today. Allowing for a *doubling* of elderly living standards provided for from the welfare budget, the relative 'burden' would still be merely the same as today. And if elderly living standards tripled in line with economic growth, the extra 'cost' would be only an additional 5 per cent of national output in 2042.

Take this upper figure of a 5 per cent increase over 50 years. What does this compare with? It is the same as the rise in British welfare spending from 1989 to 1992 due to the impact of the recession. Also 5 per cent of GDP is less than one quarter the spread of 24 per cent between the smallest (Japan) to the largest (Sweden) welfare spender in the OECD. This 5 per cent is also about the same increase which European Union countries on average added to their welfare spending between the early 1980s – at about 24 per cent – and the mid 1990s of about 29 per cent. It is also about the same as the increase in average OECD public pension expenditure from 1960 (4.3 per cent) to 1985 (8.9 percent). The point is that all these '5 per cent increases', whether demographically linked or not, have been afforded without bringing financial crisis to any of the countries involved. The assertion of the 'unaffordability' of the 5 per cent cost of ageing acquires rather less purchase when put in such perspective.

It is striking that most other detailed empirical studies of the costs arising from more old people also fail to substantiate the siren voices. As a result many of the foremost authorities in the field of demography dispute the panic. Anthea Tinker, a leading figure from the British Society of Gerontology, argues that the effects of the demographic time bomb have been exaggerated.[27]

John Ermisch, for the Joseph Rowntree Foundation, shows that 'demographic pressures on pension expenditure over the remainder of this century are very moderate in Britain, as they are in most industrialised countries'.[28] Even when the numbers of pensioners rise as the baby boomers reach retirement age he argues that the impact will not be great. In Britain if the present policy of increasing pensions only in line with the cost of living is maintained 'then the contribution rate in the mid-2030s does not need to be higher than at present'.[29] Overall he concludes that none of the implications of the demographic shift 'are of crisis proportions'.[30]

John Hills' research into the British welfare state backs up these critical voices. He provides one of the most trenchant debunkings of the ageing panic. From his investigation he concluded that the problem was grossly exaggerated:

> 'Much current debate starts from the assumption that welfare policy is boxed in by fiscal constraints. This report suggests that there is actually a range of options ... . There is no "demographic time bomb" which will cause an unsustainable explosion of welfare costs.' [31]

The next chapters, dealing with the specific arguments in favour of a pension time bomb and a health time bomb, will provide more detail of the counter-apocalyptic calculations made by Hills and Ermisch.

In a different intellectual climate from today it might be the case that this critical perspective would be more accepted. It would be assumed that any problems arising from a trend such as ageing could be absorbed. For example, in the more optimistic and dynamic 1960s, a study for the British government on welfare provision for the elderly simply assumed the anticipated greater numbers of old people could be accommodated.

The study's author, Amelia Harris, noted the expected increase in the numbers of old people from 1965 to 1976 was 20 per cent. However, unlike similar reports today this was not the occasion for tidings of woe. Instead she reported that services for the old, including residential places, sheltered housing, home helps and health visitors, were already planned to increase much more rapidly, by between 35 and 100 per cent.[32]

Occasionally the common sense observation that we are not living in a static, stagnant world creeps into the official publications. For example, the major OECD report in 1988 on the social policy implications of ageing populations did one calculation that seemed to dispel the time bomb myth. Looking at Canada, with one of the highest projected expenditure growths resulting from ageing among the OECD countries, the report showed that the average annual growth rate required to maintain a constant social expenditure share in the face of demographic change between 1980 and 2040 is only 1.05 per cent. Despite such a sober illustration reports like this from the OECD are always popularly interpreted as substantiating the demographic time bomb.[33]

A similar point about the offsetting effects of economic growth was made in the OECD's biannual *Economic Outlook* in June 1995. Focusing on health care costs, it showed that growth in real public health spending per head in an ageing society could be afforded as long as growth was ½ to 1 per cent below productivity growth. This would be in line with the sorts of increases in real health spending made in recent years. Assuming future productivity growth therefore obviates any need for real belt tightening to cope with ageing populations.[34]

To summarise so far, it can be seen that there is no evidence that even the ageing trends projected will create an unaffordable burden. A modern society's normal capacity to grow economically will provide more than sufficient resources to sustain an ageing society and allow continued increases in living standards for all. The next chapters will address the specific burden arguments which are deployed to try to justify our concerns - the welfare, and the particular pensions and health time bombs - and the way these assumptions are used to legitimise policy change in these fields. Before these issues are addressed, this chapter will conclude by reviewing some of the supplementary arguments used to try to substantiate the demographic time bomb idea.

The special burden of the older old

With the difficulty of proving the conventional case that the over 64s are such a huge burden, there has been a tendency to shift emphasis to highlight the problem of the older old - the over 74s - instead. (See chart 19.)

Since it is difficult, or impossible, to substantiate the 'unsustainable burden' represented by old people in general, the over 74s would seem to make an easier target. They are easier to be seen as dependent and burdensome.

While some alarmist demographic studies admit that the actual increase in the proportion of over 64s is not growing all that fast, they claim that fears about the social impact of ageing are still justified as a result instead of the shifts *within* the age structure of the elderly. For example, Jean Thompson wrote in the publication *Population Trends*:

> 'Even though the total numbers over age 60 may not increase by much over the next decade or two, [differential movements within this total age group mean] there will be a significant increase in the aggregate needs of this age-group to the extent that needs for care and support increase with age.'[35]

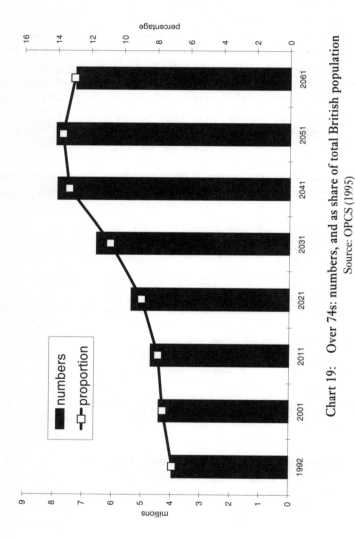

Chart 19:   Over 74s: numbers, and as share of total British population
Source: OPCS (1995)

She writes that 'what is often referred to as the ageing of the population is much in the public eye, but nonetheless the scale of the increase over the near future in numbers of the very old seems not to have been widely recognised'.[36] Her invocation seems clear that even though the pace of ageing is not that rapid, the growth in the older old population still gives plenty of grounds for genuine worry.

To substantiate her case Thompson explains that 80 year olds' care and support needs can be assumed to be four times that of 60 year olds. She draws the conclusion that 'there is likely to be a rapid rise, particularly over the near future, in the aggregate needs of the elderly population for care and support' and asserts that this assessment 'is robust to the uncertainties in projecting future numbers over the short term'.[37]

Now it is obvious that older old people are more likely to need care and support than younger old people are. As Tinker writes the very old age group 'makes the highest demands on health and social services'. For example, while about half of hospital beds are taken by over 64s, most of these – two-thirds, or nearly one third in total – are occupied by over 74s.[38] However, Tinker's qualifying caution that even with the very old 'we should be aware of generalisations' is usually ignored in this type of discussion about the older old.[39]

Thompson's argument, for example, cannot by substantiated by her statistics alone. She does not spell out assumptions that are relevant to her case about changes over time in the morbidity rates for all old people, the 60-year-olds, the 70-year-olds and the 80-year-olds. These are required before any conclusions could be drawn about 'rapid rises' in care needs. An understanding of the *relative* needs of different old age groups does not tell us anything about changes in the *absolute* needs of all elderly people.

The differentials can even widen between the needs of the old and the older old, in the way highlighted, while the care requirements of the average older person may fall as overall health and ability standards improve. Since the incidence of more elderly people tends to parallel economic and social progress, this is likely to be the case. This thesis will be explored further in the section on health in chapter 6.

The statistics themselves can be deceptive too. The proportion of the older old of over 74s has risen from 21 to 38 per cent of the old over the twentieth century up to 1991. This proportion will rise further to 41 per cent during the 1990s. This sort of rise can appear dramatic but what is happening in the nineties is not some inexorable trend. Rather it is merely another statistical product of a specific combination of fertility changes. The numbers of over 74s at the end of the twentieth century rise as a result of the high fertility rates around the First World War, while the under 75s old fall in number owing to the decline in inter-war and, especially, 1930s birth rates. In the next century the proportion of older old will tend to fluctuate rather than exhibit a further secular rise.[40] (See chart 20.)

The spectre of a new 'class war': inter-generational conflict

'Will those in work stand for it, finding an ever greater slice of their earnings going to pay for their parents' generation? After the class war and the war of the sexes, do we face a generation war?'[41]

The difficulties of substantiating a convincing financial argument that ageing is a genuine burden have not quietened the panic-mongers. Many have simply refocused their concern onto new dangers to society from ageing. Another favourite is the threat of inter-generational conflict. The statistical assumptions are the same as with the dependency ratio demographic time bomb, but the stress on inter-personal conflict seems to give the scare greater impact. This fear of tension appeals more to the individuated outlook described in the last chapter. It gives demographic worries more popular purchase than a set of dry statistical projections.

The growth in the number of elderly is supposed to undermine existing inter-generational equity. The OECD, for example, argues that the working population will not be willing or able to bear the tax levels necessary to fund societal ageing.[42] It goes on to warn:

'Under existing regulations the evolution of public pension schemes is likely to put a heavy and increasing burden on the working population in coming decades. Such a financial strain may put inter-generational solidarity - a concept on which all public retirement provisions are based - at risk.'[43]

Similarly the World Bank believes that rising payroll taxes to pay for the old 'will intensify the inter-generational conflict between old retirees (some of them rich) who are getting public pensions and young workers (some of them poor) who are paying high taxes to finance these benefits and may never recoup their contributions'.[44]

The basic argument is that the old either already are taking, or soon will take, too large a part of the national incomes of developed societies.

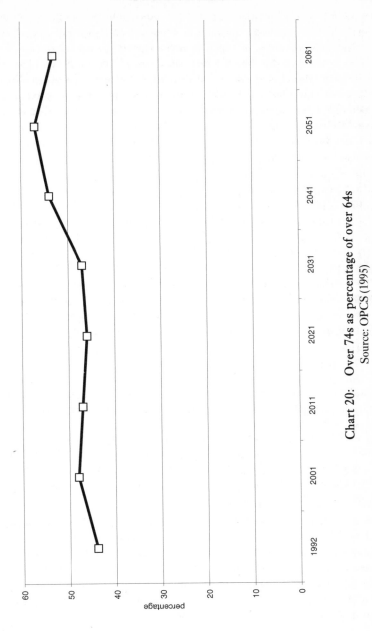

Chart 20: Over 74s as percentage of over 64s
Source: OPCS (1995)

As a result heavily taxed younger generations will be provoked to launch a destabilising backlash. Giarini and Stahel warn that: 'The real class struggle might become a struggle between age groups.'[45]

This version of the demographic panic was first raised in the US. As with other aspects of the ageing discussion it has since spread to other countries. Questions about the relative share of national economic wealth given to old people started to come to the fore in the US during Ronald Reagan's presidency.[46] The influential demographer Samuel Preston blamed the escalating costs of government entitlement programmes providing for the old for America's economic difficulties, especially the plight of the poor.[47]

Concern about conflict was promoted especially by the pressure group, Americans for Generational Equity (AGE), formed in 1985. Chaired by Republican senator David Durenberger it was supported, not surprisingly, by Medicare's private competitors: health care providers, insurance companies, banks and military contractors. (Medicare is the public health care scheme for the poor elderly, and the private sector could be expected to benefit from a reduction in public welfare provision.) In particular, AGE warned of a 'generational crisis' when the baby boom generation officially becomes old around 2030. Then it fears that the younger generation may revolt against the 'greying' of the government budget and divide politics along generational lines.

Some, especially in America, have added a race element to this vision of age wars. Because the old are disproportionately white and the young poor are mainly black, some argue that the interest of good race relations demands that the welfare costs of ageing be curtailed.[48]

In some instances the existence of institutionalised racism is used to justify the forcing through of cuts in elderly entitlements today. If nothing is done now the spectre is raised of future racist governments favouring the aged white population. Hess, for example, warns that: 'War - virtual bloody war - would break out a generation from now if today's mainly white Baby Boomers try to collect their Social Security "boodle" from a working class that will be largely black and Latino.'[49]

The basic argument about inter-generational conflict derives from the familiar belief that the old are to blame for the fiscal crisis. The particular form of this repeated notion is to stress the uneven impact of this burden on different generational cohorts. The policy recommendations return to familiar conclusions.

The consequence of the age-war vision is strikingly similar to the financial arguments about ageing and state expenditure. Minkler and Robertson describe the political agenda at work here:

'Efforts in the US to encourage divisiveness within the working class have been widely recognised as a key strategy in the war on welfare .... The creation of an ideology based on generational equity and 'age/race' wars thinking ... blames the old for poverty and economic hardship in the young.'[50]

The reforms recommended as necessary to pre-empt the threat of inter-generational conflict involve reducing the entitlements of the elderly. The predictable solution proposed is to reduce government expenditure on social security and Medicare – starting as soon as possible. AGE proposes supposedly objective and pre-emptive policies to reduce the present and future costs of retirement for future generations of youth. Once more the campaign to cut back on the state's role uses demographic arguments to justify itself, this time under the guise of preventing inter-generational conflict.

It is not difficult to show that a disproportionate amount of government and welfare expenditure goes on the elderly. AGE provided figures that show that the over 65s, although constituting only 11.5 per cent of the population, consume 28 per cent of the national budget and 51 per cent of all government expenditure on social services.[51] But is this really outrageous, or even surprising? Surely this is what a large chunk of welfare expenditure is designed for – to provide for those who are no longer able to provide for themselves.

By definition state retirement pensions are paid to the elderly. Most health expenditure also goes on the elderly but this is also to be expected and is a tribute to the improvements this century in the health status of the younger remainder of the population. The conventional assumption held by most people is that such official support in old age was what they were paying part of their taxes towards.

Far from this uneven distribution of public funds being a reason for conflict between generations, it is an expression of a civilised and reasonable coherent society. As John Walsh writes, 'It's in the way society cares for its oldest, most vulnerable citizens that its real value can be judged.'[52] In fact, the only truly effective solution to the disproportion that AGE illustrates would be to alleviate all welfare provision for the elderly through compulsory euthanasia for everyone at the time of retirement.

Another well-used weapon in the intellectual armoury of the proponents of generational equity is that the old are wealthier and more financially secure these days. This notion is designed to further delegitimise the elderly as a welfare constituency.

Not only do the old supposedly get more than their fair share but they are greedy too. The claim is that the elderly population is not just bigger but richer. Meredith Minkler described how the view emerged in America in the 1980s that the old constituted a group of developing wealth, whilst children and young people were suffering as a consequence of social programmes for their elders.[53]

In the US one of the most important early contributions to this outlook came from Samuel Preston in his 1984 Presidential Address to the Population Association of America. He pointed out the divergent trends in the incidence of poverty in the 1970s – falling among the elderly and increasing among children. He explained this in terms of the relative impact of a social security system that was too generous to the old.[54]

In Britain Johnson, Conrad and Thomson have argued a similar line: 'Welfare systems are tending to promote the interests of the increasingly wealthy retired population at the expense of poor children and parents.' They predict that a young voter 'backlash' against the elderly is on the cards.[55]

The case for inter-generational warfare takes support from the argument that an image of the elderly as poor and deserving does not hold any more. No less an institution than the World Bank has rejected the 'myth' of the elderly being poor in its research report on the old age crisis:

'In most countries poverty rates are higher among the young than among the old, and families with small children are the poorest of all. The old are even better off when comparisons are based on lifetime income rather than current income. Why? Because people with higher incomes are more likely to live long enough to become old, whereas people with low incomes are more likely to have many children and die young.'[56]

Although this World Bank 'fact' is drawn from the circumstances in developing countries the generalisation that old people are rich is held by many to be true for all countries. The British government, for example, presented a picture of the old as well off in its 1985 green paper on the Reform of Social Security and the subsequent Social Security

Act of 1986 which cut back the level of SERPS. Again, in the official Griffiths report on community care in Britain the author expressed the common opinion that a growing number of older people were reasonably well off and in a position to pay their own way in old age. It claimed that 'many of the elderly have higher incomes and levels of savings in real terms than in the past.'[57]

The next year John Moore, a former Tory Social Security minister, told the 1989 Help the Aged conference: 'It is simply no longer true that being a pensioner tends to mean being badly off ... . For most it is a time to look forward to with confidence. The modern pensioner has a great deal to be envied.'[58]

Such claims sum up the image of the emergence of Well Off Older People, the Woopies, a phenomenon which has been used by politicians to justify curbing and means-testing certain benefits and services for the elderly. They thereby claim to serve the social good of offsetting the danger of disruptive inter-generational conflict.

The reality of elderly wealth contradicts this image. For a start, the level of welfare spending per head is not generous by absolute or even by historical standards. David Thomson has researched that 'the social welfare benefits paid in Britain today are not as valuable, relative to the incomes of non-beneficiaries, as were the pensions paid during the first half of the twentieth century, and they are worth very much less than the allowances distributed by the nineteenth century Poor Law'.[59]

He concluded that 'current calls for the trimming of expenditure upon such dependent groups as the elderly come after a long period of decline in the resources allotted to elderly persons'. This is the opposite of the conventional belief that there had been a redistribution of resources to the elderly.[60] And that was in 1984. Since then the relative value of state pensions compared to average living standards has fallen much further with the de-indexing of pensions from average income levels from the start of the 1980s.

The financial position of older people is made worse by the existence of a sluggish economy that restricts employment possibilities. On the basis of his research Paul Thompson argues: 'The post-war exclusion of most older people from the labour market, combined with a level of welfare support lower in relation to average wages than it was 200 years ago, means that the relative poverty of the old in Britain has never been worse.'[61]

The government's own General Household Survey figures also tell a story about living standards for the elderly that challenges the myth of the stereotype Woopie. Official press releases have highlighted that the proportion of the old in the poorest segments of the population – having an income less than half of average earnings – has fallen. This is presented as evidence of the enrichment of the elderly. In reality this is more an indication of the extension of the number of poor in society beyond pensioners, and the widening of income inequality. The old are a smaller proportion but of an even bigger total of the statistically defined poor.

Also the reality is that the absolute numbers of poor old people have risen, even when the numbers of comfortably off old people have also grown. But in most countries including Britain the former has increased faster than the numbers of elderly overall, so that a higher proportion of the elderly are in the poor category.

Across Europe Malcolm Johnson estimates that one in three of the retired population is below the poverty line, with Britain having among the highest levels.[62] The 1996 Social Trends report confirms that pensioners in Britain are a significant element of those in permanent poverty.

Many others concur with this finding. R Walker concluded his study into the financial position of the elderly in the mid-1980s showing that 'while a small number of pensioners could be considered affluent, the majority still have incomes that place them on the margins of poverty and that any rise in incomes has been from a very low base'.[63]

Sinclair and Williams found the same phenomenon in their review of levels of pensioners' income. In 1987 pensioners' total net income ranged from £46.70 for the lowest fifth – with 90 per cent from social security – to £209.60 for the richest fifth – with only 25 per cent from social security. Overall the poorest 60 per cent of pensioners derive at least 75 per cent of income from the far from generous levels of social security payments. This confirmed to Sinclair and Williams that 'the majority of elderly people, in terms of disposable income, are not that well off'.[64]

Falkingham and Victor agree that 'it is true that the absolute position of the elderly as a group has improved over time, but it is not possible to conclude that the elderly as a whole have become a relatively more affluent group'.[65] They also explain this paradox by the growth of inequality.

About 5 per cent of the richest fifth of the population are over 65. These are the legendary Woopies, numbering about half a million. They 'are likely to be younger, male, have been employed in non-manual jobs and had access to non-state sources of income'.[66] This also means that the Woopies are not a fixed group. People tend to leave the group with greater age as their initially adequate savings are consumed with the passing of years. The existence of Woopies, therefore, is not a fiction but coexists with the widening inequalities across society over the past 20 years.

The warning about inter-generational conflict has, statistically, no more substance to it than the earlier claims about the demographic time bomb. The specific feature of this particular argument with its stress on widening generational wealth inequality does not stand up either.

Not surprisingly, inter-generational equity campaigns have found it difficult to win a mass active following. AGE, for example, is now defunct. Minkler and Robertson noted in 1991 that despite the roles of AGE and other pressure groups, and despite the arguments made by politicians and the support of the mass media, none of this vision of age, or age/race, tension is so far reflected in opinion polls.[67]

This is true on the eastern side of the Atlantic too. Walker has found 'there is no empirical basis in Britain for the growth of generational based resentment'.[68] Opinion surveys conducted by bodies ranging from the European Community to British Gas confirm that there is no basis for the claim that young people view old people as a burden. The European survey also found that 80 per cent of those in employment agreed that they had a duty to ensure, through their contributions and taxes, that older people have a decent standard of living.[69]

Nevertheless, the arguments the believers in inter-generational conflict use remain important within the wider ageing discussion. They help to support the broader sentiment that there exists a crisis of ageing. These pressure groups may not mobilise many young people onto the streets, but their propaganda does provide support for the assumptions underpinning the demographic time bomb notion. It is an argument that is likely to become more prevalent because of the way it strikes a chord with the perceptions of many people who today live individuated lives. It may well be that opinion surveys carried out in the second half of the 1990s show more resonance for this outlook.

Today the idea of a demographic calamity retains its hold and grows despite the lack of evidence. It is as if facts are powerless in the face of the conventional wisdom. It seems that a good panic rarely lets the absence of corroborating arguments or evidence get in the way. So although the intellectual argument behind the demographic time bomb thesis has been weak and equivocal the concern continues to spread.

Notes

1. See Tinker (1992).
2. World Bank (1994), p xiii.
3. *The Guardian*, 27 January 1996.
4. Royal Commission (1950b), p 53.
5. Royal Commission (1950b), p 31.
6. Royal Commission (1950a).
7. See, for example, Ermisch (1983).
8. World Bank (1994), p 343.
9. Ratios computed from OPCS (1981) and (1995).
10. Thomson (1984), p 469.
11. Faber and Wilkin (1981).
12. Moore (1987), p 295.
13. Sinclair and Williams (1990).
14. Hagemann and Nicoletti (1989), pp 14 and 45.
15. Serow and Espenshade (1978), p 55.
16. Serow and Espenshade (1978), p 58.
17. OECD (1988b) cited in World Bank (1994), p 31.
18. Sheppard and Rix (1979), p 24.
19. Gibson and Fisher (1979), pp 3-16.
20. Binstock (1985), p 440.
21. OPCS (1994), p 31.
22. Royal Commission (1950b), p 36.
23. See also Johnson and Falkingham (1992), chapter 2.
24. See, for example, OECD (1988a).
25. Jackson (1991).
26. Royal Commission (1950b), p 31.
27. Tinker (1992), p 17.
28. Ermisch (1990), p 44.
29. Ermisch (1990), p 48.
30. Ermisch (1990), p 55.
31. Hills (1993), p 5.
32. Harris (1968), p 1.
33. OECD (1988a), p 39.
34. OECD (1995).
35. Thompson (1987), p 20.
36. Thompson (1987), p 22.
37. Thompson (1987), p 21.
38. DHSS (1978).
39. Tinker (1992), p 14.
40. Tinker (1992), p 14.
41. I Traynor, 'Grey time bomb at the heart of the Western welfare state', *The Guardian*, 27 January 1996.
42. OECD (1988), p 39.
43. OECD (1988b), p 102.
44. World Bank (1994), p 4.
45. Giarini and Stahel (1989), p 79.
46. Johnson (1995), p 257; and see, for example, Preston (1984a) and (1984b), and Peterson (1988).
47. Preston (1984b).
48. Hayes-Bautista, Schinck and Chapa (1988).
49. Hess (1990).

50. Minkler and Robertson (1991), p 1.
51. Johnson (1995), p 257.
52. *The Independent*, 11 December 1998.
53. Minkler (1987).
54. Preston (1984).
55. Johnson, Conrad and Thomson (1989), p 7. They make a wide-ranging attack on the concept of the 'selfish welfare generation', which they claim has stored up serious economic and political problems for the future.
56. World Bank (1994), p 11.
57. Griffiths (1988).
58. Quoted in Falkingham and Victor (1991), p 471.
59. Thomson (1984), p 451.
60. Thomson (1984), pp 474–76.
61. Thompson (1992), p 26.
62. Johnson (1995), p 258.
63. Walker (1988), p 384.
64. Sinclair and Williams (1990), p 383.
65. Falkingham and Victor (1991), p 476.
66. Falkingham and Victor (1991), p 490.
67. Minkler and Robertson (1991).
68. Walker (1990), p 389.
69. See Midwinter (1991), and Walker (1993).

5· The Pensions Time Bomb

Chapter 3 described how the assumption of a demographic time bomb has been used extensively to legitimise an anti-welfarist and anti-statist agenda. The last chapter explained that there is no material substance to the time bomb thesis. The next two chapters will explore further the specific case of a welfare time bomb. Specifically these chapters will challenge respectively the two main forms the time bomb takes: pensions and health. They will show once again that ageing is being used to justify agendas that have non-demographic sources.

Is there any substance to the claim of a demographic constraint on welfare spending? To the extent that there is financial pressure to restructure and contain welfare spending it is illegitimate to scapegoat demographic movements. The pressure on welfare budgets arises not from demographic shifts but from wider social constraints on many industrialised countries' wealth creating capacities. The financial problem of large deficits and burgeoning government debt levels is not the burden of too many old people, but the absence of adequate productive activity to generate sufficient wealth expansion for all members of society, of every age, to live well from.

It was in the mid-1970s that mainstream questioning of the 'affordability' of the welfare state took off. It was no coincidence that this followed the climate shift brought about by the world economic recession of 1973-74. This marked the end of the long post-war economic boom and ushered in an age of more limited economic growth in the advanced industrialised countries. As Myles reports 'a protracted economic slump, characterised by declining output, rising unemployment and inflation ... brought about a radical reassessment of the post-war welfare state. Rather than a means to reinvigorate capitalism, the welfare state came to be construed as a fetter on capital accumulation'.[1] Ageing was brought into the debate to give the anti-welfare state arguments a spurious air of necessity in order to alleviate an inevitable financial crunch.

There is no doubt, of course, that a significant portion of society's resources is consumed by the old. Pampel and Williamson argue that age structure, and specifically a growing elderly population, is a 'critical factor in determining social welfare spending in Western industrial nations.'[2] But it is wrong to overstate the dominant role of elderly support in boosting welfare spending.

It appears an arithmetical fact that with population ageing, merely to maintain living standards for the over-64s a higher proportion of social spending will always have to be allocated for purposes needed by the elderly. But this is not as straightforward as it would seem. Take a look at the relative shares of social security budgets. Despite ageing, the proportion of the total social security budget going on pensions has not risen inexorably over recent years. In Britain, for example, the ratio of social security expenditure going on pensions fell from 45 per cent in 1971 to 37 per cent in 1985. And this was only partly the result of de-indexing of pensions from average earnings in favour of price increases introduced in 1980.

The reason is that the cost of providing benefits to the unemployed and other victims of the recession has grown quicker. Higher unemployment can have a much greater influence on the state welfare budget than demographic ageing. More unemployed - a social rather than a supposedly 'natural' phenomenon like ageing - increases social security payments to the unemployed and reduces the proportion of taxpayers, exacerbating levels of government deficits.

Demographic factors are less important than other economic trends in explaining increases in government social spending. Heller et al calculated that in the G7 countries demographic change accounted for only about one quarter of the real growth in social spending from 1960 to 1981.[3]

Even discounting for the impact of factors like movements in unemployment levels, the extra welfare costs for the British government resulting from the officially projected rates of ageing are relatively small. Ian Gibbs reports that looking 40 years ahead overall expenditure on health and social services would need to be only 12 per cent higher than now to maintain present levels and standards of provision[4], an increase of far less than 1 per cent of current GDP.

Colin Gillion, Director of the ILO's Social Security Department, uses OECD population projections to show that on the basis of a certain combination of assumptions – including real benefit growth of 1 per cent per year, a reversal of the earlier retirement trend, more women workers, fewer unemployed and more migrant workers – tax rates in 2040 could be either the same or lower than in 1986. These other factors 'broadly speaking ... more than offset the cost of the ageing process'.[5] He concludes 'there are a number of mechanisms and developments which might offset the rather gloomy and dramatic conclusions which are inevitable if the ageing process is envisaged as taking place in an otherwise unchanging world'.[6]

Further doubt is cast on a demographic ageing threat to the welfare state when it is recalled that the modern welfare state was established after the Second World War at a time when industrialised countries were ageing faster than today. Vincent makes the point that the rate of ageing of the British population was at its highest at precisely the time the British pension system was being established. The fact that this did not undermine either the financial integrity of the pensions system, nor dent its popularity, suggests to Vincent that, assuming economic growth continues at a reasonable pace, the British economy can well cope with the ageing projections made now for the next century.[7]

It would be wrong to suppose that the founders of the British welfare state were unaware of what was happening demographically. Although the occasional Cassandran voice at the time predicted a financial crisis would occur within a few years as a result of ageing, most specialists then were of the opinion that economic growth would suffice to fund the welfare state notwithstanding changes in the population's age structure. This reflected the more positive mood of the time about society's ability to cope with any future problems, not least through the benefits of economic growth. The change today in addressing the affordability of the ageing costs to the welfare system is not the result of the discovery of the ageing phenomenon. It is the prevalence both of an anti-state sentiment and of a more negative assessment of the human potential to overcome difficulties it encounters.

The pensions time bomb

Pensions are *the* issue of the 1990s, according to Will Hutton, editor-in-chief of *The Observer*. It is widely assumed that demographic trends lie behind pensions' higher profile of recent years. This section explains that something other than demography provides the real fuel for this discussion. Demographic fears are being used to provide legitimacy for moves to limit existing social provision for the elderly. The identification of old people as a problem serves a strategy of undermining the state's role in providing pensions for its citizens.

Pensions are an expensive business for every major economy. Their cost as a percentage of total government spending in the industrialised countries ranges from about 16 per cent to almost 40 per cent, with the UK and the US close to the average of one quarter.[8] (See table 6.) In money, this meant that in 1996–97 the British government spent £32bn on pensions, the largest element of the total welfare budget of almost £190bn. The cost of public pensions therefore represented over one third of the total social security budget of £90bn.

Pensions represent the single largest component of state spending which is indisputably attributable to older people. It is therefore not surprising that the cost of pensions has occupied a prominent role in the debate about the social burden of ageing. The common notion of increasing numbers of elderly people drawing their pension benefits and draining the resources produced by the rest of the population seems one of the most obvious confirmations of the reality of the demographic time bomb. This section will show that, as with all the welfare costs attributable to older populations, the burden from public pensions is also exaggerated.

On the one hand, then, the pensions issue is among the most graphic illustrations of the demographic time bomb. On the other, it is the area of public policy reform that is most explicitly claimed as driven by demographic necessities. By being the biggest *single* element of age-related social spending, modifying and reducing pension liabilities is presented as the most obvious means to defuse the time bomb. Some Western governments, including Britain, have used concern about ageing as the pretext for cutting back on pension levels or increasing the age of entitlement. In others major reforms are still to come. This section will explain that these reforms – of the present and the future – cannot legitimately be justified by population ageing.

Table 6:   Public pension spending as percentage of total
government expenditure

Country	Public pension spending / total government expenditure
UK	24.1
US	24.5
Germany	34.4
France	25.8
Italy	37.0
Canada	19.1
Australia	16.0
Austria	37.9
Belgium	17.6
Denmark	24.8
Finland	34.3
Greece	30.6
Ireland	15.7
Luxembourg	25.4
Netherlands	17.9
New Zealand	15.6
Norway	22.3
Portugal	18.9
Spain	23.2
Sweden	28.1
OECD average	24.7

Source: World Bank (1994),p 358.

The thrust of current British policy on pensions is unambiguous and openly admitted. The aim is to reduce the cost to the Treasury from an ageing population. In theory the government has two choices. Either reduce the spread of eligibility or reduce the level of pension. In the past it has proceeded upon the latter with the ultimate effect of bringing about in practice the former. Without officially reneging on the universality principle, the level of state pension will be allowed to fall so much in comparison with average living standards over the next couple of decades as to make it hardly worth the effort of collecting.

The emphasis now is on extending private pension provision to reduce even further reliance upon state handouts and to offload the remaining pressures on statutory pension provision. Ageing is advanced as the reason necessitating the reform of the pension system away from universal public pensions towards private provision, with the state merely retaining the residual role of providing a safety net. This chapter will further show that the crusade to move from public to private systems also cannot be legitimised by even the most extreme of the ageing projections. This is because the particular type of pension system employed - private or public, funded or pay-as-you-go - makes no difference to the amount of wealth required at any point in time to fund elderly, unproductive people to a particular standard of living. Different systems are merely different technical means for transferring this wealth to pensioners. As Gabriel Stein, an international economist with Lombard Street Research, writes 'pensions – however constructed and organised – involve a transfer of resources from the active to the retired generation'.[9]

Finally, this chapter will address the argument that economic growth is likely to be higher if pensions are funded, and, again as Stein writes, 'the resource transfers are disciplined by market pressures, rather than if pensions are simply financed on a pay-as-you-go basis through general taxation'.[10] It will show that this is an unproven argument and that the particular pension system used for distributing part of national wealth to the elderly does not affect the means of creating that wealth in the first place.

The burden of pensions

In the industrialised world in 1985 public pension spending as a percentage of GDP ranged from 5 per cent in Australia to nearly 16 percent in Italy. The UK at 6.7 per cent was below the average of 9 percent.[11] (See table 7.) The OECD forecasts, using conventional demographic projections, that by 2040 the British level will have grown to over 11 per cent and the OECD average will double to over 20 percent. Another way of illustrating the growth of the pension burden is by estimating the net present value of the future liability from the current pay-as-you-go unfunded state schemes. Calculating liabilities up to 2030 one estimate for 1994 showed the German level at 110 percent of GDP, France 105 per cent, Italy 70 per cent, with Britain at only 7 per cent.[12] (The British level is so much lower following the pension reforms already implemented over the past two decades.)

Table 7: Public pensions as percentage of GDP in selected OECD countries in 1985

Country	Public pension spending / GDP
UK	6.7
US	7.2
Japan	5.3
Germany	11.8
France	12.7
Italy	15.6
Canada	5.4
Australia	4.9
Austria	14.5
Denmark	8.5
Finland	7.1
Greece	10.7
Ireland	5.4
Netherlands	10.5
New Zealand	8.1
Norway	8.0
Portugal	7.2
Spain	8.6
Sweden	11.2
Switzerland	8.1
OECD average	8.9

Source: OECD (1988a)

These figures give weight to the notion of the old as an increasing burden upon society. It appears self-evident that more, and older, old people will mean an increasing burden upon the rest of society. In 1996 pensions consultant Adrian Kemp expressed the prevailing sentiment, which spreads far beyond the British pensions industry, when he warned: 'The population is ageing so fast that no government will be able to afford to fund pensions in the same way as today.'[13]

This British predicament is only one instance, and a less pronounced one too, of a wider problem that is said to affect all the industrialised countries. Christopher Daykin, the British government actuary since

1989, summarises: 'social security schemes around the world face problems from the ageing of the population'.[14] In 1988 the OECD warned in a major report on pensions that:

> 'Under existing regulations the evolution of public pension schemes is likely to put a heavy and increasing burden on the working population in coming decades. Such a financial strain may put inter-generational solidarity – a concept on which all public retirement provisions are based – at risk.' [15]

Another OECD study in 1989 into the implications of population ageing for the financing of public pensions concluded bluntly that pension funds across the advanced world would not cope.[16] The World Bank, in its major international survey *Averting the Old Age Crisis* published in 1994, cautioned: 'If trends continue, public spending on pensions will soar over the next fifty years.'[17]

Since the vast majority of old people are entitled to state pensions the equation of more old people with more spending on pensions seems incontrovertible. Everything else being equal, more old people must mean a bigger cost of pensions for society. Carolyn Weaver puts the case starkly: 'Holding everything else the same, a doubling of the age dependency ratio implies a doubling of tax rates required to support systems such as social security, or a halving of the level of support per beneficiary.'[18] Hence the apparently simple arithmetical base to these international warnings of unaffordable budget demands.

World Bank economists estimate that on current assumptions of coverage public pension spending in the advanced countries will rise from less than 9 per cent of GDP to over 16 per cent between 1990 and 2040.[19] Accordingly it seems so reasonable to assert that pension systems introduced in earlier times, when there was a different age structure, cannot outlive the impact of an ageing population. They must, this argument goes, be reformed to take account of the contemporary, and projected, demographic conditions.

There is no financial substance to this alarmist perspective on pension provision. All the arguments outlined earlier on the myth of the demographic time bomb apply to the specific case of pensions too: the exaggeration of demographic trends, the refusal to offset declining youth dependency in the dependency projections, the failure to extrapolate economic growth into the future and the greater significance of non-demographic factors for a country's productive capacity.

The example of what has occurred in rapidly ageing Japan provides a quick reality check for this type of concern. In just one generation Japan has coped with the advanced world's most rapidly ageing population – with the percentage of over 60 year olds rising from 9 per cent to 18 per cent – without any dramatically adverse social or economic consequences. This illustrates how sustained economic growth absorbs demographic changes with equanimity. More widely, average OECD public pension spending as a percentage of national income doubled between 1960 and 1984 without precipitating funding crises and unfair inter-generational transfers of the sort predicted for the next century.

In addition, non-demographic factors tend to have the greatest influence on overall pension expenditure. Of this substantial increase in pension spending from 1960 to 1984 only about a quarter was attributable to demographic factors. One third of the increase was the result of increases in benefits and almost two fifths can be explained by the widening of pension eligibility to groups hitherto not included in the public pension scheme. Johnson and Falkingham draw the reasonable conclusion that 'projections of future pension costs depend as much upon political as upon economic or demographic assumptions'.[20]

Some economists have already come out to try to dispel the myth of the pension time bomb but their conclusions have not yet done much to offset the wider alarmist mood. Kevin Gardiner, an economist from Morgan Stanley investment bank, for example has explained the greater significance of high unemployment than demography in assessing the affordability of present pension schemes. The trends of earlier retirement and staying longer in full-time education are substantial influences too.

Relatively small changes in the employed part of the population can have a big effect on dependency arithmetic and swamp the effects of demography. Gardiner shows that if continental European countries exhibited similar participation and employment levels as in Britain or the US today, 'old age pensions might even be funded, in an economic sense, on a pay-as-you-go basis indefinitely'.

He gives an even more striking and counter-conventional illustration from what could happen in France, where demographic alarmism is especially pronounced at the moment. He explains 'if we suppose that in the quarter-century ahead, France is able, via a combination of more flexible working practices and changes in household preferences, to approach the sort of unemployment and participation rates seen in the

UK and the US, then, instead of rising, adult dependency might actually fall by the year 2020, perhaps by as much as one-fifth'. Gardiner concludes that 'Europe has a labour market problem, not a pension problem'.[21]

Similarly, John Hills, lecturer at the London School of Economics, has shown using the case of Britain that the demographic fears expressed by the various international bodies are inflated. He has calculated that the net welfare spending effects of the ageing population, even if elderly benefit levels were to rise in line with overall living standards (which is not the current British policy), would be about 5 per cent of GDP over the next 50 years. He incorporates other 'burdening' assumptions in his calculation including the maturing of the State Earnings Related Pension Scheme and the higher basic pension entitlements which could occur (mainly owing to married women securing full pension entitlement). This 5 per cent is no more than the recession-induced rise in British welfare spending over just three years recently, between 1989 and 1992.[22] And Britain coped with that without any dramatic financial, economic or social repercussions.

The pessimistic projections for the public pension impact from ageing which remain prevalent across the industrialised world just do not stand up. Even modest rates of economic growth will make public pension schemes manageable indefinitely. With these types of calculations in mind, it would be easy to conclude there is scope for Britain to reform its public pensions in a *more* generous direction, and for this still to have negligible financial consequences. Yet all the discussion is about the demographic necessity for reducing public pensions. Why?

Either there is a generalised misunderstanding of the financial consequences of ageing upon pension liabilities, or something other than these implications is really at stake in the pensions debate. There is precedent for drawing the latter conclusion. There are plenty of instances of how myths about the burden caused by older people are manipulated for specific policy ends. Jay Ginn, for example, in a review of social policy in the 1980s describes how those who wished to justify cuts in public pensions depicted older people as threatening the viability of welfare states through their demands on resources.[23] We agree too with the argument by John Vincent that: 'The construction of the pensions issue as a demographic problem gives it the force of an impersonal inevitability backed by the scientific knowledge of demographers.'[24]

Highlighting demographic requirements seems to provide a fair, apolitical justification for cutting back on public expenditure. Not least in Britain it is conventional to claim that the ageing population has been one of if not the main driving force behind the new consensus on welfare thinking adopted across the political spectrum which endorses a move away from universal public provision.[25] This chapter argues that all the evidence points to demographic arguments being deployed for legitimising pension reforms that have other determinants – most prominently an ideological commitment to greater individual responsibility. The real agenda is the withdrawal of the state from pension provision and the promotion of privatised systems in their place.

The pensions debate

Demographic alarmism provides the underpinning to the entire pension debate. Proposals to alleviate the supposed impact of ageing include measures to raise the entitlement age, the taxing of pensions, the de-indexation of pension increases from average income rises, and basing benefits on lifetime earnings rather than the earnings level immediately prior to retirement. For example, the World Bank offers blunt advice to advanced industrialised countries on this topic: raise the retirement age, eliminate rewards for early retirement and penalties for late retirement, downsize benefit levels – which they claim are usually 'overgenerous' – and introduce a compulsory private scheme.[26]

Until recently raising the retirement age was one of the most often discussed mechanisms to reduce government pension liabilities.[27] Hamish McRae describes the feeling of many governments: 'that if retirement ages are not raised the burden of paying pensions will be so high that working people will not be prepared to pay the tax levels necessary to fund them'.[28] Pitts explains the special attraction of raising the retirement age for a PAYG system: 'Changes in the retirement age might be expected to have a particularly powerful effect on the per worker burden of social security costs because they can cause the size of the contributory and beneficiary populations to vary in opposite directions.'[29] Later retirement simultaneously should mean more workers and fewer retired dependents.

It is striking that over the past couple of years, at least in Britain, the demographic time bomb image has become less prominent around the pensions issue. Politicians, especially those associated with New Labour policies, have begun to counsel that the demographic dangers should not be exaggerated. The British Labour Party's background document to its 1997 general election manifesto, for example, was quite moderate in its statement of the ageing problem:

> 'While the scale of the "demographic time bomb" can be overstated, and can be offset by sustainable growth and high levels of employment, an ageing population will become a growing call on the resources of society. Our pension framework must ensure that these needs can be met in a manner which is affordable today and tomorrow.'[30]

What is happening here in seemingly playing down the danger of the time bomb? An overdue hint of rationality? Perhaps society will be allowed to get back to working to improve the living standards of elderly people? Unfortunately not. British government spokespeople can claim to feel relatively relaxed about the demographic element driving pension reform not least because demography has already played a sterling role in helping to win the intellectual battle for belittling public pension provision. In Britain many measures to reduce reliance on public provision have already been introduced. Hence the recent stability of the cost of pension spending in Britain. (See chart 21.)

The OECD now publishes reports about future pension provision which emphasise Britain's relative preparedness.[31] Long-range forecasts for the national debt of major economies on the basis of present pension provision and tax rates present Britain in a favourable light. On these assumptions national debt in France and Germany would double by 2030. In Japan the level of government indebtedness would soar to three times the national income. By contrast, on present trends, Britain's debt would disappear and the government would begin to accumulate assets. The reason is simple: the reduction of public pension entitlements and the massive shift to funded private provision schemes paid for by workers via private pension contributions instead of taxes.

In Britain, and the US, the demographic arguments with respect to pensions have already been at work to substantial effect for at least the past 15 years. Many practical reforms to reduce public pension provision have already been implemented, partly legitimated by the supposedly apolitical justification of concerns about ageing. As a result of the changes made, British state pensions are already the lowest of the G7 as a percentage of wages. They are declining further in relative terms

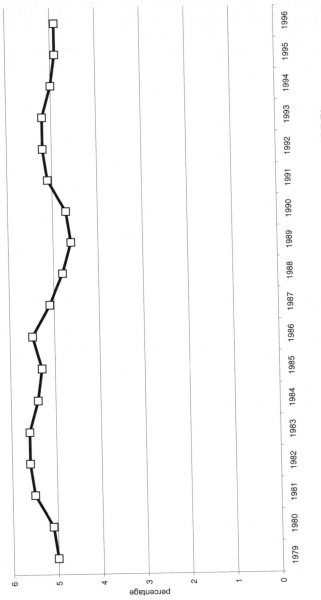

Chart 21: Public pension spending as share of national output (GDP)
Source: UK National Accounts, 1997

year on year since the change in indexation in 1980.[32] Also well over half
the British workforce now rely on occupational or personal pensions,
and the proportion is rising every year.

In the US as long ago as the late 1970s measures were being taken to
reduce future public pension entitlement. One reform was to let the real
value of pensions fall. In 1977 the US Congress de-coupled the benefit
system from the Consumer Prices Index, reversing the over-indexing
effect of the 1972 Social Security Act as implemented from 1975. The
next year the allowable retirement age was raised from 65 to 70 to
encourage later working and therefore reduced pension payments. In
1983 the American law was changed to reduce early retirement benefits
and to phase in an increase from 65 to 67 as the age at which full pension
benefits are available, implementable during the early decades of the
twenty-first century.

Meanwhile, Britain has experienced a steady succession of policy
changes since the early 1980s. All the familiar arguments about the
burden of a rising dependency ratio have been corralled in the arsenal of
attack against adequate state welfare support 'from cradle to the grave'.
In 1980 the British government changed the social security law to limit
the annual increase in state pensions to movements in prices rather than
in line with earnings. As a result the state pension has fallen way behind
the rise in living standards, and, on the basis of this policy, will wither
away to little more than pocket money for future generations. The basic
state pension fell from 20 per cent of average earnings in the late 1970s to
15 per cent in the early 1990s, and may decrease to about 6 per cent by
2040.

The 1986 Social Security Act reform of the State Earnings Related
Pension Scheme (SERPS) - whose introduction a decade earlier was
itself partly motivated by the desire to save money from the
supplementary benefits budget - was premised on the growing
'burden' of the welfare state and the worsening of the dependency
ratio:

'On the question of future pension costs the position is also clear.
According to the Government Actuary's estimate the number of
pensioners will grow from 9.3 million today to 12.3 million in 2025
and 13.2 million in 2035. The same estimate shows the ratio of
contributors paying for tomorrow's pensions falling from 2.3
contributors to every pensioner now to 1.8 contributors to every
pensioner in 2025 and 1.6 contributors in 2035.'[33]

After considering the possibility of abandoning SERPS altogether in a 1985 Green Paper the government's eventual response was substantially to reduce the level of SERPS pensions payable. The declared aim was to cut the cost of SERPS in half by 2033. The basis of the pension entitlement was made less generous by changing from the best 20 years of earnings to the lifetime average. Further reforms from 1988 also allowed more people in occupational pension schemes to contract out of SERPS and provided incentives to encourage private pension provision for retirement through personal pension schemes. The 1995 Pensions Act extended this reduction of state liability, introducing the provision for full contracting-out of SERPS. For future accruals, those who are contracted-out will not receive any additional pension in respect of the period of contracted-out service, as was previously the case.[34]

A simple cost–cutting objective is difficult to dismiss. The results of the basic pension indexation change from earnings to prices and the SERPS reforms have saved current and future British governments enormous amounts of money, which overwhelm the impact of demographic shifts.

Demographic reasons were also used to justify raising the female retirement age to 65. This was a major change in approach. Even in 1981 the Tory government had claimed in a white paper that 'when resources allow' it would introduce flexible retirement as it favoured the ability of people to choose earlier or later retirement than the statutory age. And on sexual equalisation it then favoured a 63 common retirement age, since it saw that to standardise at 65 would be seen as a 'breach of faith by many women'.[35]

These intentions were dropped by the 1990s. However, the analysis from the Equal Opportunities Commission (EOC) persuasively shows that the government's arguments for increasing the state retirement age for women to 65 spelt out in the 1993 White Paper *Equality in State Pension Age* are 'overstating the financial "crisis" facing future populations'.[36]

So in countries like Britain and the US ageing worries have already facilitated pension reductions. The ageing arguments are so ingrained that they no longer even need to be pushed hard. Expectations about future government support for pensions have been lowered systematically. This has opened up the space for the real driving forces behind further pension reforms to be made more explicit. There is a lesson here for other industrialised countries where overt fears engendered by ageing remain more in vogue.

The relative downplaying of the demographic time bomb in Britain recently has made more explicit some of these other agendas at work in the pensions' issue. The New Labour government, for example, pursues a moral campaign for individuals to take greater responsibility for themselves. With respect to pensions the argument is the need for people to assume greater personal responsibility for their future well being. As New Labour said in its agenda plans:

> 'Pensions policy, and economic policy more widely, must encourage people to save whatever their age and whatever their income. Not only is encouraging people to save better for them, it also helps to reduce the number of people forced to rely on extra state help in retirement.'[37]

This appeal to greater individual responsibility creates an apparently magic formula for government: lower levels of state benefits and lower taxes, through a scheme that is 'better' for everyone. How does this form of modern alchemy work? The new framework for 'second' pensions the Labour government is implementing is designed, it says, to encourage a higher level of personal contributions.[38] This is required because 'first' pensions, the existing public pensions, will, as we have seen, dwindle to almost nothing over the next 30 years. Whether this is done by introducing a compulsory second scheme or a formally voluntary one is immaterial, although New Labour seems reluctant to do the former out of a concern that this would be easy to brand as a new tax under a different name.

However, unless people pay into the second pension fund they will have nothing except a very rudimentary safety net from the state to live on in their old age. Personal taxes in Britain may be lower than they otherwise would be, but everyone is under pressure to pay a new replacement 'tax', even if 'voluntary' into a pensions scheme. Under the banner of individual responsibility, people are expected to pay more and the demands upon social provision are lessened.

The shift towards funded pensions
In Western Europe especially, Britain has become more than an exemplar of the pensions time bomb. As a result of what has already taken place in Britain (and the US) over the past 15 years, both

intellectually and practically, other industrialised countries have already begun to follow this lead in employing the pretext of demography to introduce pension changes. Britain has become a role model for the direction industrialised countries need to take to defuse the time bomb.

Germany, for example, passed the Pension Reform Act of 1989, which was implemented from 1992. This was driven, the German government said, by the political unacceptability of a doubling of the social insurance budget to 28 per cent by 2030 and the fear of this becoming 'a reason for inter-generational conflict'. The reforms included abolishing flexible retirement schemes. The standard retirement age for both men and women was increased to 65 from 2012, with the lowest age for early retirement raised to 62. Various penalties are to be introduced by 2001 to discourage early retirement. The index for pension increases was also switched from gross to net earnings. This means that the current ratio of pension to take home pay can no longer be improved upon.[39] France and Italy are among other European countries to begin introducing similar less generous changes since the early 1990s.

In addition to leading the way in measures to restrict pension entitlements Britain has also led the move to privatise pension provision. The shift from public pension provision to privately funded pension schemes represents the most important change in pensions systems in industrialised countries of the past half-century. An assessment of the discussion around this shift further helps to lay bare the real relationship between ageing and the pensions issue today: ageing as an excuse for changes which are driven by other political agendas.

Almost all discussion about the threat from ageing to pension systems emphasises the particular unsustainability of the pay-as-you-go (PAYG) pension scheme. The supposed seriousness of the state pensions predicament is emphasised by highlighting the technical distinction between the PAYG and the 'funded' approaches, and the former's relative defects. The distinction is another device to help make a retrenchment in state provision seem obligatory for technical and natural reasons.

PAYG is the most common government pension system used in industrialised countries. It means that current pensions are financed through current personal taxation and other deductions from salaries, sometimes supplemented by general government revenue or borrowing. Hence within the PAYG system is the inherent potential for pension liabilities to exceed the resources available. On the other hand in a funded pension system people pay into a fund which is invested to finance their pension payments. Pension benefits are technically financed by these prior savings into the fund and from the investment return on these savings. By definition liabilities can never exceed the accumulated reserves.

The features of the PAYG system are criticised as a specific illustration of the pension time bomb. The combination of relatively more old people having to be paid pensions from the wealth created by the relatively smaller current population of workers is said to herald bankruptcy for most state schemes. It is believed that liabilities for pensions will grow far beyond the means to pay for them. As Stein asserts 'pensions already promised over the foreseeable future, in most countries far exceed the payroll taxes that ostensibly finance them'.[40] Hamish McRae writes that: 'growth in state-sponsored investment funds seems inevitable as countries find that this is the only way they can fund the demands of an ageing population. The present pay-as-you-go pensions schemes, which just about work if there are four or five people of working age to every pensioner, cannot work if there are only two-and-a-half workers for each pensioner'.[41] As with all ageing concerns this dilemma is assumed to bite during the first half of the twenty-first century.

In the US concern about the necessity for at least modifying the PAYG social security system started to be voiced from the mid-1970s.[42] As with the ageing panic generally, so the PAYG pensions time bomb took some time to acquire widespread currency. Significantly much of the early 1970s discussion of the pensions burden was dismissive of those who talked up the demographic problem. For example, Robert Clark's 1977 study of the impact of ageing on the American social security system downplayed the problem. He wrote: 'All of our projections indicate that the movement toward zpg (zero population growth) will require ever greater transfers of income to support the elderly, with the Social Security System being forced to bear much of the burden'.[43] However, in conclusion he was sanguine that it could be afforded, not least because youth-related government expenditure would fall at the same time.

In similar vein W Reddaway, also writing in 1977, emphasised social over demographic factors in assessing the future viability of PAYG: 'On the whole, therefore, one should dismiss the increased pensions' bogey as quantitatively negligible, so far as it rests on demographic factors: its real basis is the general desire to improve the provision made for the elderly by raising the real value of the pension.'[44]

By the turn of the decade, though, the supposed demographic danger to PAYG schemes was becoming more widely accepted. As John Myles describes:

'The "crisis" of old age security had been discovered. In the usual formulation, the roots of the crisis are attributed to demography; the system of old age security entitlements currently in place in the capitalist democracies cannot withstand the rise in the number of old people projected for the decades ahead.' [45]

In a keynote article in 1980, 'Why Social Security is in trouble', Nathan Keyfitz compared the American PAYG system to a chain letter, which every teenager knows from experience always breaks down. The PAYG scheme collapse, he explained, was just as inevitable since the increasing ratio of retired persons to workers increased the burden on workers.[46]

In the US the demographic scare goes that while in 1950 there were 16 American workers for each retired person, by 1996 there were just three. By 2030, as more and more baby boomers reach pension age, there will only be two. It therefore appears to become more and more burdensome to finance PAYG pensions. In proportion to these demographic trends, social security taxes in the US have climbed from 2 per cent of pay in 1937 to 12.4 per cent in the mid-1990s. Although there is a cash flow surplus today, some demographic projections conclude the system will turn cash negative by about 2013. By 2030 it is estimated the accumulated trust funds invested in government bonds will be exhausted.[47] Similar alarmist predictions about the problems of unfunded schemes are now made for most other industrialised countries.

During the 1990s the argument spread across the industrialised world that the only fully effective solution to the pensions time bomb is to replace PAYG systems by funded schemes, either wholly or in part. In most cases the recommendation is for this reform to be effected through the privatisation of pensions. The model of Chile's 1981 pension reforms is the most often cited.[48]

It is striking that the funded versus pay-as-you-go distinction is only being highlighted now when demography is believed to be moving against the working population. For most of the twentieth century the number of pension recipients has been relatively small compared with the number of people of working age. Throughout that time governments have expressed little anxiety, or even pleasure, about what to do with all the 'surpluses' from the PAYG scheme.

This inconsistent approach also ignores the fact that the PAYG revenue collecting systems often encouraged the notion that pension money was being specifically accounted for in a 'fund'. This is precisely what the PAYG systems are now attacked for being deficient in. In Britain, for example, the development of national insurance-based pensions, formalised in Neville Chamberlain's Widows', Orphans' and Old Age Contributory Pensions Act of 1925, gave the impression that people in employment pay 'national insurance contributions' into the 'national insurance fund'. The reality has always been that pensions and other welfare benefits are paid for out of general tax revenue, of which the national insurance contribution is just one, notably regressive, element. Despite the terminology there never was a firewalled pension fund.

The introduction of SERPS in the 1970s put across a similar signal as with national insurance that contributors were paying into some type of fund. Why otherwise was it not going to be fully introduced until 1998? The implication was that it would take time for the 'fund' to build up. Was this gradual introduction not an example of prudent financial management? Money was being accumulated by the state on our behalf so it was unreasonable to expect a full return until this nest egg had grown. This was another deception. In 1985 the government came clean on its predecessor's real motives: 'The twenty-year postponement of the full implementation of the scheme had nothing to do with building up a fund: there is no fund. The postponement was based on the hope that the scheme could be afforded from 1998'.[49]

Today this pretence of a distinct fund has been officially abandoned. Why have governments suddenly started to come clean in the 1990s? One simple reason is that moving away from a PAYG system satisfies the prevalent desire to curb government spending. Another is that the favoured alternative to PAYG, the private funded arrangement is in line with the intellectual ascendancy of market principles and of anti-state sentiments. The problems supposedly associated with the existence of PAYG schemes in most industrialised countries are emphasised as necessitating a shift to more individual responsibility for pension provision and a reversal of the 'dependency culture'. Private funded schemes are consistent with cheaper and smaller government.

In a funded scheme personal contributions are each year invested in a pool of assets. This fund accumulates during the contributor's working life and is therefore available to be run down in order to pay the pension during the years of retirement. One of the attractions for those who promote funded schemes is that it appeals to a sense of personal responsibility, what has been called a 'prudential life course'. Some ideologues are no doubt attracted by the implication that failure to contribute fully to one's own pension can play on the guilt that people have only themselves to blame for a miserable old age. They thoughtlessly lived only for the present rather than investing wisely for the future. They should not have spent such a carefree working lifetime, and instead should have been conscientiously and responsibly building up their personal nest egg for the future. What fools they were not to think ahead to finance their twilight years.

To give weight to the ideological anti-state stance, three basic lines of argument are advanced for moving towards funded schemes as a necessary response to demographic pressures. First, funded schemes, unlike PAYG ones, cannot collapse under the weight of an excessive burden on the workforce of the future. Secondly, they are said to be more efficient. And thirdly, funded schemes are said to be beneficial for economic growth. Let us look at the substance of these arguments.

PAYG systems look good, it is said, when they are first set up and are well able to provide large benefits to those workers who were 30 to 50 years old when the schemes were introduced. However, when the schemes fully mature and everyone over statutory pension age becomes eligible for full pensions they become more expensive. Eventually in the face of present demographic trends, they must break down. By definition, on the other hand, funded schemes cannot become bankrupt in the same way.

On closer inspection this apparently self-evident contrast is not quite so clear. Despite technical differences between the operation of the two different types of schemes they have something fundamental in common. Both make their payments from the economic wealth created by the workers of the future. Whether pensions are obtained through funded or unfunded schemes is immaterial to the stock of what is available when it is needed. Under funded schemes people do not store up goods and services now for consumption in their elderly years. Nor do funds create goods and services; they simply create entitlements to a proportion of the economy, of whatever size.

As Daykin argues: 'If the economy as a whole is considered, rather than individuals within the economy, there can be no transfer of money across time. That is to say, whilst there can be sums of money set aside to which particular individuals will only become entitled at some specified time in the future, this money cannot be taken out of the economy as a whole and set aside until some future date when it is reclaimable. Unless we can find a way of investing outside of our economic system, or in economies with a quite different ageing cycle, the wealth which people are creating at any particular time is used to finance the lifestyle of people at that time. So, even with a funded pension system, it is still the workers of tomorrow who will fund the income of tomorrow's pensioners, even if the transfers take place through the dividends on the shares which the pensioners own through their pension funds.'[50]

Everything else remaining the same, a change in pensions system therefore cannot affect the financial implications of the demographic time bomb. The amount of the total social product that elderly people consume as a group is logically independent from the production of that level of output. The goods and services consumed by pensioners as a whole must be provided by the workforce of the day, however little or much has been put into pension funds.

Despite the declared theoretical differences between the two systems in the way they are organised, in practice both are the same in their reliance for their fulfilment on the productive capacity of the economy. They both require that part of the economic unit's wealth be used to support a section of the population which is not being productive. Whether these funds are distributed via taxation or via the realisation of the proceeds from previous saving is not pertinent to the requirement that pensions are paid out of the stock of economic surplus at any point in time. Whether from tax, in the case of PAYG, or from dividends, in the case of funded pensions, in both cases the money for pensions comes from current output. The 'common sense' attraction of a scheme based upon planning and saving for the future over one based on relying on the generosity of the working section of the population therefore blurs the commonality of the two approaches.

A change to a funded system also has no technical advantage for lessening the personal cost in the here and now of preparing for your old age. As Paul Johnson argues: 'If transfers [from working age to elderly people] are mediated ... through private pension schemes rather than a public social security pension, working age people may experience an equally large reduction in current consumption as private pension premiums have to rise in response to the increased number of retirement years ... . Whether [this transfer] is done publicly or privately has little bearing on the total cost.'[51]

Jan Toporowski, a reader in economics at South Bank University, similarly makes the point that there is nothing magical about the efficacy of funded pensions: 'Ultimately all modern pensions come either from taxes on employment, or from the profits generated by employment in the case of funded schemes ... . (With a stagnant economy) savings out of employment income are therefore hardly a more adequate base for future pensions, except for those who will make money from selling and mis-selling private pension schemes.'[52]

Toporowski is drawing attention to two basic deficiencies of the funded scheme. If average economic growth in the future is lower than we have become used to in the developed world, funded schemes then only 'work' at the expense of even lower living standards than at present for the future pension-maintained generations of retirees. It is self-evident that government liabilities will not rise if PAYG schemes are abandoned, or decisively watered down, in favour of personal funded schemes, but this will be at the expense of future generations. In addition the fact that most pension funds are invested in stock markets also makes future retirees dependent on the avoidance of stock market crashes, or a sustained equity bear market, or merely an end to the past two decades of bull markets. Given the artificial character of stock market valuations today, this can hardly be claimed to be a safer, more risk adverse approach than relying on the present PAYG arrangement. Social and economic circumstances in the future could precipitate the wiping out of these paper asset values.

There is even a demographic case that the strong bull stock markets, which have made for strong pension fund performance, will not be sustained in the next century. At the moment the relatively high savings level of the baby boom generation are a force behind buoyant equity prices. Daykin and many others argue that 'by the 2020s and 2030s, however, more and more people will want to disinvest and this will tend to put downward pressure on prices'.[53]

Secondly, PAYG schemes are generally criticised today as being inefficient.[54] This would only be fair comment if private funded schemes were cheaper to run than state PAYG schemes. There is no evidence for this claim. On the contrary, because most of the proposed funded schemes would be run by private, profit-driven financial institutions, running costs are much higher than state PAYG systems. In Britain, Coopers & Lybrand (now PriceWaterhouseCoopers) estimate that the administration costs for operating the state pension scheme is in the order of £15 to £20 per person each year.[55] This works out at less than 1 per cent of contributions. On the other hand the government actuary department calculates that a member of a typical personal pension plan loses about a quarter of their savings through fees and charges. On top of this is the ongoing danger of private pension institutions mis-advising the public on the best arrangement for them. In Britain in 1998 about three million people were still awaiting compensation for the mis-selling of private pension policies in the late 1980s to those who were wrongly advised to transfer from occupational pension schemes and from SERPS. This danger will always be present in a system administered by private profit-driven institutions.

The Chilean private pension scheme is often promoted as a model for changes in the West. Yet the record of its operation highlights both the dangers pointed to by Toporowski. The Chilean system was set up in 1981 as an alternative to the PAYG scheme. Under it workers are supposed to pay 13 per cent of monthly income to one of the pension fund administrators. In a country frequently held up as a model of free market economics, the privatised pension scheme is often cited by economists as a 'brilliant achievement', especially the way it has boosted savings.

However, the downside is also apparent. A pension fund linked to financial investments is not always bound to rise. As the advertising small print reads: 'The value of your investment may fall as well as rise and is not guaranteed.' After 13 years of positive returns averaging over 13 per cent, in 1995 the fund fell by 3.7 per cent, 'leaving this year's retirees high and dry'.[56]

In addition the Chilean scheme has proved costly for its members. The level of transaction costs is high, which is exacerbated by the extent of churning in the system as a result of the freedom to switch funds as often as people like. In order to attract customers from other funds, the different funds spend a lot in marketing activities 'including glossy magazines, television adverts, pretty ladies going around knocking on people's doors and so on'.[57] Barrientos calculates that the total setting up and running costs amount to about one third of contributions.[58] It seems fair to conclude that the private pension institutions in Chile, many of them US-based, are benefiting much more from the privatisation of pensions than the workers who have contributed their hard earned savings.

Having addressed the efficiency arguments, the only way a technical shift in the structure of pensions, from recycling to funding, could make a difference is if it boosted economic wealth to a level over what it would have been. This brings us to the third argument that funded schemes are better for economic growth. Johnson and Falkingham describe how this belief has spread. In the period since 1973, they write, 'Social security systems which had been seen as handmaidens of growth in the 1960s were now seen as obstacles to economic efficiency.'

In 1983, for example, the United Nations was criticising the way that the supposed generosity of state pension schemes was contributing to economic difficulties. It claimed that the increase by the US government in public programmes for the elderly and the indexation of benefits to inflation may have encouraged early retirement and therefore represented a disincentive to work.[59] The OECD's 1988 report on public pensions made the same claims.[60]

This is a dubious argument. Several factors influence decisions to take early retirement but the supposed generosity of benefits paid to early retirees is unlikely to rate highly. Early retirement is rarely a free choice when it means a substantial fall in living standards. But even if it could be shown that early pensions encourage some people to stop work early, why is this an economic problem and a cause of slower growth? The continuation of high levels of unemployment in most of the industrialised countries throughout the ups and downs of recent business cycles makes untenable the view that slower economic growth these days is caused by labour shortages.

If the labour market effects from public PAYG pensions are inconclusive, could there be an economic effect through an impact on savings? Martin Feldstein was one of the first economists to argue that public pensions tend to lower economic growth by reducing savings and investment.[61] This has now become a common theme of market economists. In its 1994 study the World Bank described a vicious circle of demographic ageing putting pressure on public pension schemes; higher public pensions commitments consume more of GDP and require higher tax revenues; these increases, in turn, tend to slow economic growth, making the public pension system even less sustainable.[62] The World Bank blames public PAYG pension systems for hindering growth: 'More basically, the system has become unsustainable because it has impeded growth.'[63]

The argument advanced is that funded schemes would result in higher levels of saving and that these would accelerate the rate of economic growth. Stein asserts that 'economic growth is likely to be higher in a country where the pension system builds up and maintains large savings which are available for investment purposes, than in a country which relies on tax revenues to pay each year's pensions'.[64] But for this to hold, first, one would have to show that funded pensions would increase the net savings rate. It is just as reasonable to suppose that people saving towards their pensions might reduce other savings to compensate.

Also even if it were shown that savings rose *as a result* of the new pension arrangements, this might only inflate the prices of financial assets and not stimulate real economic growth. Daykin notes that: 'Funding obviously creates investment of a sort, but it is not obvious that it creates real investment.' Apart from the savings substitution issue, 'It may also simply have the effect of forcing up prices in stock markets, if there are too many investors chasing a finite volume of financial instruments, unless the availability of investment monies leads to new investment projects being pursued which would otherwise not have taken place.'[65] For the latter to occur it would be necessary to establish that growth is being hampered by current shortages of savings in providing a capital fund for productive investment. Of course, many other reasons than the level of savings can be advanced for explaining the relatively low investment levels in the 1990s.

No one has yet convincingly established either of these arguments. Despite much research into the savings–growth link, it has proved impossible to substantiate the assertion that funded schemes are better for growth. Johnson and Falkingham report that no empirical proof exists for this claim.[66] Even Feldstein concluded his argument with the qualification that the case is 'not strong'.[67] Gravelle comes to the same conclusion. His review of the 20-year debate in the US on the link between savings and personal pension schemes shows that it has been largely inconclusive.[68] Daykin agrees and reports that 'many of the studies that have been carried out by academic economists, particularly in North America, suggest that there is no benefit at all from funding because it simply substitutes for other forms of saving'.[69] Significantly even the World Bank - one of the most vocal advocates of funded schemes - admits that it is difficult to substantiate the claim that PAYG systems lower the level of savings and adversely affect the rate of capital accumulation and growth.[70]

Conclusion

The embedded character of the demographic threat to the state pension system within public imagination is such that in some countries, such as Britain, the demographic time bomb argument can now be relatively downplayed. This is not because they have concluded that a demographic threat is a myth but because the deep-rooted nature of this assumption provides a secure platform for other arguments in favour of the need for pension reform.

This fosters a multidimensional case for pension reform. Fears about demography making state pensions unaffordable are supplemented by fears of inadequate economic growth. Complementing the demographic case is the argument for greater individual responsibility. And with this argument for assuming greater personal responsibility, playing upon fears for the future widens the case. A climate of lower expectations makes it easier for politicians to call for sacrifices to pay for the dependent elderly today and in the future. Saving for 'the future you do not know' is more than a successful advertising jingle. It sums up the sense of risk and uncertainty about the future that has become so prevalent today.

So John Denham, the pensions minister in the Labour government, argues for private pension provision because of the unsure world we now inhabit, not because New Labour has renounced the principles behind Beveridge's welfare state. In a changed world state pensions are too insecure and uncertain. A 20-year-old needs security over 60 years. Relying on the state to provide is too risky. Denham explains that one's future public benefits would depend upon a high level of inter-generational trust. That trust can no longer be guaranteed since the previous Conservative government has destroyed it. Such a possibility, he claims, is endemic in a democracy because future governments can always renege on the promises and decisions made by the present one.

The necessity for personal responsibility is now framed in terms of coping with risk and uncertainty, rather than consistency with free market principles. The consequence is the same. Demographic fears are still played upon. But different, more caring, mediating arguments are deployed to justify the move away from social, collective provision to personal responsibility.

The form of the British pensions debate has implications elsewhere and is worthy of more detailed study than is within the ambit of this book. As Will Hutton forecast, it still has much scope to run in Britain. But whatever the form or pace of the discussion in different countries it is clear that demographic assumptions and pensions discussions are inextricably linked. The successful argument of the case against the pension time bomb can only serve rational debate on this matter.

Notes

1.   Myles (1983), pp 467-8.
2.   Pampel and Williamson (1989), p 7.
3.   Heller et al (1986), p 20.
4.   Gibbs (1991), p 376.
5.   Gillion (1991), p 120.
6.   Gillion (1991), p 124.
7.   Vincent (1996), p 9.
8.   Cited in World Bank (1994), p 358.
9.   Stein (1997), p 2.
10. Stein (1997), p 3.
11. OECD (1988a).
12. Stein (1997), p 5.
13. *Independent on Sunday*, 3 March 1996.
14. Daykin (1998), p 1.
15. OECD (1988b), p 102.
16. Hagemann and Nicoletti (1989), p 60.
17. World Bank (1994), p 7.
18. Weaver (1987), p 277.
19. World Bank (1994), p 7.
20. Johnson and Falkingham (1992), p 141.
21. *The Independent*, 17 February 1996.
22. Hills (1993), p 14.
23. Ginn (1993).
24. Vincent (1996), p 22.
25. Nicholas Timmins, 'Hail the welfare revolution; *The Independent*, 9 May 1996.
26. World Bank (1994), p 21-22.
27. OECD (1989), p 74.
28. McRae (1994), p 103.
29. Pitts (1978), p 180.
30. Labour Party (1996), p 3.
31. See OECD (1995).
32. Johnson and Falkingham (1992), p 56.
33. DHSS, (1985b).
34. Daykin (1998), p 23.
35. DHSS (1981).
36. EOC (1995), p 36.
37. Labour Party (1996), p 7.
38. Labour Party (1996), p 3.
39. Schmahl (1993).
40. Stein (1997), p 4.
41. *The Independent*, 9 January 1996.
42. See Rejda and Shepler (1973), Hogan (1974), Turchi (1975), Clark (1977).

43. Clark (1977), p 53.
44. Reddaway (1977), p 29.
45. Myles (1983), pp 462–3.
46. Keyfitz (1980), p 107.
47. *Financial Times*, 26 October 1996.
48. See Carter and Shipman (1996).
49. DHSS (1985a).
50. Daykin (1998), p 32.
51. Lloyd–Sherlock and Johnson (1996), p 14.
52. *Financial Times*, 23 May 1996.
53. Daykin (1998), p 32.
54. World Bank (1994), p 12.
55. Association of British Insurers (1997), p 40.
56. *Business Week*, 18 December 1995.
57. Daykin (1998), p 26.
58. Barrientos (1996), p 55.
59. United Nations (1983).
60. OECD (1988b), p 10.
61. Feldstein (1974).
62. World Bank (1994), p 120.
63. World Bank (1994), p 157.
64. Stein (1997), p 16.
65. Daykin (1998), p 30.
66. Johnson and Falkingham (1992), pp 126–8.
67. Feldstein (1974), p 61.
68. Gravelle (1990).
69. Daykin (1998), p 31.
70. World Bank (1994), pp 307–8.

6· The Health Time Bomb

The conventional equation of ageing with worsening health provides ample scope for the ubiquitous demographic time bomb. As populations age it is assumed that the costs of health and social care must increase rapidly as people live longer and require greater care for a proportionately greater part of their lives. A fear in most industrialised countries is that increasing numbers of elderly people carrying a progressively heavier burden of disease and disability will swamp health services and consume an increasing proportion of the health and social services budgets. As Raymond Tallis describes the British situation: 'There are already signs of panic, with ill-judged attempts by health managers to ration health care according to age.'[1]

This chapter on health will not engage the rationing debate head-on. Nor will it repeat the argument that economic growth is the best antidote to any increased social costs associated with ageing. Instead the main aim here is to shake the popular belief that ageing populations must mean significantly more disease and disability, and therefore must create sharply increasing demands on the provision of health and other social services. Specifically it addresses the validity of the notions that old people are highly prone to illness, and that greater longevity must mean increasing disease and therefore demand for health care. In meeting this aim it will provide a more balanced perspective on the ageing/health relationship which, hopefully, others will use within the wider discussion on health rationing.

This chapter will show that much of the assumed arithmetic around health service costs and ageing is distorted. To take the extreme case, it is sometimes thought that health care costs will rise in proportion to the growth of the elderly population. This is far from the truth. Take the usual assumption that the elderly population in Britain will grow by about 50 per cent over the next half century. In contrast, health services costs of about 6 per cent of GDP in Britain today will not grow by anything like 50 per cent as a result of population ageing. This is for a combination of reasons that this chapter will explore:

a) About a half of the health budget still goes on the non-elderly, below 65 year olds, so, other things being equal, health spending cannot rise in proportion to population ageing as this takes no account of what is happening to the health spending on younger cohorts.

b) The health demands of the non-elderly population as a group (if not as individuals) may fall, offsetting any rising demand from the elderly. An older population structure means relatively fewer younger people, especially infants, requiring medical treatment.

c) Reaching old age does not bring on permanent morbidity. Most over-64s are fit and healthy.

d) The old are becoming healthier generation by generation, as a result of both their early life experiences and medical advances. We are not just living longer, but staying healthy longer.

e) There is mounting evidence that serious disease tends to be concentrated in a shorter time at the end of one's life. This is known as the compression of morbidity.

f) Increased longevity does not increase morbidity and disability. Morbidity and age do not rise in strict proportion. By some measures the older old are healthier than the younger old.

How much does health care cost?

Polly Toynbee, the liberal and acclaimed social affairs journalist, summed up the conventional wisdom about the limits of health care provision in the final months of the last British Conservative government. 'Bevan's ringing promise, so fine, perhaps unrealisable, to care for all of us, forever, from the cradle to the grave' she began, and continued: 'Already that promise is being broken in health authorities all over the country, not necessarily because of bad management, not necessarily because of Tory cuts either, but because it is a promise inherently unaffordable.'[2] Toynbee, among many others, claims that one of the prime explanations for such an assertion is the financial impact of an ageing population. Conventional thinking contains two elements: a public health care system is unaffordable, and ageing is one of the contributory factors.

Before the second point about ageing is addressed, it will be useful to establish the extent of the health service's financial crisis. It is not as grave as many think. By Toynbee's tone, one would assume that health care costs are spiralling out of control in Britain. This is not so. For the past 20 years the government's health budget has been growing at about 1.5 per cent a year in real terms. This is not a negligible increase but it still means that as a percentage of national output health expenditure has been falling since the trend growth rate of GDP is about 2.25 per cent.

By international comparison too, the cost of health care in Britain is relatively low. Spending on health as a percentage of GDP varies widely across the advanced industrial economies of the G7. This is true both for the levels of public provision by the state and total spending across the economy.

Table 8:   Health spending as a share of GDP

	Total	Public
Japan	6.6	4.7
UK	6.6	5.5
Italy	8.3	6.5
Germany	8.5	6.1
France	9.1	6.7
Canada	10.0	7.2
US	13.4	5.9

Source: OECD (1993a)

By this measure Britain has either one of the most efficient or one the most rudimentary state health services within the G7. Either way it is at present the least costly to the national economy, equal with Japan, and the second cheapest to the national exchequer. So for the health crisis discussion to be proceeding with such gusto in Britain implies that something other than material necessity, whether demographically or otherwise determined, is at its root.

The fact that a liberal such as Toynbee now questions if a functioning National Health Service (NHS) was *ever* realisable in Britain seems to represent a dramatic lowering of expectations from the post-war assumptions. In the 1950s and 1960s Conservatives, Labour and Liberals all gave their backing to universal health care provision. The shared belief was that an expanding economy could well afford an extensive health care service. This became an unquestioned assumption of modern living. Today, though, everyone seems to have adjusted downwards his or her expectations of what an advanced developed country can afford. It would appear reasonable to conclude that it is society's expectations that have changed rather than some significant increase in the practical cost of universal health provision.

This inflated assessment of the crisis facing the modern health service provides the context for the even more dramatised discussion about the ageing burden on the health budget. In a climate where there is a tendency to exaggerate problems, the ageing dimension is bound to attain a high profile. Once the guns are out for public health care it is not surprising that old people figure prominently in the sights since the elderly are indisputably disproportionate consumers of health care.

Over half of health service spending in Britain and in most other industrialised countries is regularly devoted to the over 64s.[3] Giarini and Stahel go further and claim that 'In some "advanced" countries 50 per cent of the overall health expenses are absorbed by people during the last three weeks of their life'.[4] In Britain the elderly take over 40 per cent of acute hospital beds.[5] McRae reports that in the US, it has been estimated that Medicare spends six times as much for recipients in the last year of their life as it does for its average members.[6] Johnson and Falkingham claim that people over 75 on average cost the British health service nine times as much as persons aged 16-64.[7]

The World Bank makes a similar comparison in stating that public health spending per person over age 65 can exceed 10 times that on under 15s. It reports the certain fact that 'the demand for health services increases as countries grow older, since health problems and costly medical technologies are concentrated among the old'.[8]

So there is a strong financial basis for old people to feature strongly in the health discussion. In Britain today it seems every row about the future of the NHS incorporates reference to the impact of ageing. With respect to the NHS's finances Toynbee explains: 'The funds are limited, the demands on it are growing at twice the rate of inflation, partly because of the ageing population, partly because of the galloping costs of new treatments.'[9]

And this is not some fixation of Toynbee alone. Most media discussion of the relationship of ageing to health is made in rather pejorative terms: the 'elderly health disaster' (*British Medical Journal*), or, the 'elderly health burden' (*New Society*).[10] Hunt, *The Independent's* medical correspondent, sums up the way perceived pressures on the health care system focus on the consequences of ageing:

'First, there are the demands of the elderly, the most prolific consumers of health care. By 2001 there will be a 26 per cent rise in the number of people over 85 in England and Wales. This group uses about 14 times as many resources as those aged 16–44. Second, chronic diseases such as heart disease, cancer and stroke put more pressure on resources because medical advances allow people to live longer. Third, new procedures, diagnostic tests and drugs, are often very expensive.'[11]

From the shortage of intensive-care beds to the stretching of the accident and emergency services there is usually someone to lay at least part of the fault at the door of demography. The belief is that an increase in numbers of old people will bankrupt health systems, and that additional years of health expectancy would simply be years of poor health which would cost society as a result, for example, of repeated hospitalisation.[12]

Rice and Feldman speak for many when they claim that as a result of the forecast increase in the number of elderly 'it is near certain that we shall be facing an increasing demand for medical services for at least the next several decades'.[13] The belief is that the demands on the health service posed by an ageing population and medical advances are not just rising, but increasing too fast. It is such a commonplace notion that few see any need to argue the case. Instead the frequent unsubstantiated assertion is that as a result of ageing, health care costs will rise 'exponentially'.[14]

Simon Jenkins, in his otherwise well argued survey of Tory policy on the state during the 1980s and early 1990s, uncritically throws in the burden of ageing. He writes that falling confidence in the NHS was partly because 'the hospitalisation of the elderly and mentally ill, all living longer, was ... escalating costs'.[15] He claims this led NHS officials to ponder: 'Should greater life expectancy - presumably incurring more care - be regarded as a good thing irrespective of cost?'[16] The message is clear. The elderly are living longer and thereby incurring greater and possibly socially harmful costs. Butler, from the US National Institute on Aging, emphasises this view that increased longevity is a major contributor to extra costs. He forecasts that 'the drop in mortality rates means a growing burden of serious sickness problems in the oldest population groups'.[17]

Returning to Britain, an ageing population is said to undermine the NHS as a tax-funded, free-at-the-point-of-use service, and necessitate its replacement by a slimmed down 'core NHS' with new charges and other payments. The implications of ageing are often believed to be exacerbated by medical advances, many of which it is claimed, almost contemptuously, merely keep chronically ill, old people alive. McRae argues that:

> 'All industrial countries already find it hard to contain medical costs. They will find it harder to do so as their populations age, for this will inevitably increase the demand for medical services. This demographic shift makes it all the more vital that countries take control of their medical costs.'[18]

Sinclair and Williams in recognising the truism that old people are less healthy than the average adult highlight what is often ignored by others in the discussion. The increased number and proportion of elderly needs to be set against the decreased health expenditure on children as a result of the decline in the birth rate.[19] But a wider point needs to be made on the relation between age structure and morbidity.

The demographic alarmists use the statistic that the proportion of health spending going on over 64s is rising. For example, in Britain the proportion of hospital and community health service expenditure directed to people above this age rose from 43 per cent in 1974 to 51 per cent in 1983.[20] But this should be viewed as a positive development for the health of the overall population, of all ages. The greater concentration of illness and disability within elderly sections of the population is the product of reduced morbidity among younger age groups, not a result of greater elderly morbidity – this chapter will show the latter is falling too. The increasing proportion of health spending attributed to the elderly is highlighted in many reviews, when what should be emphasised is the declining absolute level of illness that manifests itself in that rising proportion. The demographic alarmists herald as a cause for despair a statistic that should be welcomed as a sign of progress.

The same pessimistic interpretation is put on the fact that the elderly take up a higher proportion of hospital beds these days. But as Tinker et al report, this disguises the real drop in the number of beds available overall. And for the elderly themselves between 1987 and 1991 there were 10 per cent fewer geriatric beds.[21] In this way the myth about ageing destroying the health service provides a cover for the decline in resources available for everyone.

Overall ageing seems to be playing its usual prominent role as the inevitable, non-political excuse by those in favour of cutting back on state health care provision. Ageing is being used to legitimise measures to cut back on government health spending. In this specific area of public expenditure one form of the attack which has been prominent in Britain is the redefinition of medical care as a social service. While in the past nursing care for the old was seen as an extension of the NHS, today the distinction between medical and social help is emphasised. From the government's perspective there is a sound financial basis for this shift. Social care, unlike health care, is not mainly free at the point of use. Governments committed to cost cutting have had an interest in seeking to redefine what used to be seen as appropriate, and free, NHS services, as means-tested social services. Dependent, bedridden old people who in the past would have been regarded as hospital patients are re-categorised as nursing home residents.

For example, the 1993 Community Care Act, which followed on from the Griffiths' commission and the 1990 NHS and Community Care Act, shifted responsibility for long-term care of the elderly in residential and nursing homes from central government - the NHS - to local authorities. Funding for care of the old via social security spending was stopped. Cash limits were imposed on the resources available. Now local authorities use means tests to determine payments. The consequence is a shift of financial cost from the state - whether central or local - to the individual.

As with the pension issue the shift in policy is away from collective provision towards personal responsibility. And again it is the supposed impact of the ageing population that is used to justify these changes, as politically neutral and unavoidable. This chapter will now address the validity of the common assumptions about morbidity and old age that underlie this discussion.

Are old people likely to be ill?

The underlying assumption of most understanding of the relationship between ageing and health service needs is that old people tend to be ill, and therefore more old people means more ill people and greater demands upon the health services. At first sight this seems self-evident. There is a positive correlation between age and disability reflecting the strong association between age and chronic cardiovascular, musculoskeletal and neurological diseases. Tinker et al report fairly that 'the number of people with severe physical disability increases sharply with age and there is a similar increase in the number suffering from dementia'.[22] The British General Household Surveys (GHS) consistently confirm that there is a greater incidence of both acute and chronic sickness among elderly people than among any other age group.

The misconceptions arise when the extrapolation is made that all, or most, old people are disabled or ill in some way. It is a major distortion to translate a valid age component of relative morbidity levels between the young, the middle aged and the elderly, into the belief that old age means absolute morbidity. Nor is it legitimate, as the World Bank does, to try to give this relative measure a value judgement which implies that old people are being too demanding because of their specific care needs: 'The kind of medical care required for old people often involves more expensive technology, hospitalization, and long-term nursing care than does medical care for younger people.'[23] The implication is clear; the old are in some way to blame for excessive demands on the health system because of the special type of treatment they require.

The dominant stereotype then is that to be old means to be unhealthy and to require expensive medical treatment. This is very different to the valid observation upon which it is based, that an older person is relatively more likely to have a health problem than a younger person. Christina Victor shows vividly what happens when this distinction is elided: 'Later life and ill health are perceived to be synonymous.'[24] The assumption made, she continues, is that 'the greying of nations is presented as a world-wide pandemic from which there is no escape'. The logic extends that more infirm and demented old people are seen to present 'an insatiable demand for health and social care'.[25]

The image that most old people are ill remains one of the most distorted expressions of the social construction of 'elderly dependency'. Social gerontologists such as Alan Walker and Chris Phillipson have always challenged this prejudice and emphasised that most old people are not unhealthy. In their critique of ageism they reject the way that old age is pathologized as a process of infirmity and illness, when this is not true for most elderly people.[26]

The idea of 'dependence in old age', and therefore of the drain which older people put on society's resources, is even less valid in a medical than in an economic context. Many elderly people are able to and would like to work and be economic contributors, but are prevented from doing so by legislation and social attitudes. Therefore, their economic dependence is often real but it is often involuntary and unnecessary. Though most elderly people are prevented from engaging in economic activity they are biologically and physiologically capable of pursuing active lives.

The fact is that most old people are not ill or disabled. Also the morbidity that old people do face is usually concentrated in the last few years of their lives. Only one in five people ever requires institutionalised elderly care. Paul Thompson substantiates that the image of the elderly all being ill and dependent is a vast exaggeration: 'A mere one in twenty of those over 65 live in hospital or an institution, and even among those over 75, two-thirds have no physical difficulties with ordinary daily activities.'[27] Even over a decade ago the American National Institute on Aging said about half of the 85+ population were fully independent.[28] A more recent British study of those 90+ found that 'many functioned satisfactorily at a simple level with the help of family members and domiciliary services'.[29] It is therefore illegitimate to hold to some static homogenous model of the elderly, who automatically develop chronic illness at year 65 (or 60 if a woman) – or whatever the official retirement age happens to be.

The circumstance that most old people are not ill today puts into perspective the health cost of coping with the usual projections for population ageing. Even assuming no change in morbidity levels or in real expenditures per person in each age group, Ermisch estimates that in 2026 British health and personal social service expenditure would only need to be 12 per cent higher than in the mid-1980s. As Ermisch concludes: 'This is a trivial increase in expenditure compared with the 14 per cent increase in real expenditure on these services during 1980–88.'[30]

Moreover, this is probably the worst case scenario. It is unrealistic to assume that average rates of health service use by over 64s stay the same over time. This book has already discussed the plasticity of biological ageing, between generations and within generations. Christina Victor explains that although it is true that morbidity increases with age, it is striking that there is no automatic relationship between a particular age and a particular health status. On the contrary health status varies between sexes and between social classes. She continues: 'There are profound age, gender and class differences in health status in later life and these represent the continuation of inequalities observed within the non-retired population.'[31]

Professor Tom Kirkwood, professor of biological gerontology at the University of Manchester, has developed the 'disposable soma theory' to explain the relationship between ageing and health. This says that people age because their bodies have evolved in a way as to put only a limited investment into those cells (somatic, or body cells) that are not involved in reproduction. He believes:

'The ageing process works through the life-long accumulation of damage to the body, rather than being clock-driven. Damage can occur in a number of ways, such as oxidation by free radicals, mutations and accumulation of faulty proteins. The body keeps repairing the damage for as long as possible, but eventually too much damage accumulates.'[32]

The consequence of this understanding is that there is no determinate age for particular symptoms of ageing to appear. There is a positive relationship between age, cell damage and disease. However, the age of the onset of morbidity and how long people live is determined by an interaction between genes and environment. The notion of old age as a time of mass ill health and the stereotype of a biological concept of old age as a time of inevitable and universal biological decline can therefore be rejected.

Today's elderly population is therefore healthier than ever before, reflecting the improved levels of nutrition and other aspects of living standards and better medical support that they have enjoyed throughout their lives compared with earlier generations. Unsurprisingly the same factors that have contributed to the post-war improvement in late age mortality, thereby giving an impetus to demographic fears, are also benefiting old age morbidity levels.

Victor's investigation into health status differences between different generations of older people comes to the same conclusion of an improvement in elderly health. Using cross section surveys from the GHS at different times she is able to show a declining prevalence of chronic health problems at the same age.[33] Some studies even show a decline in the prevalence of dementia.[34]

Bowling and Farquhar recognise that the rise in the absolute number of over 85s means there is likely to be more age-related chronic illness. However, they explain that healthier 'younger' elderly people offset this. They also report evidence from the GHS of 1977 and 1987 which 'indicates that people aged 60+ and 70+ today have fewer severe disabling conditions than people in these age groups a decade ago'.[35] So overall elderly health is getting better.

The demographic fact is that people stay much fitter and healthier to older ages than in the past. This is mainly the product of better experiences in those critical early years of life - a point verified by the British Medical Association. They claim that almost certainly, early life experiences will be reflected in the people's health status in their elderly years.[36]

With great bearing for projections for future health care needs, tomorrow's elderly will be even healthier than today's. The baby boomers, who start to reach their 60s from the second decade of the twenty-first century, are the first generation to have been brought up with the advantage of universal health care. Growing up in the higher living standards of the post-Second World War years meant fitter and healthier young people at the time. Child and youth morbidity (as well as mortality) rates fell substantially in most industrialised countries in the second half compared to the first half of the century. Fitter and healthier young people keep that advantage with them into their older years. As Raymond Jack explains about health prospects for the elderly: 'At the other end of the life span improved ante natal screening will reduce the numbers of people entering old age with a handicap as will better peri- and post-natal care and improved childhood nutrition.'[37]

Hence the prognosis for the health of old people in the twenty-first century - born after 1950 - is not likely to be comparable to that of old people living at the end of the twentieth century - born before 1935.

In addition better living standards, including medical care, for older people today and in the future helps keep them healthier still. Ironically the cost of health care for old people in the future would rise most if the present attempts to cut back on health treatment today - for young and old people - were successful. In these circumstances, others things being equal, the fear of mounting elderly health bills could be realised precisely as a result of the actions taken to cut provisions now – justified by today's false fears. To conclude, the notion that more old people means many more, or even proportionately more, sick, dependent old people simply does not hold.

Nor is it legitimate to claim that there is a rational reason for rationing treatment to over 64s because it is less effective and old people cannot effectively benefit from such care. Michael Rivlin, writing in the *British Medical Journal*, shows there is not a genuine basis to the idea that elderly people gain less from treatment.[38] He explains that in many cases elderly people's response to treatment is as good as young people's. He quotes Brandstetter's review of studies into how elderly people cope in intensive care units: 'The percentage of survivors fully recovered, freely ambulatory, fully alert and productive, was the same in the elderly [over 65] compared with two other groups [under 41 and 41-65].'[39] Jecker and Schneiderman confirm this: 'Evidence is mounting that no significant age difference exists in mortality or morbidity outcomes associated with various interventions, including survival after CPR [cardiopulmonary resuscitation] ... coronary artiography and coronary bypass surgery, liver and kidney transplantation, other surgeries, chemotherapy, and dialysis.'[40]

Does greater longevity increase health care need?
Chapter 2 has already explained that population ageing is not primarily the result of greater life expectancy for the elderly. The factors of falling and low fertility affecting the population structure, and of greater proportions of previous generations reaching old age, are much more important in understanding demographic ageing. Nevertheless, it has also been shown that the life expectancy of older people has begun to rise more rapidly since the 1960s, by over two years in just two decades, the same as the gain during the whole of the rest of the twentieth century. Old people are beginning to live longer old lives. It is widely remarked, for example, that the growth rate of the over 74s is higher than for the over 64s (though this is partly a result of the cohort effect from the survivors of the larger numbers born in the first decades of the twentieth century). The phenomenon of increased longevity is a tribute to social and economic progress in the twentieth century. Such advances will continue, if at a slower rate, into the next century.

Although this development only marginally affects the dominant reasons for ageing in the twenty-first century, it could be much more important for the expected costs of health and social care. Given that so much of health and social services spending goes on the elderly already, it is widely thought that the impact of greater longevity could have a disproportionate, and even overwhelming, consequence for the health budget. This is why the statistic most often presented as evidence of the unaffordable cost of an ageing population burden is the growth of the proportion of very old people in their eighties. Whereas in 1946 at the start of the NHS only one per cent of the population was aged 80 or more, by the 1980s this figure had risen to almost 3 per cent. The usual projections show a doubling by early next century. The relevant question for us is, will this increasing longevity be bought at the expense of more prolonged morbidity and disability?

The current situation is that the average elderly person remains free of prolonged morbidity or disability until the early seventies, after which they have an increasing and accelerating burden of disability until they die at about 75. There are three possible ways this could develop in the future as old people live longer beyond 75 [41]:

(1) The 'nightmare' scenario where the age at which disease and disability strikes remains as at present, but death is postponed. This is the basis for the claims of an 'exponential' growth of health need, and encouraged Kramer famously to articulate his fear of a 'pandemic of mental disorders and associated chronic diseases and disabilities'. [42]

(2) The receding horizon model, where the onset and progress of disease and disability is postponed to precisely the same extent as death itself, so that the number of years of diseased and disabled existence remains unchanged.

(3) The 'compressed morbidity' scenario, where both disability and death are postponed but the former more than the latter, so that the interval between the onset of chronic disease or disability, and death is shortened. This idea was initially postulated by Fries in 1980 [43] and has been widely discussed ever since. It is linked to the idea of the trend to the relatively painless and disability-free death from old age, and the progressive approximation of the health span to the life span.

The evidence of recent trends points somewhere around the second scenario, and is much more likely to be moving towards the third, than receding to the first. We can say with confidence from recent experience that the nightmare 'exponential' growth scenario is unfounded. It is striking that while few specialists accept Fries' theory of compressed morbidity wholeheartedly even some of his critics, such as Emily Grundy, have had to concede that on average old people today are healthier than in the past, putting paid to the first scenario.[44]

What is the evidence for each scenario? We have already described the wider trend to healthier old people. By definition this rules out the first scenario. But there are also indications that the relative health of the elderly is improving faster than life expectancy is improving. Disability-free life expectancy is rising faster than life expectancy. An increase of life expectancy without serious chronic disease or disability at every age would provide some indication of a tendency towards the compression of morbidity.

Bowling and Farquhar explain why it is inaccurate to stereotype the older old as invariably ill: 'There are increasing reports that very elderly people living at home are the healthy survivors of their cohort in that they do not have more of the same major morbidities of younger elderly people or have a poorer perceived health status.'[45] Manton and Soldo make the further observation that the oldest old can exhibit lower morbidity rates than one might expect because by very old age high risk individuals have been removed by mortality selection. For example, cancer rates fall with age because the most susceptible part of the population has already been done for.[46]

The GHS in Britain reveals that although there has been an increase in the proportion of people of all ages reporting a long standing illness (given the overall improvements in levels of morbidity, this suggests a higher proclivity to pronouncing oneself ill), the upward slope is flattest in the oldest. In the last two decades, the percentage of the overall population reporting long standing illness has increased from 21 to 34 per cent, while for the over-75s it has increased from 62 to 69 per cent – proportionately much less.[47] It would appear that there has been a relative improvement in the health of the more elderly compared to the rest of the population.

Kirkwood also reports, 'Evidence suggests that people are reaching 85 in much better shape than previously, which is why the death rate among that age group is still falling… We are living longer because the conditions to which we are exposed today are less severe than they used to be. We are enjoying better nutrition, less exposure to infectious diseases, and less physical stress.'[48] The same social changes mean that people both live longer and stay healthy longer.

For American society, Thomas et al found in the mid-1980s, that 'individuals who reach old age in good health tend to maintain their good health until shortly before death'. They concluded that two conventional assumptions were decidedly misplaced: 'old age and illness are not synonymous' and it is not true that people 'accumulate one disability after another as they age'. Instead they calculated that the average duration of terminal illness was only 4.9 months, giving support to Fries' perspective.[49]

Fries' own studies seem to confirm that the average age of first appearance of chronic disease symptoms is increasing more rapidly than life expectancy. That is, morbidity rates are falling faster than mortality rates. He reports, 'emerging data demonstrate a slowing of increases in life expectancy and a delay in the age of onset of major chronic illnesses', for atherosclerosis (the main cause of death) and lung cancer (the most frequent major malignancy).[50]

Arber and Ginn have also identified this trend: 'In every age group, the proportion of people with a given disability has decreased over time, with a corresponding increase in "expectation of life without disability".'[51] Bebbington, Wells and Freer, and Rogers et al all provide supporting evidence.[52] The later make the interesting observation that the most widely used model to measure the health of the population at any time is bound to give pessimistic results because it excludes recovery from dependency. Yet as medical treatment increasingly serves to bring about recovery, the improvements in active life expectancy are partially obscured.[53]

National long-term care surveys in the US record a decline in the total prevalence of chronically disabled community dwelling and institutionalised old people for all three age strata employed: 65-74, 75-84, and 85+. The proportion of non-disabled persons who became disabled after two and five years was also significantly lower in the later than the earlier time interval. Increases in life expectancy above 65 were therefore associated with declines in the age specific prevalence of chronic disability, further confirmation that things are moving in the direction of Fries' thesis.[54]

In Britain the direction of change is the same. The evidence is most compelling with respect to severe disability. Emily Grundy reports from the GHS that in 1991 some 80 per cent of men and 79 per cent of women aged 85 and over and living in private households were able to bathe themselves, feed themselves, get in and out of bed and get to the toilet without help from another person. In 1980 the equivalent percentages were only 69 per cent and 64 per cent. Although the proportion of this age group in institutions (who are excluded from the GHS) increased during the 1980s, this increase is not sufficient to account for the change. Calculations adjusted to allow for the institutional population show that for the very old life expectancy with a more serious inability to undertake personal care tasks independently decreased between 1980 and 1991.[55] Studies from other European countries suggest similar decreases in the extent of serious disability as longevity increases.[56]

Raymond Jack is among those who believe these improvements are likely to continue. He explains that: 'New medical techniques – such as the 25 000 plus hip replacements per year, and coronary by-pass operations – could reduce the rate of disability among future generations of old people, and improved health promotion and preventative medicine may lead to a "rectangularization" of the morbidity curve such that disability will be postponed until the very end of the life span.'[57] Manton and Soldo agree that it is reasonable to anticipate further progress in controlling the rate of chronic disease progression and therefore a reduction of disease manifest at any age.[58] The Association of the British Pharmaceutical Industry has drawn similar conclusions: 'Recent research confirms that many people who live beyond 65 remain healthy and active until very late in their lives. What seems to be clear is that the period of ill health and heavy dependency is being compressed into the last three to four years before death – whether it occurs at 65+, 75+, 85+ or 90+.'[59]

All in all the evidence seems to be growing that serious illness will be increasingly concentrated into a shorter period towards the end of one's life, a more 'rectangular' morbidity curve. Fries may therefore be correct in his thesis. Certainly the numbers of aged ill will not rise as fast as some predict. Fears of health service and elderly care overload are sure to be inflated when such real improvements in elderly health and abilities are ignored.

Linked to greater longevity one of the supplementary arguments employed by those fearful of the impact of ageing upon the demand for health care is that expensive high technology medical techniques are keeping chronically sick elderly people alive. Technology is thereby said to be perpetuating the burden older people place on the health and care budgets. One of Fries' most ardent critics, E Gruenberg, claims, 'The net effect of successful technological innovations used in disease control has been to raise the prevalence of certain diseases and disabilities by prolonging their average duration...the net contribution of our success has actually been to worsen the people's health.'[60]

The World Bank also spells out the vicious spiral it sees costly medical progress spawning. It attributes rapid population ageing to the consequence of 'medical improvements' which then undermines the integrity of the health service: 'Richer countries have more expensive health facilities that keep people alive longer, increasing the demands on their pension systems. Conversely, an ageing population places increasing strains on the health care system of a country, since health problems and costly medical technologies are concentrated among the old.'[61]

The idea that technological improvements in medicine are to blame for a crisis in health care reveals a perverse logic. Traditionally medicine is seen as having three linked aims: the overcoming of disease, the relief of suffering caused by disease, and the prolongation of life. Under the anti-medical technology argument allowing people to live longer becomes a problem for the health service because it keeps alive more people who by the definition of being alive are susceptible to disease. Keeping people alive means more people to be treated at some point. So stopping people dying 'escalates costs' and squeezes the resources for health care that can be offered. But that begs the question of what type of health care is to be offered if it is not to keep people alive and free from disease or suffering. You could take this form of argument further and claim that preventative medicine is not such a good thing after all because people are prevented from having one health disorder only to develop another.

Leaving this peculiar logic to one side and returning to the facts, there are some strong counter arguments. For a start the costs of medical technology used with old people are exaggerated. The main costs of treating elderly people are not in the use of sophisticated technology but in routine treatment and in caring.[62] Levensky explains: 'Contrary to conventional wisdom, the savings will be small if we eliminate intensive, high technology care for the aged.... Probably no more than 1 or 2 per cent of the [US] national health care expenditure for the elderly is devoted to high-cost medical admissions.'[63]

Even more importantly, medical technology has the opposite effect on health spending that these critics believe. It tends to reduce rather than inflate expenditure. In the labour intensive area which health care represents, new technology usually works to reduce costs. Jack argues that as a result medical developments tend to offset rather than intensify the health cost impact of older populations.[64]

A report in 1996 from the Institute of Public Policy Research also explains why the suggestion that new technologies place an increasing burden on a cash-strapped NHS is misplaced. It says that new technologies may increases costs in some areas but will reduce costs in others, as techniques become commonplace and doctors gain expertise.[65]

Tallis's review of probable medical advances also emphasises their cost reducing benefits. He explains: 'Most of the feasible medical advances seem likely to make a disproportionate impact on disabling conditions – such as arthritis and stroke – rather than life threatening ones, and one might expect their net effect to be to reduce, rather than increase or merely postpone, chronic morbidity and disability.' [66]

The signs are that medical technology tends to reduce the more costly forms of disease, making it an even more cheapening influence on health budgets. The rational conclusion is that there are too few resources going into, and applying high technology medicine, not too much.

The implications of population ageing for health service costs are grossly distorted and inflated in most discussion about the future of public health care. As with the pensions issue it appears that in the health discussion demography is being made to play patsy as the ideologically and politically neutral pretext for containing state expenditure on health.

Recently a few more critical voices have begun to question the conventional assertions. For example, a report from the Institute of Public Policy Research in late 1996 questioned the scale of the financial crisis for the NHS precipitated, supposedly, by ageing (and new technology). It concluded that 'the projected increase in the elderly population and the consequences for the NHS have been exaggerated, as there is little correlation between ageing and increased health care costs'.[67]

With the prevalent state of received wisdom on this issue, many more critical reports like this will be needed before the health care time bomb is effectively dealt a death.

Notes

1. Tallis (1994), p 77. See Callaghan (1990) and Zweibel et al (1993) for discussion about rationing on the basis of age.
2. Toynbee (1996), p 29.
3. Tinker et al (1994).
4. Giarini and Stahel (1989), p 129.
5. Tinker (1992), p 77.
6. McRae (1994), p 287.
7. Johnson and Falkingham (1992), p 133.
8. World Bank (1994), p 2.
9. Toynbee (1996), p 50.
10. Giles and Condor (1988).
11. *The Independent*, 12 June 1995.
12. Zook et al (1980).
13. Rice and Feldman (1983), p 393.
14. World Bank (1994); 'Grey timebomb at the heart of the Western welfare state', *The Guardian*, 27 January 1996, p 14.
15. Jenkins (1995), p 72.
16. Jenkins (1995), p 71.
17. Butler (1983b).
18. McRae (1994), p 39.
19. Sinclair and Williams (1990).
20. Johnson and Falkingham (1992), p 133.
21. Tinker et al (1994), p 13.
22. Tinker et al (1994), p 13.
23. World Bank (1994), p 46.
24. Victor (1991), p 23.
25. Victor (1991), p 24.
26. See Henwood (1992).
27. Thompson (1992), p 27. See also Tinker et al (1994).
28. *Milbank Memorial Fund Quarterly* special issue 'The oldest old' (1985), p 178.
29. O'Connor et al (1989), p 411.
30. Ermisch (1990), p 43.
31. Victor (1991), p 23.
32. Quoted in *The Independent*, 8 September 1998.
33. Victor (1991).
34. Hagnell et al (1983).
35. Bowling and Farquhar (1991), pp 275-6.
36. Barker (1992).
37. Jack (1991), pp 290-1.
38. Rivlin (1995), p 1180.
39. Brandstetter (1992), pp 175-6.
40. Jecker and Schneiderman (1992), p 191.
41. These variations are usefully reviewed in Tallis (1994), pp 80-81.
42. Kramer (1980).
43. Fries (1980).
44. Grundy (1984), pp 663-4.
45. Bowling and Farquhar (1991), p 276, and see Johnson et al (1990)
46. Manton and Soldo (1985), p 233.
47. OPCS (1992).
48. *The Independent*, 8 September 1998.

49. Thomas et al (1986), pp 105-9.
50. Fries (1989), p 209.
51. Arber and Ginn (1990), p 431.
52. Bebbington (1988), Wells and Freer (1989), and Rogers et al (1990).
53. Rogers et al (1990), p 646.
54. Manton et al (1993).
55. Grundy (1996), pp17-18, and Bone et al (1995).
56. Boshuizen and van de Water (1994).
57. Jack (1991), pp 290-91.
58. Manton and Soldo (1985), p 277.
59. Association of British Pharmaceutical Industry (1991), p 4.
60. Gruenberg (1977), p 24.
61. World Bank (1994), pp 3, 43.
62. Rivlin (1995), p 1181.
63. Levensky (1990), pp 1813-16.
64. Jack (1991).
65. *Daily Telegraph*, 4 September 1996.
66. Tallis (1994), p 83.
67. Wordsworth at al (1996), as quoted in the *Daily Telegraph*, 4 September 1996.

7· Can Ageing Stunt Economic Growth?

The last three chapters have established that there is no economic or material basis to the demographic time bomb. They have explained that assuming the sorts of levels of secular economic growth experienced even by the weakest of the industrialised countries over the past couple of decades, there will be no resource shortage for coping with ageing populations.

This leaves one question to address. Could it be that the ageing phenomenon would prevent such adequate growth rates to be achieved in the future? This chapter will show that this is a popular prejudice among some economists and other opinion formers. It is beyond the scope of this book to make predictions about how fast the developed economies will advance in the future. However, this chapter will establish through a review of economic literature that it is spurious to attempt to establish any determinate relationship between the pace of ageing and the pace of growth.

One of the difficulties with countering the thesis that ageing populations represent a constraint on economic growth is that it is so infrequently spelt out. Johnson and Falkingham are representative of conventional thinking in beginning their study *Ageing and Economic Welfare* with the apparently uncontroversial statement that 'The age structure of a country's population ... can have an enormous impact on the performance of the economy and the welfare of individuals.'[1]

However, towards the end of their book and having failed to substantiate this assertion they have to admit: 'Our understanding of the processes of economic growth and of innovation is really too primitive to permit confident long-term predictions to be made.' Nevertheless this honest admission of their inability to prove the economic case does not prevent their repeating their opening assertion: 'Economic analysis shows that population ageing is *not* just a social security issue ... . It is a demographic force that will impinge on all aspects of economic performance – on the way we work and produce, spend and save, invest, inherit and bequeath.'[2]

This approach to the discussion of the economic implications of ageing is typical. The *assumption* that ageing holds back growth is ubiquitous, but it is unusual to find a clear exposition of how this cause-effect relationship works. The rarity of attempts to substantiate the argument is striking.

The OECD, for example, in a recent extended survey of the impact of ageing populations simply asserts, 'potential GDP growth is projected to slow down as a result of ageing'.[3] That is all that is said on the matter of the consequences for growth. No explanation is attempted.

Hamish McRae makes the same unsubstantiated claim:

'An older industrial world will inevitably be a slower-growing one. There is no doubt that economies with a large proportion of old people, and the prospect of a shrinking population, have a lower capacity for growth (and maybe a lower appetite for it) than "young" countries.'[4]

Why 'inevitably'? Why is there 'no doubt'? If there were an absolute shortage of workers this might conceivably represent a hypothesis to be tested. But when there is unemployment, including especially among young people, across the industrialised world labour capacity is clearly no constraint on growth of economic output.

The dubious character of McRae's belief was highlighted even more in an article he wrote on ageing and economics. His main argument was that the relatively slower pace of ageing in Britain compared to other European countries meant that 'demography alone should ensure a better relative performance' by the British economy.

Wishful thinking, many would think. But getting carried away with this theme McRae finishes the piece this way:

'Look at Japan: the fastest growing developed economy of the 1960s, 1970s and 1980s has in the 1990s become the slowest. It is also, incidentally, becoming the "oldest" of the G7 countries. That is surely no coincidence.'[5]

Well, yes, it is a coincidence. And it is also a play on words. The term 'becoming' old disguises the fact that in the 1990s Japan still had one of the youngest population structures of the G7.[6] One could assert, with an equal lack of substance, but a much stronger circumstantial case, that Japan's slow growth in the 1990s was the product of too *young* a population.

So unless McRae thinks that the *anticipation* of a more aged population 10 or 20 years hence is an explanation for sluggish growth *now*, this example is certainly no evidence for the thesis. And if this were his argument, it would undermine his earlier case about Britain's bright prospects since, as we have noted, ageing is anticipated to accelerate again in Britain in 20 or 30 years' time.

Paul Kennedy puts a more chronologically coherent version of the relationship between Japanese demography and economic growth. He foresees that Japan's shift as the industrialised country with the lowest to the highest elderly dependency ratio between now and 2025 will tend to weaken 'long-term economic growth' in the next century.[7] However, he too provides no explanation for this prediction.

Reviewing much of the current discussion of the growth/ageing relationship, it is as if the *more* that people assert that ageing is bad for growth the *less* anyone feels compelled to substantiate or even spell out the inter-linking reasons. Many writers present it just as self-evident that demographic movements will affect the economy. Therefore, it is worth stating that this intuitive view does not even stand the test of history. Empirically, there is no correlation between the pace of economic growth in the short or long term and ageing. (See charts 22 and 23.) A reasonably steady rate of ageing coexists with a variety of economic experiences: booms, recessions and depressions. Also the size of economic wealth has over the long term expanded much faster than the pace of ageing – at about double the rate. Historically, both the fluctuations of the business cycle and long-term growth rates seem unconnected to the secular trend in ageing.

Some writers do try to advance a more reasoned case of ageing's negative influence on growth employing familiar economic theory. For example, some argue that too many old people as 'unproductive consumers' will be bad for the economy. Keyfitz describes the 'common sense, classical theory' that the burden of consumers who do not produce wealth, such as the elderly, will tend to hold back development (though, he adds, this is a difficult thing to show statistically).[8]

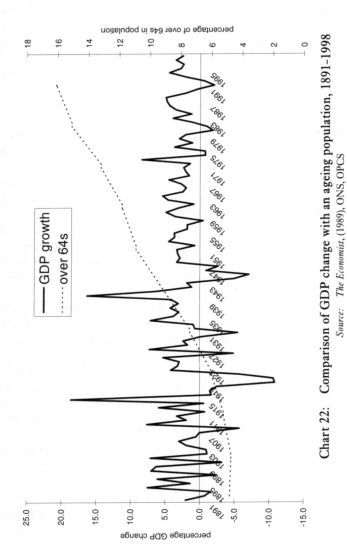

Chart 22:   Comparison of GDP change with an ageing population, 1891–1998
Source: The Economist, (1989), ONS, OPCS

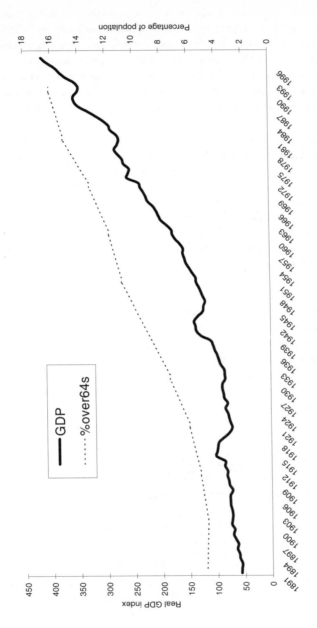

Chart 23: Growing level of economic wealth as the population ages, 1891–1998

Source: The Economist, ONS, OPCS

Paul Kennedy also views the connection between ageing and economic growth from the perspective of proportions of consumers and savers. This takes us back to the old demographic favourite: dependency ratios. Kennedy argues that a rise in the elderly dependency ratio will tend to increase consumption at the expense of investment. In his view 15-64s create wealth and the rest consume it. Too much consumption by an ageing economy 'may be a drag upon overall production increases.'[9]

Others argue that ageing's negative impact on growth is mediated through its influence in boosting state spending. Ageing is presented as the cause of higher state spending which is then projected as the cause of economic slowdown and crisis. The World Bank, for example, claims that as old age financial security systems mature 'they may actually hinder growth – through higher wage taxes, which cause evasion and push labor into the less efficient informal sector; through rising fiscal deficits, which fuel inflation; by squeezing out growth-promoting public spending, such as education or health services for the young; or through a combination of all three'.[10]

Elsewhere the same World Bank study tries to link the state spending argument to the problem of inadequate savings: social security arrangements for the elderly in the advanced industrialised countries 'may ... have discouraged work, saving, and productive capital formation – thus contributing to economic stagnation'.[11]

Although the bank repeats this conjecture at least a further five times in its study it is forced ultimately to admit that there is no empirical evidence for it:

'Numerous empirical investigations (most of them based on US data) have been unable to prove conclusively that saving did, indeed, drop once pay-as-you-go programs were established ... . Analyses of savings rates in other countries yield similar conflicting results. Studies of programs in Canada, France, the Federal Republic of Germany, Japan, Sweden, and the United Kingdom found no significant impact, except for a slightly positive impact in Sweden, where the pension program is heavily funded.'[12]

This brings to mind the somewhat cynical assessment from the OECD in 1988, 'As other explanations for moderate growth and persistent labour market problems seem to fail, social security arrangements have apparently become one of the explanations of last resort.'[13]

To find a more substantial case for the assumed inverse relationship between growth and ageing it is necessary to examine earlier economic discussions. One of the first proponents of the thesis of the negative economic impact of ageing was no minor figure. He was the man usually regarded as the greatest economist of the twentieth century, John Maynard Keynes. Ironically, his argument was based on the under-consumption of ageing populations, rather than today's more fashionable theory of over-consumption.

Keynes believed that demographic ageing went with the protracted character of the 1930s depression. His argument focused more on the size, than the age of the population, but the falling birth rate with which he was concerned inevitably meant an ageing population too.

He argued that falling-fertility, and ageing, populations tend to harm the economy. A declining population would lead to a lower level of effective demand, lower aggregate savings, less capital accumulation and ultimately a higher level of unemployment. As well as the direct effect on demand, Keynes assumed that the impact on confidence would be a further negative factor.[14]

Taking off from Keynes' arguments from the 1930s, Julian Simons developed this thesis for post-war conditions. He argues that low fertility is bad for the economy via its impact on the level of demand. Employing the fashionable under-consumptionist assumptions of the post-war Keynesian orthodoxy he explains that lower birth rates and fewer younger people weakens demand. This leads to a fall in business confidence, lower investment and hence lower national income.

This argument fell out of vogue during the late 1960s discussion about the return to low fertility levels after the baby boom. In conditions of economic boom it would have seemed bizarre to hold to the view that falling birth rates were bad for the economy. Adapting to the benevolent economic circumstances of the time the argument switched. The convention became the reverse of the 1930s. Declining fertility was now seen as positive for business and the economy.

Joseph Spengler, for example, argued that the zero population growth resulting from falling fertility was on balance good for economic welfare. He disputed Keynes' argument about the negative impact of an ageing population upon demand, instead stressing the positive way slowing population growth boosts savings.[15]

This was consistent with the Coale-Hoover thesis that was influential in population studies in the 1950s and 1960s. Addressing what was regarded as the opposite problem of too fast population growth in developing countries Coale and Hoover argued that rapid population growth in conditions of high fertility reduced saving and investment and, therefore, the pace of economic growth. By implication – though it was not their specific area of interest – low fertility and ageing should be by this reasoning be positive for the economy.

To similar conclusion, but employing different economics, the US Commission on Population argued in its 1972 report that low fertility was good for an economy by increasing income growth and demand levels.[16]

After 1973 the 'golden age' of the post-war boom ended and the industrialised economies shifted into the much slower tempo of growth which has been the case ever since. In these circumstances the sanguine view of falling fertility began to fall away. However, since the economic orthodoxy was changing too, this coloured the form of the economic discussion about demography.

When the negative economic assessment about ageing later re-emerged most specialists tended to incorporate the pro-free market critique of the Keynesian emphasis on demand deficiency that has flourished since the 1970s. They have favoured a neo-classical framework, concentrating on the impact of demography on the *supply* of savings rather than on *demand* factors. Economists recently have tended to stress the detrimental economic effect upon investment and long-term growth that results from the impact ageing was assumed to have on relative levels of savings and consumption.

This was a version of Alvin Hansen's secular stagnation thesis from the 1930s, which had incorporated demographic factors. He had argued that slow population growth was a central cause of the investment shortfall that underlay the 1930s depression.[17] Since the mid-1970s the basic position has therefore changed to argue that an older population consumes more than a younger population. This is almost the reverse of Keynes's assumption that had stressed the deficiency of consumption.

According to neo-classical theory, more consumption means less savings, and less savings is assumed to mean lower investment. So using a different economic model an ageing population, once again, results in lower national income.

It is intriguing how today most economists come to the same conclusion as Keynes that ageing is bad economically while using apparently opposite reasoning to substantiate their case, given their different economic theories. It is as if the assumption that ageing is bad economically assumes precedence over any particular school of economics.

The inconsistency in economic thinking does not end here. There can also be very different views on the implications of ageing for savings and consumption levels. Some say it is detrimental to savings, others say it is positive. Again the conclusion is usually the same that ageing is bad.

The UN, for example, in its 1990 world survey, asserts that in the 1980s 'demographic changes in the industrial countries served to lower savings rates', helping to keep interest rates high, thereby stunting investment and economic growth.[18]

In similar vein many specialists use the 'life cycle model' to substantiate their negative view of ageing. This model assumes that one saves in one's working years, especially after the children leave home, and one dissaves in retirement. With more old people acting as consumers rather than savers the claim is that population ageing means there is not sufficient saving going on.

Jackson provides a useful summary of the implications of the theory. From the life cycle perspective ageing is harmful, economically, because the larger proportion of inactive elderly can raise the demand for goods and services relative to productive potential. This can intensify the problem of allocating scarce resources and thereby weakens economic growth.[19]

On the other hand McRae, while equally pessimistic about the economic impact of ageing, believes that older countries tend to be savings–dominated societies in that they rely more on savings for safeguarding their standard of living.[20] He argues that a society that is aware it is ageing will tend to put more resources aside in saving for the future. The American economist Thomas Gale Moore agrees that an older population tends to mean a higher savings rate.[21] Worries about their own later lives makes the middle aged cautious spenders and bigger savers, more concerned to top up pensions and other insurance for their old age than spend in the present.

Some economists emphasise the growth in the number of over-45s - 'the wrinklies' - as positive for consumption levels because they no longer have children to save for. Ermisch on the other hand regards the 45 to 64s as the biggest savers. He notes that this group fell from 32 per cent to 27 per cent from 1970 to 1986 (due to the large baby boom generation), but is likely to rise again to about 34 per cent by 2015 (as the boomers mature).[22]

Although there is no consensus on ageing's implications for the national savings level, this does not prevent a much wider consensus that ageing is detrimental. What is striking from this survey is that the real economic conditions experienced seem to be more influential than the specific economic theory of the day in determining thinking about the economic effects of demographic changes. When the economic dynamic is weak there will always be some that blame demography. Depending on the dominant economic discourse though they will use different arguments to make the same case.

Given these conflicting theories it should not be a surprise that the economic argument about the impact of ageing has been difficult for anyone to substantiate convincingly. This is why a tendency runs through the literature that is sceptical of drawing definite and firm conclusions about the relationship between demographic change and economic growth.

This inconsistency in argument has led some to a more ambivalent stance on the economic impact of demography. Most tend to employ the traditional device of the two-handed economist: 'On the one hand demography has this effect, on the other hand it has the opposite one too.' The conclusion is often that no firm conclusion can be drawn.

Kennedy, for example, admits that the evidence on the savings issue is ambiguous: 'An ageing population may ... save more, and thus increase aggregate national savings – although the evidence here is not conclusive, since old people might also draw down their personal savings over time.'[23]

Others have adopted the same ambivalent approach. For example, evidence to the 1949 Royal Commission on Population did not come down decisively either way on the savings issue. On the one hand, it was argued that lower fertility tended to raise savings among family households, due to the lower consumption needs of smaller families, while on the other hand the ageing population tended to lower savings. The overall impact on savings was deemed to be uncertain.[24]

Geoffrey McNicoll's submission to a Hoover Institution seminar at Stanford University in 1985 also dismissed the one-sided negative discourse about falling fertility, and therefore, population ageing. Interestingly, though, he tended to the view that too much was being made of the impact of low fertility on the economy in general. He concluded that the net effect of changing fertility on economic activity was minimal.

He argued that 'the effects of low fertility on labour supply, technological change, and investment and consumption appear relatively slight'.[25] Reviewing the research literature he concluded that, excluding the distributional effects, 'low fertility ... presents no great difficulty for a modern economy. Its effects are likely to be small compared with business cycle fluctuations in economic performance'.[26]

Thomas Gale Moore shared McNicoll's ambivalence on the economic impact of different population structures. Against the mainstream view that ageing is bad economically he cautiously argued that ageing could be slightly positive for economic growth, but concluded that the effects either way were limited.

At the Stanford University seminar on falling fertility he commented: 'Overall, an older population probably means a slightly higher growth rate and gross national product ... . On balance, declining population size probably reduces growth and gross national product. Therefore, given the offsetting effects of age distribution and size of the population, it is to be expected that below-replacement fertility would have a negligible effect on growth.'[27]

Mason concluded his survey of the arguments to state that the relationships between demographic change, savings levels and economic growth are much less determinate than many believe. He confirmed that empirical evidence from a number of countries confirmed that 'reduced fertility and slower population growth have contributed to higher rates of savings'.[28] However, he qualified that one cannot draw any accurate conclusions from this as 'the processes involved are complex and because circumstances vary widely from country to country'.[29]

Mason summarised the relevant work of James Tobin (1967) and Nathaniel Leff (1969) in developing the life cycle model:

'At the household level, declining fertility and, hence, a reduced "burden" of childbearing lead to reduced consumption and higher saving. At the same time, the population ageing that accompanies reduced fertility increases the relative number of older households, which have lower rates of saving. The first effect, termed the dependency effect, implies that rapid population growth discourages saving. The second effect, the rate of growth effect, implies that rapid population growth encourages saving. Depending on which effect dominates, then, aggregate saving can be either positively or negatively related to the population growth effect.'[30]

Mason also claims that most empirical studies confirm this 'theoretically' variable effect of different rates of fertility and ageing. However, one could conclude that instead of the 'theory' allowing variable results, the theory is simply deficient.

When Jackson reviewed the literature he was even more sceptical of the possible economic impact of ageing. He concluded with the intellectual critique that mainstream economics is too narrow and restrictive to substantiate the belief that population ageing has adverse economic consequences however common that belief is.[31]

In similar vein Eric Midwinter, the director of the Centre for Policy on Ageing, reviewed the implications of the ageing world at the start of the 1990s. Surveying the evidence he refused to draw any firm conclusions about causality: 'The cause-and-effect relationship of socio-economic activity and demographic expansion is complex and controversial ... . (It) must be said that the relation between demographics and economics is a confused and confusing one.'[32]

So even among economists who share worries about ageing there is no consensus on the precise way in which the economy is affected. This inability to sustain a coherent argument helps account for Geoffrey McNicoll's observation in 1985 - before the demographic panic really became pervasive - that with respect to declining population 'concern (about the impact on demand and investment) is almost totally absent in more recent writings on economic consequences'.[33] With so much conflicting opinion it was an area many economists steered clear of until the heightened profile on ageing forced more of them to comment.

Given this ambiguity about the economic impact of ageing, it is legitimate to go further than just state that the economic effects of ageing may be variable. There is no determinate relationship between demography in general, and in particular population ageing, and economic activity.

Both the Keynesian and neo-classical arguments lack weight because they tend to overstate the significance of demand or supply factors over the prevailing conditions existing in production. It is well recognised that in an open economy demand factors might have little impact on domestic production. If consumer demand is weak a strong productive economy can grow through exports instead. Alternatively strong domestic demand may lead to increasing imports if they are more competitive than those from ailing domestic producers.

Meanwhile, the availability or otherwise of saved funds for investment is not the main determinate of actual levels of investment. Available funds can be used elsewhere than in financing increases and improvements in productive capacity. They can be invested abroad or be used for buying financial assets and for speculation. Circumstances in the area of production are logically prior to demand or supply conditions in determining the pace of economic growth.

What about any more direct effect ageing might have on the workforce and the labour process? Some argue that ageing impairs productivity growth. A higher proportion of older workers in the workforce is said to be detrimental because on average older workers are less efficient and productive. In fact, economists have been as divided on this issue as on the savings/ageing relationship.

Thompson gives the sort of assessment traditionally associated with those two-handed economists: 'On the one hand a labour force might gain in productivity by being an older and more experienced one; on the other hand this advantage might be eroded by less flexibility, or reduced physical or mental capacity, with a dampening effect on the growth in average productivity.'[34] It is striking how one or other of these views tends to dominate in different economic and labour market circumstances.

Up to the early 1970s Serow and Espenshade reported that most research tended to show that there was little relationship between ageing and productivity.[35] Although it is possible to show that successful companies had younger workforces Alan Sweezy and Aaron Owens explained that this was the consequence, not the cause, of their higher productivity levels, since competitive companies grow and are recruiting workers regularly.[36]

The early studies of age and working ability conducted during the post-war boom, including Alan Welford's classic study showing age's deleterious impact via the nervous system, generally concluded that the effect of age on productivity prior to age 60 is insignificant. Chronological age was found to be a poor predictor of work performance, with job experience and the impact of longer training seen to offset any physiological decline.[37]

The US Department of Labor reported in 1965 that the available medical and psychological evidence revealed no support for the broad age lines that had been drawn on the basis of claimed physical requirements.[38] Spengler argued that the individual worker's ability usually far exceeded the demands of the job so that any negative effects from ageing on performance are not usually relevant.

In 1981 Alan Walker summarised the pre-existing body of research: 'There is no evidence ... of a decline over time in the productive capacity of older workers at any given age.' He concluded that 'the emergence and forceful application of age-barrier retirement must be explained primarily in terms of social and economic factors'.[39]

However, from the 1970s more economists adopted a negative view of ageing's impact upon the productivity of the workforce. This change in sentiment tended to coincide with the end of the post-war era of full employment following on from the 1973 world recession. Labour force participation among older workers began to fall, justified by the prevalence of negative attitudes concerning the role of older workers. Older workers were now assumed to be less valuable and less productive.

There was some precedence for this view. Kuznets, for example, who challenged the negative views about population growth in the Third World in the 1960s, had argued that younger workers had advantages over older ones. Older workers, he claimed, were a bit of a drag on economic dynamism because they tended to be less mobile, since they would be more committed to family, housing and established patterns.[40]

In the early 1970s Leibenstein was one of the first to worry openly that older workers may be less productive. Their greater experience was seen as insufficient to offset their lack of mobility and declining physical strength.[41]

James Schulz, writing in 1974, found the revival of compulsory retirement was justified by this assumption and the belief that older workers were less productive and more inflexible because of work rules, seniority and pay scales.[42] In Germany earlier retirement was justified because it was believed that older workers tended to become ill more frequently while their qualifications could easily become obsolete as a result of technical progress. And owing to the shortness of their potential further working life it was argued that it would be a waste of resources to retrain them.[43]

The UN in the mid-1980s identified greater inflexibility as one problem arising from an ageing of the workforce:

'An older labour force may exhibit less flexibility and obsolescence of skills. Rising old-age dependency burdens may cause new structural problems, such as increased regional immobility of an ageing labour force. Company pension plans, for instance, are hard to transfer from one employer to another; older workers are therefore averse to changing jobs and thus the job market becomes less flexible.'[44]

John Ermisch, too, assumes that the shift to an older workforce in the next century will itself reduce the pace of productivity growth. He speculates that an ageing workforce means less investment, less innovative thinking and a preponderance of older workers handicapped by obsolescent skills. He summarises that 'the productivity of the labour force could grow more slowly with fewer new entrants'.[45]

By the second half of the 1980s, however, a more positive view of older workers regained ground in some quarters. It is surely no coincidence that this took place at a time when the public pensions costs of early retirement inspired an official turn against this trend.[46] The World Bank spelt out this reasoning, 'Raising the retirement age – regularly, as longevity increases – is probably the single most important reform to improve the financial prospects of the public pension plan. It will also raise the supply of experienced labor in the economy.'[47]

At the 1985 Stanford University seminar Thomas Gale Moore argued the benefits of older workers over younger: 'An older workforce will bring with it more expertise through on-the-job training and will be a more stable workforce with less job turnover. This implies a higher level of productivity.'[48]

Heller et al in their 1986 report to the IMF were sympathetic with this view, though rather more equivocal. They recognised that there existed no clear view of the effect of ageing on productivity but noted there was some empirical evidence 'that suggests that productivity increases with ageing in the labour force'.[49]

In 1987 the official British publication, *Population Trends*, also still retained an equivocal position on the pros and cons of older workers: 'On the one hand a labour force might gain in productivity by being an older and more experienced one; on the other hand this advantage might be eroded by less flexibility, or reduced physical or mental capacity, with a dampening effect on the growth in average productivity.'[50]

However, by the 1990s the UK's Department of Employment was encouraging British business to employ more older workers, emphasising their greater skills and experience.[51] It argued that:

'Valuable skills and experience of older workers may be lost if they face barriers to work or are made unemployed ... . Older workers are as adaptable and trainable as younger workers, and tend to be more committed.'[52]

Supporting this view, in 1996 the Employers Forum on Age was launched, involving a number of leading companies including Cadbury, British Airways and Midland Bank, co-ordinated by Age Concern. The purpose was to promote the business value of attracting and retaining experienced staff regardless of age. The Forum's chair Howard Davies, former Deputy Governor of the Bank of England, former head of the CBI, noted: 'In recent years, many employers, under pressure to cut their workforces, have operated a simple policy of removing the over-fifties, taking the costs on the pension fund.' Employers, he says, are now beginning to realise the true cost of releasing mature staff - not only in terms of redundancy and early retirement payments, but also the loss of experience, reliability and empathy with customers.

From all these conflicting arguments it can be concluded that no case has been proven that a higher proportion of older workers slows down productivity and output growth.

Johnson came to the same conclusion in his review of studies into the relationship between ageing and productivity: 'Overall, therefore, we have no real idea whether an ageing of the working population will have a positive or negative effect on labour productivity and aggregate output.'[53] A review in 1993 from the medical journal *The Lancet* of medical investigations into the relationship came to a similar conclusion:

> 'In modern industry, people are seldom called upon to sustain work near their maximum capacity and many age-related changes will therefore have little effect on work performance.... The evidence suggests that the accepted conventions about ageing (as negative for productivity) are pessimistic and that older workers offer many advantages to industrial employers through their experience, attitudes and commitment.' [54]

To finish the arguments about ageing's impact upon economic growth, this chapter will spend little time on the more traditional belief about ageing and the labour market. This is that a relative excess of older people and a relative dearth of younger workers will create economic difficulties because of creating a labour shortage. Suffice to say that it would be difficult to make a convincing case that we face an impending labour shortage when just about every international gathering emphasises the problem of high unemployment and the shortage of jobs in most industrialised economies.

However, here is an apocryphal tale of an earlier demographic time bomb that anticipated such a labour shortage. In the mid-1980s the British prime minister Margaret Thatcher argued that as a result of the falling birth rate there would be a shortage of young workers and students by 1995.

In fact, labour participation rates over this period fell. Instead of there being the forecast under-supply of young people there were not enough jobs for young workers to go around. From 1984 to 1995 activity rates for 16–19 year olds fell from 71.5 per cent to 60.2 per cent, and from 77.7 per cent to 75.7 per cent for 20–24 year olds.[55]

Labour market demand was so weak that not only were there fewer workers but the government was encouraging more young people into higher education. This served the beneficial political effect for the government of keeping youth unemployment levels down. The proportion of school leavers in higher education has risen from one in eight in 1984 to about one in three at the end of the 1990s. Given how wrong Thatcher's prediction turned out, it is perhaps not surprising that it is difficult today to find many who advance the idea that ageing will create debilitating labour shortages.

The official labour force projections carried out until 2006 indicate that slack labour market conditions are not expected to improve. Incorporating the OPCS population projections they assume that labour market pressures will remain so slack that the economic activity rate for men aged 16 to 64 will continue its secular fall since the early 1970s, by another 2.7 per cent between 1993 and 2006.[56] If ageing were expected to cause some shortfall in available workers one would expect male economic activity rates to be rising not falling.

The UN has also rejected any labour shortage case about the dangers of ageing. As noted earlier the UN has generally shared the negative view of ageing. However, in the mid-1980s it pragmatically welcomed the baby bust, the very phenomenon that has contributed significantly to the contemporary ageing trend. The reason for the UN in effect welcoming a boost to population ageing was that it hoped the consequent decline in the number of young workers could help to reduce levels of unemployment.[57] In times of mass, and seemingly permanent unemployment, the problem for the UN and others seems to be one of too many workers, not too few. Ageing's supposed negative effect on the economy via the creation of labour shortages therefore seems rather too fanciful to be argued seriously in today's economic circumstances of steady, high unemployment.

This review of the economic case against ageing leads to the charitable conclusion that we can, at a minimum, endorse the views the economist William Reddaway expressed at the end of the 1930s: 'The economic importance of population changes is often grossly exaggerated.'[58]

Notes

1.   Johnson and Falkingham (1992), p 1.
2.   Johnson and Falkingham (1992), p 176.
3.   OECD (1995), p 33.
4.   McRae (1995), p102.
5.   *Independent on Sunday*, 23 July 1995.
6.   See World Bank (1994), p 343.
7.   Kennedy (1993), p 154.
8.   Keyfitz (1975), p 280.
9.   Kennedy (1993), p 38.
10. World Bank (1994), pp xiii–xiv.
11. World Bank (1994), pp 4, 13, 92, 125–6, 158, 307.
12. World Bank (1994), p 307.
13. OECD (1988b), p 43.
14. Keynes (1937).
15. Spengler (1971).
16. Quoted in McNicoll (1987), p 223.
17. Ridker (1978), p 103.
18. UN (1990).
19. See Jackson (1991), pp 59–68.
20. McRae (1994), p 111.
21. Moore (1987), p 244.
22. Ermisch (1990), p 50.
23. Kennedy (1993), p 38.
24. Royal Commission (1950b), p 43.
25. McNicoll (1987), p 217.
26. McNicoll (1987), p 224.
27. Moore (1987), p 244.
28. Mason (1988), p 137.
29. Mason (1988), p 114.
30. Mason (1988), p 123.
31. Jackson (1991), pp 59–68.
32. Midwinter (1990), pp 222–3.
33. McNicoll (1987), p 223.
34. Thompson (1987), p 20.
35. Serow and Espenshade (1978), p 29.
36. See Sweezy and Owens, quoted in Serow and Espenshade (1978), p 29.
37. Clark, Kreps and Spengler (1978), p 927.
38. US Department of Labor (1965), p 9.

39. Walker (1981), p 89.
40. See Kuznets (1965), chapter 'Population growth and aggregate output'.
41. Serow and Espenshade (1978).
42. Schulz (1974).
43. Kohli, Rosenow and Wolf (1983), p 40.
44. UN (1987), p 143.
45. Ermisch (1990), p 33.
46. OECD (1988b), p 58.
47. World Bank (1994), p 147.
48. Moore (1987), p 244.
49. Heller et al (1986), p 10.
50. Thompson (1987), p 20.
51. Department of Employment (1993), p 41.
52. Department of Employment (1995b), p 40.
53. Johnson (1996), p 12.
54. *The Lancet*, No 8837, 9 January 1993, p 88.
55. Employment Department (1994), pp 120-21.
56. Employment Department (1994), p 121.
57. UN (1987), p 142.
58. Reddaway (1939), p 233.

8· Conclusion

It is indisputable that all advanced industrialised societies are ageing. This book, though, has challenged the way this social fact has become a kind of mantra for opponents of the welfare state and for a collection of alarmists. These are people who worry about the demographic impact on economic growth, and about how society will pay for pensions, health treatment and long-term care for the elderly.

This work has explained that population ageing is not natural, nor inexorable nor unalterable. Even the inevitability of ageing, that appears to make it an appropriate concern in our pessimistic, fatalist, fin-de-siècle times, is not well founded.

It has shown that demographic ageing has no determinate relationship to national economic activity. Moreover, modest levels of future economic growth will be more than sufficient to create the wealth required to sustain the costs brought on by greater numbers of elderly dependents. This is true however positive one is about elderly mortality trends and negative about the morbidity ones. The changes being made to public welfare operations around the world, and especially to pension systems, are not necessitated by the population projections.

There is no demographic time bomb. The anxiety about ageing that has become almost endemic in the 1990s is misplaced. It is certainly exaggerated. Sometimes commentators with particular obsessions or vested interests have manipulated it.

This book has argued that more is at issue than a mistaken concern. Demographic ageing has not just become the fashionable prism for discussing and interpreting a vast range of society's difficulties. Though the ageing trend itself is not problematic, the obsession with it is. The preoccupation contributes to creating genuine dangers.

It distracts attention from the real roots of modern societies' problems. This is bad enough in a world where the pursuit of rational inquiry and the search for solutions to the big problems of poverty, social inequality and oppression is increasingly regarded as futile.

Moreover, the promotion of a scapegoat such as ageing, a phenomenon that appears natural and unalterable, can deepen this mood of fatalism. The repercussions of an unchallenged ageing panic will be to lower people's aspirations of what is possible and of the sort of world we should expect for the future, for our generation, our children's and those that come after.

In particular, there are worrying implications of demographic alarmism for a society where trust already seems in short supply. Chapter 4 illustrated the lack of evidence that inter-generational trust has been eroded by the impact of a changing population structure. Opinion surveys today would probably be less clear cut in their interpretation. This is not because of the real economic and financial implications of ageing but because of the perception of mounting difficulties.

In an era which is already marked by fear of the future, the cumulative effect of using demographic ageing to issue warnings about the time ahead can become a self fulfilling prophecy. This especially applies to its impact upon how individuals view one another. Playing upon the supposed dangers from ageing can erode inter-generational trust.

The ageing discussion has made such an impact in the 1990s because its fears correspond to the individuated way we approach life and its pressures. People worry about what they can do about the future, not as part of a possible collective solution but as relatively isolated individuals and families. Concerns about the consequences of personal ageing - how people will cope when they have no salaries coming in after retirement, who will look after them then - makes society susceptible to the demographic time bomb scenario.

Real developments have influenced this mentality. The erosion of old solidarities and communities foster the individuated reaction to difficulties. Changes in the labour market may mean many decades of post-work life without a salary to live on. Changes to the family structure accentuate concerns about being cared for by those closest to us.

There already is a greater consciousness of age groups, symptomatic of the wider fragmentation of society. This generational consciousness is not a result of the scale of resource transfer, as the demographic alarmists predict, but it exists nevertheless for other reasons. These factors may even represent the opposite of what the alarmists have forecast. For example, far from them being more dependent on their children for care, most old people are now more independent than ever. More elderly people tend to live alone, a trend that has been more pronounced since the 1950s. Surveys show that this tends to be by choice.[1]

Generational relations have been changing recently. This is not entirely novel. But in the past, people had a greater resilience and aptitude to renegotiate the terms of these relationships to make them work reasonably effectively.

Today, however, these relations are themselves deemed to be the problem. The ageing discussion promotes the idea that these problematic inter-relationships are bound to exist, and will worsen. Inexorable demographic trends are believed to make them insoluble. Precisely as a consequence of a widespread attachment to this sort of outlook, inter-generational tensions can be aggravated. Alarmism about ageing can reinforce the fragmentation of society and aggravate individuated responses. It can make people less capable of grappling with and resolving genuine social problems

The 'demographic time bomb' is a warning. It is a warning not of population trends to come, but of the danger of naturalising social problems and playing upon individual fears and uncertainties. It can reinforce divisions and make society less trustful of one another.

Note

1.   Johnson and Falkingham (1992), p 36.

Bibliography

S Arber and J Ginn, 'The meaning of informal care: gender and the contribution of elderly people', *Ageing and Society*, vol 10, 1990.

Association of British Insurers, *Pensions – a long-term strategy*, London, June 1997.

Association of the British Pharmaceutical Industry, *Agenda for Health: the Challenges of Ageing*, London, 1991.

R Bacon and W Eltis, *Britain's Economic Problem: Too Few Producers*, London: Macmillan, 1976.

J Baldock and A Evers, 'Innovations and care of the elderly: the cutting-edge of change for social welfare systems. Examples from Sweden, the Netherlands and the United Kingdom', *Ageing and Society*, vol 12, 1992.

S Baldwin, G Parker and R Walker, 'The financial resources of the elderly or paying your way in old age', *Social Security and Community Care*, Aldershot: Avebury, 1988.

DJP Barker (ed), *Fetal and Infant Origins of Adult Disease*, London: British Medical Association, 1992.

A Barrientos, 'Ageing and personal pensions in Chile', in Lloyd-Sherlock and Johnson (1996).

A Bebbington, 'The expectation of life without disability in England and Wales', *Social Science and Medicine*, vol 27, no 4, 1988.

B Benjamin and J Pollard, *The Analysis of Mortality and other Actuarial Statistics*, London: Heinemann, 1980.

W Beveridge, *Social Insurance and Allied Services*, Cmnd 6404, London: HMSO, 1942.

R Binstock, 'The oldest old: a fresh perspective or compassionate ageism revisited?', *Milbank Memorial Fund Quarterly / Health and Society*, 63(2), 1985.

A Blaikie, 'The emerging political power of the elderly in Britain 1908–1948', *Ageing and Society*, vol 10, 1990.

F Block, R Cloward, B Ehrenreich and F Piven, *The Mean Season: the Attack on the Welfare State*, 1987.

P Blyton, 'Partial pension scheme insights from the Swedish partial pensions scheme', *Ageing and Society*, vol 4, 1984.

MR Bone, AC Bebbington, C Jagger, K Morgan and G Nicolaas, *Health Expectancy and Its Uses*, London: HMSO, 1995.

N Bosanquet, *A Future for Old Age*, London: Temple-Smith/New Society, 1978.

E Boserup, 'Comment', in Davis (1987).

HC Boshuizen and WPA van de Water, *An International Comparison of Health Expectancies*, Leiden: TNO Health Research, 1994.

P Bourdelais, *Le Nouvel Age de la Viellesse: Histoire du Viellissement de la Population*, Paris: Odile Jacob, 1993.

A Bowling and M Farquhar, 'Psychiatric morbidity and service use among elderly people', *Ageing and Society*, vol 11, 1991.

RD Brandstetter, 'Intensive care for the elderly: should the gates remain open?' *New York State Journal of Medicine*, no 92, 1992.

C F Brockington, *A Short History of Public Health*, London: Churchill, 1956.

R Butler, 'An overview of research on aging and the status of gerontology today', *Milbank Memorial Fund Quarterly*, vol 61, no 3, summer 1983a.

R Butler, 'The relation of extended life to extended employment since the passage of Social Security in 1935', *Milbank Memorial Fund Quarterly*, vol 61, no 3, Summer 1983b.

K Button and D Swann (eds), *The Age of Regulatory Reform*, Oxford: Clarendon Press, 1989.

D Callaghan, 'Rationing medical progress: the way to affordable health care', *New England Journal of Medicine*, no 322, 1990.

J Callaghan, *Time and Chance*, London: Collins, 1987.

M Carter and W Shipman, *Promises to Keep: Saving Social Security's Dream*, Washington: Regnery Publishing, 1996.

V Carver and P Liddiard (eds), *An ageing population*, Open University Press, 1978.

Central Health Services Council, *Collaboration in Community Care - a discussion document*, London: HMSO, 1978.

R Clark, 'Increasing income transfers to the elderly implied by ZPG', *Review of Social Economy*, no 35, April 1977.

R Clark, 'Policy implications and future research needs', in Espenshade and Serow (1978).

R Clark, J Kreps, and J Spengler, 'Economics of aging: a survey', *The Journal of Economic Literature*, September 1978.

R Clark and J Spangler, *The Economics of Individual and Population Ageing*, Cambridge: Cambridge University Press, 1980.

A Coale and P Demeny, *Regional life tables and stable populations*, Princeton: University Press, 1966.

A Coale and E Hoover, *Population Growth and Economic Development in Low-income Countries*, Princeton: University Press, 1958.

J Cooper, 'The divergence between period and cohort measures of fertility', *Population Trends*, no 63, 1991.

Council of Europe, *The projection of the very old*, Strasbourg: Council of Europe, 1984.

F Cribier, 'Changing retirement patterns: the experience of a cohort of Parisian salaried workers', *Ageing and Society*, vol 1, 1981.

S O Daatland, 'Ideals lost? Current trends in Scandinavian welfare policies in ageing', *Journal of European Social Policy*, vol 2, no1, 1992.

S David and C Meyer, *Blur*, London: Capstone, 1998.

J Davidson and W Rees-Mogg, *The Great Reckoning*, London: Sidgwick and Jackson, 1993.

K Davis, 'Low fertility in evolutionary perspective', in Davis et al (1987).

K Davis, M Bernstam and R Ricardo-Campbell, *Below-replacement fertility in industrial societies: causes, consequences, policies*, Cambridge: Cambridge University Press, 1987.

L Day, *The Future of Low-Birthrate Populations*, London: Routledge, 1992.

C Daykin, *Funding the Future? Problems in Pension Reform*, London: Politeia, 1998.

Department of Health and Social Services (DHSS), *A Happier Old Age*, London: HMSO, 1978.

DHSS, *Growing Older*, Cmnd 8173, London: HMSO, 1981.

DHSS, *Reform of Social Security*, Cmnd 9517, London: HMSO, 1985a.

DHSS, *Reform of Social Security: programme for action*, Cmnd 9691, London: HMSO, 1985b.

DHSS, *Caring for People: Community Care in the Next Decade and Beyond*, Cm 849, London: HMSO, 1989.

Peter Dicken, *Global Shift* (Second edition), London: Paul Chapman Publishing, 1992.

R Easterlin, 'The conflict between aspirations and resources', *Population and Development Review*, vol 1, no 3/4, September/December 1976.

R Easterlin, M Wachter and S Wachter, 'Demographic influences on economic stability: the US experience', *Population and Development Review*, vol 4, no 1, March 1978.

The Economist (compiled by Thelmer Liesner), *One hundred years of economic statistics*, London: Economist Publications, 1989

Employment Department, *Employment Gazette: Historical Supplement*, no 3, London: HMSO, June 1992.

Employment Department, 'British labour force projections: 1994 to 2006', *Employment Gazette*, London: HMSO, April 1994.

Employment Department, *Labour Market and Skill Trends 1993*, London: HMSO, 1993.

Employment Department, *Employment Gazette*, London: HMSO, July 1995a.

Employment Department, *Labour Market and Skill Trends 1995/96*, London: HMSO, 1995b.

Equal Opportunities Commission, *Equalisation of State Pension Ages: The Gender Impact*, Manchester, 1995.

J Ermisch, *The political economy of demographic change: causes and implications of population trends in Great Britain*, London: Policy Studies Institute, 1983.

J Ermisch, 'Economic influences on birth rates', *National Institute Economic Review*, November 1988.

J Ermisch, *Fewer Babies, Longer Lives*, York: Joseph Rowntree Foundation, 1990.

T Espenshade and W Serow (eds), *The Economic Consequences of Slowing Population Growth*, New York: Academic Press, 1978.

C Estes, 'Social Security: the social construction of a crisis', *Milbank Memorial Fund Quarterly*, vol 61, no 3, summer 1983.

C Estes, 'The politics of ageing in America', *Ageing and Society*, vol 6, 1986.

F Faber and J Wilkin, *Social security area population projections, 1981*, Washington: Social Security Administration, 1981.

J Falkingham, 'Dependency and ageing in Britain: a re-examination of the evidence', *Journal of Social Policy*, vol 18, no 2, 1989.

J Falkingham and C Victor, 'The myth of the Woopie? incomes, the elderly, and targeting welfare', *Ageing and Society*, vol 11, 1991.

M Feldstein, 'Social security, induced retirement and aggregate capital accumulation', *Journal of Political Economy*, no 82, September 1974.

JF Fries, 'Ageing, natural death, and the compression of morbidity', *New England Journal of Medicine*, no 303, 1980.

JF Fries, 'The compression of morbidity: near or far?' *Milbank Memorial Fund Quarterly*, vol 67, no 2, 1989.

F Furedi, *Population and Development*, London: Polity Press, 1997.

X Gaullier, 'Economic crisis and old age: old age policies in France', *Ageing and Society*, vol 2, 1982.

L Gavrilov and N Gavrilov, *The Biology of Life Span: A Quantitative Approach*, Switzerland: Harwood Academic Publishers, 1991.

O Giarini and W Stahel, *The Limits to Certainty: Facing Risks in the New Service Economy*, Dordrecht: Kluwer, 1989.

I Gibbs, 'Income, capital and the cost of care in old age', *Ageing and Society*, vol 11, 1991.

R M Gibson and C R Fisher, 'Age differences in health care spending, fiscal year 1977', *Social Security Bulletin*, 42(1), 1979.

A Giddens, *Beyond Left and Right*, London: Polity Press, 1994.

H Giles and S Condor, 'Ageing, technology and society: an introduction and future priorities', *Social Behaviour*, vol 3, 1988.

C Gillion, 'Ageing populations: spreading the costs', *Journal of European Social Policy*, vol 1(2), 1991.

J Ginn, 'Grey power: age-based organisations' response to structured inequalities', *Critical Social Policy*, vol 13, no 2, 1993.

D Glass and E Grebenak, 'World population 1800-1950', in Habakkuk and Postan (1966).

J Gravelle, 'Do individual retirement accounts increase savings?' *Journal of Economic Perspectives*, vol 5, no 2.

R Griffiths, *Community Care: Agenda for Action*, (The Griffiths Report), London: HMSO, 1988.

E Gruenberg, 'The failures of success', *Milbank Memorial Fund Quarterly*, vol 55, no 1, 1977.

E Grundy, 'Mortality and morbidity among the old', *British Medical Journal*, vol 288, 1984.

E Grundy, 'Population review: (5) The population aged 60 and over', *Population Trends*, no 84, 1996.

A-M Guillemard, 'The social dynamics of early withdrawal from the labour force in France', *Ageing and Society*, vol 5, no 4, 1985.

A-M Guillemard, *Le declin du social formation et crise des politiques de la viellesse*, Paris: Presses Universitaires de France, 1986.

H Habakkuk and M Postan, *The Cambridge Economic History of Europe*, vol 6, Cambridge: Cambridge University Press, 1966.

R Hagemann and G Nicoletti, *Ageing Populations: Economic Effects and Implications for Public Finance*, OECD Department of Economics and Statistics, Working Paper 61, Paris: OECD, 1989.

O Hagnell, J Lanke, B Rorsman, R Ohman and I Ojesjo, 'Current trends in the incidence of senile and multi-infarct dementia: a prospective study of a total population followed over 25 years: the Lundby study', *Arch Psychiatr Nervenke*, vol 233, 1983.

A Harris, *Social Welfare for the Elderly*, London: HMSO, 1968.

D Hayes-Bautista, W Schinck and J Chapa, *The Burden of Support: the Young Latino Population in an Aging Society*, Palo Alto: Stanford University Press, 1988.

P Heller, R Hemming, P Kolmert, *Ageing and social expenditure in the major industrialised countries 1980-2025*, Occasional Paper 47, Washington: IMF, 1986.

M Henwood, *Through a Glass Darkly: Community Care and Older People*, London: Kings Fund, 1992.

J Hess, 'Confessions of a greedy geezer', *The Nation*, April 1990.

J Hills, *The Future of Welfare: a guide to the debate*, York: Joseph Rowntree Trust, 1993.

T Hogan, 'The implications of population stationarity for the Social Security system', *Social Science Quarterly*, no 55, June 1974.

HM Treasury, *Public Expenditure*, London: HMSO, 1979.

HM Treasury, *Public Expenditure*, London: HMSO, 1993.

ILO, *Into the twenty-first century: the development of social security*, Geneva: ILO, 1984.

IMF, *World Economic Outlook*, Washington: IMF, May 1995.

IMF, *World Economic Outlook*, Washington: IMF, May 1997.

R Jack, 'Social services and the ageing population 1970–1990', *Social Policy and Administration*, vol 25, no 4, December 1991.

W Jackson, 'On the treatment of population ageing in economic theory', *Ageing and Society*, vol 11, 1991.

NS Jecker and LJ Schneidermann, 'Futility and rationing', *American Journal of Medicine*, no 92, 1992.

S Jenkins, *Accountable to None: The Tory Nationalisation of Britain*, London: Hamish Hamilton, 1995.

M Johnson, 'Interdependency and the generational contract', *Ageing and Society*, vol 15, June 1995.

P Johnson, 'The assessment: inequality', *Oxford Review of Economic Policy*, vol 12, no 1, 1996.

P Johnson, C Conrad and D Thomson (eds), *Workers versus pensioners: inter-generational justice in an ageing world*, Manchester: Manchester University Press, 1989.

P Johnson and J Falkingham, 'Inter-generational transfers and public expenditure on the elderly in modern Britain', *Ageing and Society*, vol 8, 1988.

P Johnson and J Falkingham, *Ageing and Economic Welfare*, London: Sage, 1992.

P Johnson and G Stears, 'Pensioner Income Inequality', *Fiscal Studies*, vol 16, no 4, 1995.

R Johnson et al, 'Morbidity and health care utilisation of old and very old persons', *Health Services Research*, vol 25, 1990.

Joseph Rowntree Foundation, *Income and Wealth*, vol 2, York: Joseph Rowntree Foundation, 1995.

P Kennedy, *Preparing for the Twenty-first Century*, London: Harper Collins, 1993.

N Keyfitz, 'How do we know the facts of demography?', *Population and Development Review*, vol 1, no 2, December 1975.

N Keyfitz, 'Why social security is in trouble', *Public Interest*, no 58, 1980.

N Keyfitz and W Flieger, *World Population: an analysis of vital data*, Chicago: University of Chicago, 1968.

N Keyfitz and W Flieger, *World Population Growth and Ageing: demographic trends in the late twentieth century*, Chicago: University of Chicago, 1990.

J M Keynes, 'Some economic consequences of a declining population', *Eugenics Review*, vol 29, no 1, 1937.

H Kirk, 'Geriatric medicine and the categorisation of old age - the historical linkage', *Ageing and Society*, vol 12, 1992.

M Kohli, J Rosenow, and J Wolf, 'The social construction of ageing through work: economic structure and life-world', *Ageing and Society*, vol 3, 1983.

M Kramer, 'The rising pandemic of mental disorders and associated diseases and disabilities', *Acta Psychiatricia Scandinavica*, 1980, vol 62, supplement 285.

S Kuznets, *Economic Growth and Structure*, London: Heinemann, 1966.

S Kuznets, *Growth, Population and Income Distribution*, London: WW Norton, 1979.

Labour Party, *Road to the Manifesto: Security in Retirement*, London: Labour Party, 1996.

P Laslett, 'The significance of the past in the study of ageing', *Ageing and Society*, vol 4, 1984.

P Laslett, 'The emergence of the Third Age', *Ageing and Society*, vol 7, 1987.

P Laslett, *A Fresh Map of Life: the Emergence of the Third Age*, London: Weidenfeld & Nicolson, 1989.

N Leff, 'Dependency rates and savings rates', *American Economic Review*, vol 59, December 1969.

P Lellouche, *Le Nouveau Monde*, Paris: Bernard Grasset, 1992.

NG Levensky, 'Age as a criterion for rationing health care', *New England Journal of Medicine*, no 322, 1990.

J Lewis, 'The ideology and politics of birth control in inter-war England', *Women's Studies International Quarterly*, vol 2, 1979.

P Lloyd-Sherlock and P Johnson, *Ageing and Social Policy: Global Comparisons*, London: Suntory and Toyota International Centres for Economics and Related Disciplines at the London School of Economics, 1996.

G McNicoll, 'Economic growth with below-replacement fertility', in Davis et al (1987).

H McRae, *The World in 2020*, London: Harper Collins, 1995.

KG Manton, LS Corder and E Stallard, 'Estimates of changes in chronic disability and institutional incidence and prevalence rates in the US elderly population from the 1982, 1984, and 1989 national long-term care survey', *Journal of Gerontology*, vol 48, 1993.

KG Manton and B Soldo, 'Dynamics of health changes in the oldest old: new perspectives and evidence', *Milbank Memorial Fund Quarterly/Health and Society*, vol 63, no 3, 1985.

J Marchant, *Cradles or Coffins?*, London: National Life, 1916.

A Mason, 'Saving, economic growth, and demographic change', *Population and Development Review*, vol 14, no 1, March 1988.

E Midwinter, 'An ageing world: the equivocal response', *Ageing and Society*, vol 10, 1990.

E Midwinter, *The British Gas Report on Attitudes to Ageing*, London: British Gas, 1991.

'Special issue: The Oldest Old', *Milbank Memorial Fund Quarterly/ Health and Society* (in collaboration with the American National Institute on Aging), vol 63, no 3, 1985.

M Minkler, 'The politics of generational equity', *Social Policy*, Winter 1987.

M Minkler and A Robertson, 'The ideology of "Age/Race wars": deconstructing a social problem', *Ageing and Society*, vol 11, 1991.

TG Moore, 'Comment', in Davis et al (1987).

C Murray, *The Emerging British Underclass*, London: Institute of Economic Affairs, 1990.

J Myles, 'Conflict, crisis and the future of old age security', *Milbank Memorial Fund Quarterly*, vol 61, no 3, 1983.

I Nascher, *Geriatrics. The Diseases of Old Age and their Treatment*, Philadelphia: Blakiston, 1914.

D O'Connor, P Pollitt, C Brook and B Reiss, 'A community survey of mental and physical infirmity in nonagenarians', *Age and Ageing*, vol 18, 1989.

Office of Population Censuses and Surveys (OPCS), *Population Trends*, London: HMSO, Autumn 1975.

OPCS, *Population Projections 1979-2019*, London: HMSO, 1981.

OPCS, *1981 Census Guide 1: Britain's Elderly Population*, London: HMSO, 1984.

OPCS, *Population Trends*, London: HMSO, Summer 1987.

OPCS, *The general household survey 1990*, London: HMSO, 1992.

OPCS, *1991-based National Population Projections*, London: HMSO, 1993.

OPCS, *Population Trends*, London: HMSO, Autumn 1994.

OPCS, *1992 - based National Population Projections*, London: HMSO, 1995.

OPCS, *Population Trends*, London: HMSO, Spring 1995.

OPCS, *Population Trends*, London: HMSO, Winter 1995.

OPCS, *Population Trends*, London: HMSO, Summer 1997.

OECD, *Demographic Trends 1965-1980 in Western Europe and North America*, Paris: OECD, 1966.

OECD, *Ageing Populations: The Social Policy Implications*, Paris: OECD, 1988a.

OECD, *Reforming Public Pensions*, Paris: OECD, 1988b.

OECD, *Health and pension policies under economic and demographic constraints*, Paris: OECD, 1988c.

OECD, *OECD Health Systems: Facts and Trends 1960–91*, Paris: OECD, 1993a.

OECD, *Statistical Tables on Public Expenditure on Social Protection*, Paris: OECD, 1993b.

OECD, *Jobs Study*, Paris: OECD, 1994

OECD, *Economic Outlook*, Paris: OECD, June 1995.

F Pampel and J Williamson, *Age, class, politics and the welfare state*, Cambridge: Cambridge University Press, 1989.

S Parker, *Work and Retirement*, London: George Allen & Unwin, 1982.

B Peterson, 'A note on old age pensions: demography and the distribution between generations', *Journal of Institutional and Theoretical Economics*, vol 144, 1988.

P Peterson, 'The salvation of Social Security', *New York Review*, 17 March 1982.

M Peterson and C Rose, 'Historical antecedents of normative vs pathological perspectives in aging', *Journal of American Geriatrics Society*, vol 30, 1983.

Phillips Committee, *Economic and Financial Problems of the Provision for Old Age*, Cmd 9333, London: HMSO, 1954.

C Phillipson, *The Emergence of Retirement*, Durham: University of Durham, 1977.

C Phillipson, 'Pre-retirement education: the British and American experience', *Ageing and Society*, vol 1, 1981.

C Phillipson, *Capitalism and the Construction of Old Age*, London: Macmillan, 1982.

A Pitts, 'Social security and aging populations', in Espenshade and Serow (1978).

The Population Institute, *First Conference on Population, 1965*, Philippines: University of the Philippines Press, 1966.

H Pratt, *Gray Agendas: Interest Groups and Public Pensions in Canada, Britain and the US*, Ann Arbor: University of Michigan Press, 1994.

S Preston, 'Children and the elderly: divergent paths for America's dependents', *Demography*, vol 21, no 4, 1984a.

S Preston, 'Children and the elderly in the US', *Scientific American*, vol 251, 1984b.

S Preston, 'Changing values and falling birth rates', in Davis et al (1987).

A Rappapart, 'Prepare for the world of post-65 (and early retirement)', *Harvard Business Review*, July–August 1978.

W Reddaway, *The Economics of a Declining Population*, London: George Allen & Unwin, 1939.

W Reddaway, 'The economic consequences of ZPG', *Lloyds Bank Review*, no 124, April 1977.

G Rejda and R Shepler, 'The impact of Zero Population Growth on the Old Age, Survivors, Disability, and Health Insurance program', *Journal of Risk and Insurance*, no 40, September 1973.

R Ricardo-Campbell, 'US Social Security under low fertility', in Davis et al (1987).

D Rice and J Feldman, 'Living longer in the US', *Milbank Memorial Fund Quarterly*, vol 61, no 3, 1983.

S Riddle, 'Age, obsolescence and unemployment: older men in the British industrial system 1920–1939: a research note', *Ageing and Society*, vol 4, 1984.

R Ridker, 'The effects of slowing population growth on long-run economic growth in the US during the next half-century', in Espenshade and Serow (1978).

MM Rivlin, 'Protecting elderly people: flaws in ageist arguments', *British Medical Journal*, vol 310, 1995.

J Roebuck, 'When does Old Age begin?: the evolution of the English definition', *Journal of Social History*, vol 12, no 3, Spring 1979.

A Rogers, R Rogers and A Belanger, 'Longer life but worse health? Measurement and dynamics', *The Gerontologist*, vol 30, no 5, 1990.

B Rosen and T Jerdee, 'Too old or not too old?' *Harvard Business Review*, November–December 1977.

Royal Commission, *Report of the Royal Commission on Population*, Cmd 7695, London: HMSO, 1949.

Royal Commission, *Papers of the Royal Commission on Population*, vol 2 (Reports and Selected Papers of the Statistics Committee), London: HMSO, 1950a.

Royal Commission, *Papers of the Royal Commission on Population*, vol 3 (Report of the Economics Committee), London: HMSO, 1950b.

Royal Commission, *Papers of the Royal Commission on Population*, vol 5 (Memoranda presented to the Royal Commission), London: HMSO, 1950c.

W Schmahl, 'The "1992 reform" of public pensions in Germany: main elements and some effects', *Journal of European Social Policy*, vol 3, no 1, 1993.

J Schulz, 'The economics of compulsory retirement', *Industrial Gerontology*, Winter 1974.

K Sen, 'Old Age Security and Pensions in India: A critique of the current paradigms', in Lloyd–Sherlock and Johnson (1996).

W Serow and T Espenshade, 'The economics of declining population growth: an assessment of the current literature', in Espenshade and Serow (1978).

H L Sheppard and S E Rix, *The graying of working America*, New York: Free Press, 1979.

I Sinclair and J Williams, 'Demography, health and personal services', *The Kaleidoscope of Care*, London: HMSO, 1990.

H Singer, 'Economic progress in underdeveloped countries', *Social Research*, vol 16, 1949.

R Smith, 'The structured dependency of the elderly as a recent development', *Ageing and Society*, vol 4, 1984.

Social Trends, no 23, London: HMSO, 1993.

J Spengler, *Declining Population Growth Revisited*, Chapel Hill: Carolina Population Centre, 1971.

J Spengler, *Zero Population Growth: Reactions and Implications, Past and Present*, Durham NC: Duke University Press, 1978.

G Stein, *Mounting Debts: the coming European pension crisis*, London: Politeia, 1997.

H Sutherland, *Birth Control*, London: Harding and Mare, 1922.

H Sutherland, *Control of Life*, London: Burn, Oates and Washbourne, 1944.

A Svanborg, 'The health of the elderly population: results from longitudinal studies', *Research and the Ageing Population*, CIBA Research Foundation, 1988.

A Sweezy and A Owens, 'The impact of population growth on employment', *American Economic Review*, no 64, May 1974.

R Tallis, 'Medical advances and the future of old age', in M Marinker (ed), *Controversies in Health Care Policies: Challenges to Practice*, London: British Medical Journal Publishing, 1994.

G Therborn, *European Modernity and Beyond: The Trajectory of European Societies 1945-2000*, London: Sage, 1995.

P Thomas, P Garry and J Goodwin, 'Morbidity and mortality in an initially healthy elderly sample: findings after five years of follow-up', *Age and Ageing*, vol 15, 1986.

J Thompson, 'Ageing of the population: contemporary trends and issues', *Population Trends*, no 50, London: HMSO, Winter 1987.

P Thompson, '"I don't feel old": subjective ageing and the search for meaning in later life', *Ageing and Society*, vol 12, 1992.

D Thomson, 'The decline of social welfare: falling state support for the elderly since early Victorian times', *Ageing and Society*, vol 4, 1984.

A Tinker, *Elderly People in Modern Society*, London: Longman, 1992.

A Tinker, C McCreadie, F Wright and A Salvage, *The Care of Frail Elderly People in the United Kingdom*, London: HMSO, 1994.

J Tobin, 'Life cycle saving and balanced economic growth', in W Fellner (ed), *Ten Economic Studies in the Tradition of Irving Fisher*, York: Wiley Press, 1967.

P Townsend, 'The structural dependency of the elderly: a creation of social policy in the twentieth century', *Ageing and Society*, vol 1, 1981.

P Townsend and D Wedderburn, *The Aged in the Welfare State*, London: G Bell and Sons, 1965.

P Toynbee, *The Future of Care for Older People*, London: Lemos and Crane, 1996.

B Turchi, 'Stationary populations: pensions and social security', in Spengler (1978).

United Nations (UN), *World Economic Survey 1983*, New York: UN, 1983.

UN, *World Economic Survey 1987*, New York: UN, 1987.

UN, *World Economic Survey 1988*, New York: UN, 1988.

UN, *World Economic Survey 1989*, New York: UN, 1989.

UN, *World Economic Survey 1990*, New York: UN, 1990.

UN, *Demographic Yearbook. Special issue: population ageing and the situation of elderly persons*, New York: UN, 1993.

UN, *World Economic Survey 1994*, New York: UN, 1994.

US Department of Labor, *The Older American Worker: age discrimination in employment*, Washington: Department of Labor, 1965.

US President, 'Long range effects of population change on the US budget', cited in *Population and Development Review*, June 1979.

C Victor, 'Continuity or change: inequalities in health in later life', *Ageing and Society*, vol 11, 1991.

J Vincent, 'Who's afraid of an ageing population', *Critical Social Policy*, no 47, 1996.

A Walker, 'Towards a political economy of old age', *Ageing and Society*, vol 1, 1981.

A Walker, 'Review' of Phillipson (1982), *Ageing and Society*, vol 3, 1983.

A Walker, 'The economic "burden" of ageing and the prospect of inter-generational conflict', *Ageing and Society*, vol 10, 1990.

A Walker, *Age and Attitudes: Main Results from a Eurobarometer Survey*, Brussels: Commission of the European Communities, 1993.

R Walker, 'The financial resources of the elderly or paying your own way in old age', in Baldwin, Parker and Walker (1998).

A Warnes, 'Being old, old people, and the burdens of burden', *Ageing and Society*, vol 13, 1993.

C Weaver, 'Social security in aging societies', in Davis *et al* (1987).

A Welford, *Ageing and Human Skill*, Oxford: Oxford University Press, 1958.

N Wells and C Freer, *The Ageing Population: Burden or Challenge?* London: Macmillan, 1989.

J Williamson, 'Drugs in old age: new perspectives', *British Medical Bulletin*, vol 46, no 1, January 1990.

World Bank, *Averting the Old Age Crisis: policies to protect the old and promote growth*, New York: Oxford University Press, 1994.

World Health Organisation, *Ageing and Work Capacity*, Geneva: WHO, 1993.

E Wrigley and R Schofield, *The Population History of England 1541–1871: a Reconstruction*, Cambridge: Cambridge University Press, 1989.

CJ Zook, SF Savickis, FD Moore, 'Repeated hospitalisation for the same disease: a multiplier of national health cost', *Milbank Memorial Fund Quarterly/Health and Society*, 1980, vol 58, no 3.

N Zweibel et al, 'Public attitudes about the use of chronological age as a criterion for allocating scarce health care resources', *The Gerontologist*, vol 33, no 1, 1993.

Index